Christ Exalted

Monographs in Baptist History

VOLUME 12

SERIES EDITOR
Michael A. G. Haykin, The Southern Baptist Theological Seminary

EDITORIAL BOARD
Matthew Barrett, Midwestern Baptist Theological Seminary
Peter Beck, Charleston Southern University
Anthony L. Chute, California Baptist University
Jason G. Duesing, Midwest Baptist Theological Seminary
Nathan A. Finn, Union University
Crawford Gribben, Queen's University, Belfast
Gordon L. Heath, McMaster Divinity College
Barry Howson, Heritage Theological Seminary
Jason K. Lee, Cedarville University
Thomas J. Nettles, The Southern Baptist Theological Seminary, retired
James A. Patterson, Union University
James M. Renihan, Institute of Reformed Baptist Studies
Jeffrey P. Straub, Central Seminary
Brian R. Talbot, Broughty Ferry Baptist Church, Scotland
Malcolm B. Yarnell III, Southwestern Baptist Theological Seminary

Ours is a day in which not only the gaze of western culture but also increasingly that of Evangelicals is riveted to the present. The past seems to be nowhere in view and hence it is disparagingly dismissed as being of little value for our rapidly changing world. Such historical amnesia is fatal for any culture, but particularly so for Christian communities whose identity is profoundly bound up with their history. The goal of this new series of monographs, *Monographs in Baptist History*, seeks to provide one of these Christian communities, that of evangelical Baptists, with reasons and resources for remembering the past. The editors are deeply convinced that Baptist history contains rich resources of theological reflection, praxis and spirituality that can help Baptists, as well as other Christians, live more Christianly in the present. The monographs in this series will therefore aim at illuminating various aspects of the Baptist tradition and in the process provide Baptists with a usable past.

Christ Exalted

Pastoral Writings of Hanserd Knollys with an Essay on His Eschatological Thought

EDITED BY
Barry H. Howson

☞PICKWICK *Publications* • Eugene, Oregon

CHRIST EXALTED
Pastoral Writings of Hanserd Knollys with an Essay
on His Eschatological Thought

Monographs in Baptist History 12

Copyright © 2019 Barry H. Howson. All rights reserved. Except for brief quotations in critical publications or reviews, no part of this book may be reproduced in any manner without prior written permission from the publisher. Write: Permissions, Wipf and Stock Publishers, 199 W. 8th Ave., Suite 3, Eugene, OR 97401.

Pickwick Publications
An Imprint of Wipf and Stock Publishers
199 W. 8th Ave., Suite 3
Eugene, OR 97401

www.wipfandstock.com

PAPERBACK ISBN: 978-1-60608-165-5
HARDCOVER ISBN: 978-1-4982-8786-9
EBOOK ISBN: 978-1-4982-4107-6

Cataloguing-in-Publication data:

Names: Howson, Barry H., editor.

Title: Christ exalted : pastoral writings of Hanserd Knollys with an essay on his eschatological thought / edited by Barry H. Howson.

Description: Eugene, OR: Pickwick Publications, 2019 | Series: Monographs in Baptist History 12 | Includes bibliographical references and index.

Identifiers: ISBN 978-1-60608-165-5 (paperback) | ISBN 978-1-4982-8786-9 (hardcover) | ISBN 978-1-4982-4107-6 (ebook)

Subjects: LCSH: Knollys, Hanserd, 1599?–1691. | Dissenters, Religious–England–History–17th century. | Baptists–Doctrines–History–17th century. | Theology, Doctrinal–England–History–17th century.

Classification: BX6495.K63 H69 2019 (print) | BX6495.K63 (ebook)

Manufactured in the U.S.A.   08/19/19

Contents

Preface | vii
Timeline of Hanserd Knollys's Life | ix
Introduction | xi

1. The Life and Death of that Old Disciple of Jesus Christ and Eminent Minister of the Gospel, Hanserd Knollys | 1
2. Christ Exalted | 29
3. The Parable of the Kingdom of Heaven Expounded | 77
4. The World that Now Is and the World that Is to Come | 145
5. The Eschatology of Hanserd Knollys with Special Reference to His Commentary on the Book of Revelation | 211

Select Bibliography | 233

Preface

It has been a great privilege for me to have walked with Hanserd Knollys over these past twenty years. Dr. Dennis Bustin and I both wrote our PhD dissertations on Knollys and both were published by Paternoster and Brill respectively. We were very grateful for their willingness to publish them. However, not many people, other than scholars, will likely buy and/or read these works partly due to their cost. So we published through the generosity of Pickwick Publications and its Baptist series editor, Michael Haykin, a much briefer work on Hanserd Knollys's life and thought entitled, *Zealous for the Lord: The Life and Thought of the Seventeenth-Century Baptist Hanserd Knollys*.

In order to compliment that volume and to allow readers to read Knollys directly, I have edited this book which contains four of his pastoral writings that I believe reflect who the man was as a Christian and as a pastor. I have also added a final chapter on Knollys's eschatological thought with special reference to his commentary on the Book of Revelation. Eschatology was an important part of his thought, having written six works that fall into this category. Some of the works are repetitious and some of them, like the two I have included in this selection for this book,[1] are more pastoral but have some emphasis on eschatology. Consequently, I have included an essay summarizing his eschatological thought for those readers interested it.

There are several people that I want to thank for this book. The first is my dear friend Ruth Engler who transcribed Knollys's seventeenth-century published works into Word format. This work would not have made it into print were it not for her. Also I am grateful to my friend Roy Paul who

---

1. *The Parable of the Kingdom of Heaven expounded* and *the World that now is and the World that is to Come*.

edited and formatted this book for the publisher. Also I want to thank Heritage College and Seminary for providing me with an eight month sabbatical that gave me time to work on this book and get it ready for publication. Also my gratitude to Pickwick Publications and especially to Michael Haykin for accepting and publishing both of these works on Knollys. Michael has been a dear friend and encouragement to me over the many years that we have known each other. Last but not least I want to thank my wife Sharon who has been my friend and partner for over thirty-five years of marriage. In the providence of God my life would not be what it is without her.

I dedicate this book to my parents-in-law who both passed away into the presence of Jesus last year only six weeks apart, both in their 90s. I knew them for almost forty years and they were a great encouragement to me in my walk with Christ. Both of them would agree with Knollys's pastoral passion and his doctrinal commitments, and I know would have enjoyed reading his writings contained herein.

Timeline of Hanserd Knollys's Life

1599 or 1609	Knollys is born
1627	Knollys matriculates from St Katherine's Hall Cambridge
1631	Knollys is appointed vicar in the Church of England at Humberstone
1632	Knollys marries Anne Cheney
1633	Birth of their son Cheney Knollys, the first of ten children
1633	Knollys resigns his Church of England living
1635/36	Knollys's conversion to the free grace of salvation in Christ through the ministry of John Wheelright
1638	Knollys arrives in Boston, New England, and is embroiled in Antinomian controversy
1641	Knollys returns to England
1642	The English Civil War between Parliament and King begins
1642?	Knollys becomes a member of Henry Jessey's Independent/Congregationalist church
1644	The First London Confession of Faith is written and signed by seven London Baptist churches
1644/45	Knollys is baptized
1645	Knollys and several others plant a Baptist church in London near Great St. Helens
1646	Knollys signs the revision of the 1644 London Confession

Timeline of Hanserd Knollys's Life

1649	Charles I is beheaded and the Commonwealth under the Parliament rules England
1651	The Civil War ends
1653	Oliver Cromwell becomes Lord Protector and Knollys serves in the government
1660	The Protectorate falls, and Charles II is restored to the throne
1661	Knollys is imprisoned in Newgate Prison for eighteen weeks
1662	The Act of Uniformity is passed and dissenters resign from their pulpits
1670	Knollys is imprisoned in Bishopsgate
1671	Anne Knollys dies
1677	The Second London Confession of Faith is written and signed by Calvinistic Baptists
1684	Knollys is imprisoned in Newgate Prison again for at least six months
1689	James II flees; William and Mary become King and Queen of England; the Act of Toleration is passed
1689	The Second London Confession is published; the first Calvinistic Baptist General Assembly is held
1691	Knollys dies

Introduction

HANSERD KNOLLYS'S LIFE NEARLY covered the whole of the seventeenth century, beginning as a member of the Church of England, then becoming an Independent, and finally a Particular Baptist. In addition, he was an educated pastor and one of the leaders of the Particular Baptist association of churches throughout its first fifty years of existence. Moreover, he had travelled beyond the borders of England spending four years in New England and some other time on the Continent. He is, therefore, an interesting and important figure of early Baptist History.

Knollys was born at Cawkwell near Louth in Lincolnshire, England about the year 1599.[1] His father, Richard Knollys, was probably "the resident

---

1. For his life see his autobiography entitled, *The Life and Death of that Old Disciple of Jesus Christ, and Eminent Minister of the Gospel, Mr. Hanserd Knollys, who died in the Ninety-third Year of His Age written with his own hand to the year 1672, and continued in general, in an epistle by Mr William Kiffin*; Stephen and Lee, "Knollys, Hanserd"; Brown, "Hanserd Knollys, 1638–1641," 1–7; Brackney, *The Baptists*, 214–15; White, "Knollys, Hanserd (c. 1599–1691)," 2:160–62; Wilson, *The History and Antiquities of Dissenting Churches and Meeting Houses*, 562-71; Culross, *Hanserd Knollys*; White, *Hanserd Knollys and Radical Dissent in the Seventeenth Century*; Duncan, *Hanserd Knollys*; and James, *Religious Liberty on Trial*; Howson, *Erroneous and Schismatical Opinions*; Dennis Bustin, *Paradox and Perseverance*.

Knollys's birthdate could be either 1598 or 1599. According to his autobiography he died on September 16, 1691 in his ninety-third year (Knollys, *Life and Death*, 4, 7). Knollys's name was spelled in seventeenth-century documents variously including: Knollys, Knowles, Knolles, Knolies, Nowles, Noles, Knollis, Knowls and Knoles.

Muriel James has studied the Parish records of Cawkwell and notes that Knollys was not baptized until November 13, 1609 (*Religious Liberty*, 26–27). On account of this baptismal date Dennis Bustin has challenged the previously accepted date of Knollys's birth. He makes a very strong case for a 1609 date for Knollys's birth. I remain uncertain. The 1599 date comes from William Kiffin who knew Knollys for some 54 years, and clearly states in the "Epistle to the reader" in Knollys's *Autobiography* that he died in

xi

clergy man of the parish," a God-fearing man. At the age of ten Hanserd was tutored at home and later briefly attended Grimsby free school. When he was fourteen years old his father was appointed the Church of England rector of Scartho near Market Grimsby; consequently, the family moved to Scartho, only a short distance from Cawkwell. Sometime afterwards he studied at Puritan Cambridge and, in particular, St. Katherine's Hall College where such Puritans as William Strong, John Arrowsmith and Thomas Goodwin, his contemporaries, also attended.

On March 30, 1629, he became a pensioner at St. Katherine's Hall, Cambridge with a view to ordination in the Church of England. During his time at St. Katherine's he was under the Mastership of the Puritan Richard Sibbes. After only three months Knollys was ordained a Deacon and the following day ordained Presbyter of the Church of England by the bishop of Peterborough, Dr. Dove.

Two years later, on August 24th, the bishop of Lincoln, John Williams, gave Knollys a small living at Humberstone, near his father's parish in Scartho.

In 1631 Knollys married Anne Cheney, a woman ten years younger than himself, the daughter of John Cheney Esq. of Bennington. Knollys tells us she "was a holy, discreet woman, and a meet help for me in the ways of her household, and also in the way of holiness." Shortly after his marriage Knollys became convinced that some of the practices of the Church, including the wearing of the surplice, the signing of the cross in baptism, and the admitting of wicked persons to the Lord's Supper were sinful. Consequently, he resigned his living sometime after March 1633 but was permitted for several years to continue preaching. About 1635 or 1636 he became convinced that his ordination was false and that he "had not received any seal from Christ of [his] ministry; for though many had been reformed and moralized, yet [he] knew not that [he] had been instrumental to convert any souls to God." He resolved not to preach anymore "until [he] had a clear call and commission from Christ to preach the gospel."[2] Consequently, he began to pray "day and night" for several weeks asking "that Christ would count me worthy, and put me into the ministry."

One day after praying in the woods at Anderby in Lincolnshire his prayers were answered while he was walking home and meditating. Not hearing any voice, nor seeing any vision but only those words which were "plainly and articulately spoken" into his "ears and understanding" Knollys

---

his ninety-third year (1691). On the other hand, why would Richard Knollys, a minister of the church of England, wait ten years to baptise his son, and not matriculate until 28 years of age? Bustin, *Paradox and Perseverance*, 29, 324ff.

2. Knollys, *Life and Death*, 17.

was told to "go to Mr. Wheelwright³, and he shall tell thee, and shew thee how to glorify God in the ministry." The next morning he went to see Wheelwright who, unbeknown to Knollys, had just moved to a village three miles from Humberstone. He told Wheelwright of his case, and that the Lord had sent him. After some conversation together Wheelwright told Knollys that the latter could not glorify God in the ministry because he was building his "soul upon a covenant of works, and was a stranger to the covenant of grace." Wheelwright then explained to him the covenant of free grace. Upon hearing this, Knollys tells us, he considered himself "a stranger to [free grace] in great measure, having [been] only under legal convictions and a spirit of bondage." He went on to confess, "And though I had some discoveries of my want of Christ, yet I had sought righteousness as it were by the works of the law, and got my peace by performing duties, and rested on them." Knollys then went home and prayed and "begged of God to teach [him] the covenant of grace." He searched the Scriptures and one day, hearing a message by a Mr. How⁴ on Galatians 2:20, he came to understand that he had lived a "life of works, not of faith." Now he began "to see the necessity of believing in Christ for pardon and salvation." How had explained that "Christ was the author, root, and only foundation of saving faith, and that God did give the faith of evidence, Heb. xi. 1, in some new covenant promise, Gal. iii. 14; and that those promises were given of God, 2 Pet. i 4." For that night and the next day Knollys prayed that God would give him such a promise. The following day he locked himself in the church and while he was praying "mourning and bemoaning" himself and his "soul's condition, fearing ... that God would leave" him and "forsake" him, he was given the promise "I will never leave thee, nor forsake thee." He then confessed,

> Lord who am I! I am a vile sinful sinner, the chief of sinners, most unworthy of pardon and salvation! How, Lord! never leave thee nor forsake thee? Oh, infinite mercy! Oh free grace! who am I? I have been a graceless soul, a formal professor, a legal performer of holy duties, and have gone about to establish mine own righteousness, which I now see is but filthy rags.

---

3. John Wheelwright was born about 1592, entered Sidney Sussex College in Cambridge in 1611. He was ordained a deacon and priest in December 1619. In April 1623 he was instituted as the vicar of Bilsby. He served as vicar for ten years at which time he was removed from his office for the charge of simony. Sometime after this he was preaching at Belleau in Lincolnshire but was eventually silenced by the Church authorities for his Puritan opinions. In 1636 he left for New England. It is likely during these years 1633–1636 that Knollys came in contact with him.

4. This is likely Samuel How who wrote *The Sufficiencie of the Spirits Teaching without Human Learning*.

Then God gave him two promises from Isaiah 43:22–25 and 54:9–10, assuring him of the forgiveness of his sins, and of his place in the covenant of peace. He records that he experienced "joy and peace in believing."

The next day he saw Wheelwright who told him he was now "somewhat prepared to preach Jesus Christ and the gospel of free grace to others, having been taught it of God." He instructed Knollys to wait upon God, and the Holy Spirit through the word would teach him how to preach. Knollys went home and began to pray for this. One day, while he was praying, these words were spoken to his heart by the Spirit, "I have appeared unto thee for this purpose, to make thee a minister and a witness both of those things which thou hast seen, and of those things in the which I will appear unto thee."[5] Upon hearing these words from the Lord he felt called and commissioned to preach the gospel. For the next three or four years Knollys experienced the blessing of the Lord on his preaching "whereby very many sinners were converted and many believers were established in the faith."[6]

In 1633 the situation worsened for the Puritans in England with the elevation of William Laud to the Archbishopric of Canterbury. Laud aggressively pursued a policy of uniformity of worship for all citizens. He left no room for dissent and persecuted those who rebelled. This policy had its effect upon the newly converted Puritan, Hanserd Knollys. While he was preaching in Lincolnshire in 1636 he was arrested on a warrant from the Court of High Commission. He convinced the man who issued the warrant to let him go. Knollys and his family then went to London for a time. From there they set off for Boston, Massachusetts on a twelve-week voyage during which they suffered much hardship including the loss of their only child. They probably reached Boston in the summer of 1638, and remained there, returning to London on December 24, 1641 in the midst of the struggle between King and Parliament that shortly led to Civil War the following year.

It was around this time that the London Particular Baptist group of churches was forming. Between the years 1638 and 1644, seven churches joined together to form a fellowship of Calvinistic Baptist churches; and in 1644 they declared their orthodoxy and Baptist convictions in a *Confession of Faith*. About this time Knollys came to Baptist convictions, and joined this young group of churches as one of its pastors.

Sometime after his return to London from Boston, Knollys became a member of Henry Jessey's Independent congregation.[7] It was during this

---

5. Taken from Paul's conversion testimony in Acts 26.

6. Knollys, *Life and Death*, 17-24.

7. Henry Jessey was born in 1603 and died in 1663. He was an English Dissenter under the reign of Charles I and a founding member of the Puritan religious sect, the church that was founded by Henry Jacob in 1616.

time that Knollys seriously began to question infant baptism and considered that only believers were the proper recipients of this ordinance. In January 1643/44 he told Jessey that he was not prepared to have his child baptized and requested that some meetings take place that "they [the church] might satisfye him, or he rectify them if amiss herein." The discussions were carried on for two months at which time sixteen members felt it was wrong to have their infants baptized and had removed themselves "not satisfyed we ware [sic] baptized as a true Church." At the same time, some of those who held to believer's baptism scrupled over the adminstrator of baptism.

Knollys's congregation in 1645 met next door to Great St. Helen's Church where it was reported by some neighbours that as many as a thousand attended his services. He was eventually turned out of there by his landlord and moved to Finsbury Fields.

In 1646 Knollys signed the second edition of the *First London Confession of Faith*. This second edition contained a few changes made to the first as a result of some criticisms made by the Presbyterian Daniel Featley.

In the 1640s and 1650s, the Particular Baptists were to experience tremendous growth as they spread their message beyond London. Knollys was quite involved in this expansion. For example, in 1649 Kiffin and Knollys were authorized by Parliament to go to Ipswich to preach. And in the early 1650s he went to Wales as an evangelist probably appointed by the London churches.

During the 1660s he published the first of six eschatological works. This first book, written in 1667, was *Apocalyptical Mysteries*. In it, he expounded the historicist view of the Book of Revelation in three parts discussing the seven trumpets, the seven vials, and the kingdom of Christ to come.

We know a little more of Knollys's activities in the 1670s. During the early 1670s his wife, one grand-child, three sons, and possibly another grandchild and a daughter-in-law, all died. Moreover, he thought he was about to die as well. However, believing the Lord could heal him, he called for Kiffin and Vavasor Powell to pray over him and anoint him with oil according to James 5:14, 15. As a result of this and the prayers of others, he recovered. His wife, however, did not recover from her illness and died in 1671 in her sixty-third year, after forty years of marriage.

In 1674 Knollys wrote his second eschatological work, *The Parable of the Kingdom of God Expounded*. In it, he sought to encourage Christian professors and sinners to be ready for the Coming of the Lord, which he believed was to be very soon. In this work he also clearly taught a postmillennial eschatology where Christ will come at the beginning of the millennium, spiritually and powerfully, and at the end, physically and personally. Five years later, after the Popish Plot scare, he published two more eschatological works, *Mystical Babylon Unvailed* and *An Exposition of the Eleventh Chapter of Revelation*. Both of these works boldly taught that Papal Rome was the great enemy of God's people. At the end of the former treatise he calls people to come out of Papal Rome, and in the latter he states that he believes the end will occur around 1688 (9 years from the time of these works).

In addition to the above works of the 1670s, Knollys and the London Particular Baptist churches anonymously published a new *Confession of Faith* in 1677. It was made public in 1689 when William and Mary came to the throne and a measure of toleration was given to Dissenters under the *Act of Toleration*. At that time Knollys, with thirty-six others, signed this *Confession* which was a Baptist revision of the *Westminster Confession* and *Savoy Declaration*. No doubt Knollys and others would have signed this *Confession* in 1677 but refrained from doing so because of persecution. In 1689 Kiffin and Knollys were the only Particular Baptists who had been a part of the movement in its early years, and signatories to this *Confession*; and they were the only two to sign both the *First* and *Second London Confessions*.

In 1681 Knollys wrote his fifth eschatological work, *The World that now is and the World that is to Come*. This treatise is divided into two parts dealing with the two Comings of Christ. The first part teaches that the first Coming of Christ was to save sinners, to build up the church of God, and to institute the gospel ordinances for his people to worship the Lord in spirit and truth. The second part deals with the millennial kingdom, the Second Coming of Christ, the resurrection of the dead, and the eternal judgment.

Dissenters in general experienced difficult persecution from 1682 until 1688. During the Spring of 1684, Knollys was imprisoned in Newgate for breaking the Conventicle Act. He was eighty-six at the time and remained there for sixteen months. Four years later Knollys published his last and crowning work on eschatology, his *Exposition of the Book of the Revelation*. It was formed from the messages he preached to his congregation in past years. In it he also gives an invitation to the people of God to come out of Papal Rome and again suggests the time of the end to be around 1688.

On September 19, 1691 he died in his ninety-third year. He was buried in Bunhill Fields.[8]

This collection of Knollys's writings gives the reader a view into his theological thought and into the thought of his Particular Baptist colleagues of the 17th century. Knollys had published over 25 different works but this collection focuses primarily on his theology, and in particular, on his soteriology and ecclesiology. The first of the writings is his autobiography entitled,

---

8. For a much more detailed survey of Knollys's life and thought, see the companion volume by Dennis Bustin and Barry Howson entitled, *Zealous for the Lord: The Life and Thought of the Seventeenth-Century Baptist Hanserd Knollys*.

The Life and Death of that Old Disciple of Jesus Christ and Eminent Minister of the Gospel, Mr. Hanserd Knollys, covering his life from birth to 1672. It was published by his close friend and colleague William Kiffin[9] shortly after his death in 1691. This is the main source for our knowledge of Knollys's life and is quite invaluable, particularly regarding his conversion, and his movement from Independency to baptistic belief.

The second work is *Christ Exalted: A Lost Sinner sought and saved by Christ: God's people are a holy people. Being the sum of diverse sermons preached in Suffolk*. The first edition was published in 1645 containing two sermons and then a second edition came out a year later with three sermons. The edition in this collection is the second one. In this publication we get an understanding of Knollys's soteriological thought. We see his understanding of conversion and the Christian life following conversion.

The third work in this collection was written in 1674 during the Restoration period in which Baptists were under persecution for their beliefs. It is entitled, *The Parable of the Kingdom of Heaven expounded*, which expounds the Matthew 25:1–13 passage on the Ten Virgins. In this work Knollys is concerned that many who profess faith in Christ in this time of crisis are not true followers of Christ, and so calls them to repentance.

The fourth work is written seven years later in the same period of persecution entitled, *The World that Now is and the World that is to Come*. This treatise deals with the first and second comings of Christ. The first part deals with the church in the present time, and the second part looks forward to the new era after Christ returns.

I have concluded this work with a summary of Knollys's eschatological writings of which he wrote six during the Restoration period. This flurry of eschatological writing by him was not unusual for the time because many puritans believed the end was near. In fact, as noted earlier, Knollys believed that the end would occur in 1688. This essay on Knollys's eschatology draws from these six works beginning with a general survey of his eschatology and concluding with a survey of his commentary of the Book of Revelation. I have chosen to put his thought in summary form so that the reader doesn't have to wade through all of the often repetitive and long discussion on the subject.

I have sought to be faithful to the original publications of Knollys's writings in this volume. However, I have modernized the spelling, phraseology or words that are peculiar to the seventeenth century, none of which take away from the true sense of the text. Also italics are often prolific in the

---

9. William Kiffin was born in 1616 and died in 1701. He was a Baptist minister in London during the same time that Knollys ministered in London. He was also a wealthy and successful merchant in the woollen trade.

original text, and I have chosen to remove most of them and leave them in regular print. In addition, I have removed most of the Latin and Greek from the text because its function for understanding Knollys is unnecessary. I have also inserted paragraph breaks where there were none before in order to help the reader follow Knollys's thought.

1

The Life and Death of that Old Disciple of Jesus Christ and Eminent Minister of the Gospel Hanserd Knollys

Introduction

KNOLLYS'S AUTOBIOGRAPHY ENTITLED, *The Life and Death of that Old Disciple of Jesus Christ and eminent minister of the Gospel Hanserd Knollys* that is provided in this collection of his works is a reprint of the original publication from the 1690s. The bulk of the work covers his life from birth to 1672 which places it in the middle of the Restoration period when Dissenters, like the Baptists, were considered an illegal religious group and so were persecuted by the authorities for preaching or gathering for study or worship. This is a brief autobiography and only covers some of the particulars of his life. It is really a spiritual autobiography, giving details of his conversion, calling to preach, and highlighting God's sovereign leading and care in his life. The work ends in 1672 because the autobiographical record of his final years was "unhappily lost." His close friend and fellow Baptist William Kiffin, who published the work, concludes the last 19 years of his life with these words:

> Thus far was written with his own hand, and there we must be forced to break off, though abruptly; the remaining part of his life, written by himself as this was, being (as Mr. Kiffin mentions in his preface) unhappily lost; which, because it is impossible to be supplied by any hand so particularly as his own, must be done in general, by letting the Christian reader know that this holy man's life was all of a piece, and that he maintained his zeal, fidelity, and integrity in the latter part of it as well as in the former, even to the end of it. He was not very long sick; not keeping

his chamber above five weeks, nor his bed above ten days. All the time of his sickness, he behaved himself with extraordinary patience and resignation to the divine will, longing to be dissolved and to be with Christ—not so much to be freed from pain and trouble, as from sinning, which he expressed to one near him, with a more than ordinary transport of joy. A little before his death, he wrote the following epistle, which he left as his last legacy to the church.

William Kiffin in his "Epistle to the Reader" makes clear the purpose of its publication as an encouragement to Knollys's flock upon his death. He writes, "It was the special charge God gave to his people of old, that the many signal providences and mercies that they had received from him should by them be recorded and left to their children's children, to the end that the memorial of his goodness might cause them to love and fear his name."

The publication ends with "Mr. Knollys's Last Legacy to the Church, written a little before his death," by his own hand, as an encouragement to the church with words of counsel for them.

The
Life and Death
of that Old Disciple of Jesus Christ, and
Eminent Minister of the Gospel,
Mr. Hanserd Knollys,
who died in the ninety-third year of his age.

Written with his own hand to the year 1672, and
continued in general, in an epistle by
Mr. William Kiffin.

To which he added Hanserd Knolly's
Last Legacy to the Church.

Mark the perfect, and behold the upright, for the end of that
man is peace. Psal. 37:37

LONDON:
Published by E. Huntington, High Street, Bloomsbury.

1812.

EPISTLE to the READER

It was the special charge God gave to his people of old, that the many signal providences and mercies that they had received from him should by them be recorded and left to their children's children, to the end that the memorial of his goodness might cause them to love and fear his name. Therefore, they are required to bless the Lord from the fountain of Israel, from the very beginning of all his favours towards them. It is no small favour the servants of God are made partakers of, that his people of old have left so many testimonies of the gracious goodness and providences of God toward them; being a means to strengthen the faith of his people in a dependency upon him in all those variety of dispensations that do attend them in this world: that whatever troubles they meet withal in this life, they may know that God deals no otherwise with them than he has done to those that formerly have feared his name; and may be comforted with the same comforts and supports which his servants formerly have received from God. The author of these ensuing experiences was that ancient and faithful servant of God, Mr. Hanserd Knollys, who departed this life in the ninety-third year of his age, having been employed in the works and service of Christ as a faithful minister for above sixty years. In this time he laboured without fainting under all the discouragements that attended him, being contented in all conditions, though never so poor this world; under all persecutions and sufferings, so he might therein serve his blessed Lord and Saviour. I have myself known him for above fifty-four years, and can witness to the truth of many things let by him under his own hand. It is a great pity that the last twenty years of his life cannot be found amongst his writings, which to the knowledge of many were attended with the same sufferings as formerly, and with the same holy behaviour under them. He was in that time a prisoner in the New Prison for the truth's sake many months, where with great cheerfulness he remained, comforting and encouraging all that came to visit him with many blessed exhortations to cleave to the Lord. None were sent empty away without some spiritual instructions, and many of his fellow-prisoners were greatly strengthened and comforted by the heavenly counsel that dropped from his lips. He spent much of his time there in prayer and study of the word of God, daily preaching to them the things that concern the kingdom of God.

He was chosen an Elder to a congregation in London, with whom he laboured for near fifty years, under many difficulties that attended him. Neither the poverty of the church, nor the persecutions that he endured, were any temptation to him to neglect his duty toward them, but he was willing to be poor with them in their poverty and to suffer with them in their sufferings. He was willing to labour for his own and his family's bread by keeping a school when the church were not able to supply his wants, although he wanted not opportunities to have advanced himself in the world if he would have accepted of them. But like a faithful Pastor, he chose rather to be poor and suffer affliction than to leave the duty and work he was called unto, until he arrived to the age of above ninety years. When he found weaknesses attending him, his love and affection to that poor church was such that he was daily exercising his thoughts to find an able minister for them in his room; declaring to several of his friends what great satisfaction it would be to him to see one settled amongst them; and that he would be willing to part with something of that little which he had (if there was need) for his maintenance from the church (towards his support). It pleased God to provide one for them, to their great satisfaction and rejoicing. So great was his natural affection and tender care for his daughter and grandchildren, who he knew were like to come to some distress, that he did accordingly at that great age again undertake the teaching of a school, that he might do to the uttermost of his ability to provide for them.

And having finished his work, he fell asleep in the Lord on September 19, 1691. That these experiences may be of use to all those that read the same is the desire and prayer of yours in the Lord,

WILLIAM KIFFIN.

The Life and Death of Mr. Hanserd Knollys

I, Hanserd Knollys, was born at Cawkwell, near Louth, in Lincolnshire, and was removed from there with my parents to Scarthe, near Market Grimsby, in the same County. About the sixth year of my age, I fell into a great pond, and was preserved from being drowned by the water bearing up my clothes till my father came, leaped in, and pulled me out. About the tenth year of my age, I having construed the thirty-fifth chapter of Jeremiah in my Latin Bible to my father, he took occasion to dissuade me from the love and use of strong drink, and said he would give me twenty pounds if I would drink water, but withal told me he would not have me do it to the prejudice of my health. He charged me to make no vow to God so to do, for I did not understand how sacred a thing a vow is, how it binds the soul, and that it would be sin not to perform my vow. Whereupon I drank water eleven years, and never in all that time drank any wine or strong drink.

About that time, my father kept a tutor in his house to teach me and my brother, who was a godly and conscientious young man. He gave us good instruction for our souls and convinced us of the sin of Sabbath-breaking and of disobedience to our parents. After my father had preferred our tutor to a place of greater profit, we went a little while to Grimsby free school till my father got another tutor for us into his house. One day going to the free school, we fell out and fought; upon which I was much convinced that we had sinned against God, and against our father, who had often told us we were brethren, and ought not to fall out by the way. I said, "Brother, we have sinned, come let us be friends, and pray God to pardon this and our other sins;" whereupon we both knelt down upon the ploughed land, and I prayed, wept, and made supplication to God as well as I could. I found so great assistance from God at that time that I never used any set form of prayer afterwards. This done, we both kissed each other, and went to school.

Afterwards I went to Cambridge, and there a godly minister preached on Hosea 4:17. His doctrine was that the joining to sin by often committing it after conviction of conscience for it did provoke God to give over many to the power of their corruptions and let them alone to die in their sins. I was thereby convinced that it was my case, for I had oftentimes broken the Sabbath after conviction, had disobeyed my parents, and had often told untruths. The same Lord's day at night, another godly minister preached at five o'clock upon Ephesians 2:3; and thereby I was much more convinced of my sinful condition, and that I was a child of wrath without Christ and grace, etc. which work of conviction remained strongly upon me above one year; under which I was filled with great horror, fears of hell, sore buffetings, and temptations of the devil, and made to possess the sins of my youth. Yet I prayed daily, heard all the godly ministers I could, read and searched the holy scriptures, read good books, got acquainted with gracious Christians then called Puritans, kept several days of fasting and prayer alone (wherein I did humble my soul for my sins and begged pardon and the grace of God for Christ's sake); grew strict in performing holy duties and in reformation of my own life (examining myself every night, confessing my sins and mourning for them); and had a great zeal for God and an indignation against actual sins, both committed by myself and others.

On June 29, 1629, I was ordained Deacon, and the next day, I was also ordained Presbyter by the Bishop of Peterborough, having preached above sixteen sermons before I would be ordained by way of trial of my ability for that great work of the ministry.

After my ordination, the Bishop of Lincoln gave me a small living at Humberstone, where I preached twice every Lord's day and once every holy-day. That which made me strict and laborious in preaching was partly the work of conviction upon my conscience, but more especially a providential acquaintance that I had gotten with a very godly old widow in Gainsborough, where I taught the free school before I came to Humberstone, who told me of one called a Brownist[1] who used to pray and expound scriptures in his family, whom I went sometimes to hear and with whom I had conference and very good counsel. While I was at Humberstone, there lived a very religious widow, who falling sick sent for me, and charged me that I would not depart her house in the day-time until she ended or mended, lest Satan should tempt her above her strength. The Doctor of physic had given her over; some godly ministers, friends and relations did take leave of her as a dying woman. She received nothing for several days but a little julep, which was put in her mouth with a spoon and most of it ran out again, and lay speechless two or three days with her family mourning over her and expecting her death every hour. I had brought some of my books

---

1. Brownists were those who gathered as independent separatist churches in the 1690s onward. Robert Browne formed the first Brownist church in 1581. At this time any Brownist gathering was meeting illegally.

to her house, and was studying her funeral sermon, and when I had almost finished the same, the devil set upon me with a violent suggestion that the scriptures are not the word of God. He had suggested this temptation to me diverse times before, but prevailed not. Now the tempter assaulted me with this argument: whatever you ask in the name of Christ, God will do it, but scripture was not true; and if I would put it now upon trial, I should find it not to be true, for if I would ask the woman's life in the name of Christ, God will not grant it and thereby I should know the scriptures were not true; nor are they the word of God, for his word is true. To which I answered, "Satan, you are a liar, a deceiver, and a false accuser. The holy scriptures are the word of God, and the scriptures of truth; and seeing you have often tempted me in this kind, and now do assault me again, that I may forever silence you, you wicked and lying devil, I will trust in God, and act faith in the name of Christ in that very word of his truth which you have now suggested. I will leave my study, and go and pray for her, and believe that God will hear my prayers through the intercession of Jesus Christ, and restore her life and health, that you may be found a liar." Whereupon I went into the parlour where she lay speechless without any visible motion or use of any senses; and having locked the door (candles being in the room), I knelt down by her bedside and prayed above half an hour, using my voice. Then she began to stir, toss, and struggle so much that I was constrained to stand up, and holding her in her bed, still prayed over her. Satan then gave me a great interruption, and suggested to me she was dying, and that these were the pangs of death upon her. I, notwithstanding this assault of the devil, was assisted by the Holy Spirit to pray and believe still, and in a short time she lay very quietly. I knelt down again and prayed fervently, and within half an hour, while I was yet praying, she said, "The Lord has healed me; I am restored to health." Then I returned praises to God, in which she joined with me, lifting up her eyes and hands, still saying, "I am healed."

    I rose up from my knees, and asked her how she did; "O Sir," said she, "God has heard your prayers, and has made me whole. Blessed be his holy name." Then I unlocked the door, and some of her kinsfolk and servants being at the door came in and asked me if she were dead, to whom I answered, "No." Then they asked me how she did, I bade them go to her and ask her. They replied she had been speechless for four days. I told them she could speak now; and as soon as they came to her bedside, she lifted herself up and said, "I am well, the Lord has heard prayer and healed me, I am very weak and sore in my bones, but I am in health, I pray you give me something to eat." As soon as they brought her some broth, she sat up and ate it, and took some of her julep; and from that time received strength. The next day she rose and walked with a staff; which being heard of, many godly ministers and Christians came to visit her, and to know the truth of what was told them touching her recovery. I told them it was not anything in me, but it was the Lord that had done it for his own glory, and to silence Satan, who was never suffered to tempt me in that kind afterwards. God bruised Satan under my feet, and my Lord Jesus Christ made a conquest of him, and gave me the victory, and helped me to give him the glory of it.

The next year after this I married a wife, with whom I lived forty years, and by whom I had issue seven sons and three daughters. She was a holy, discreet woman, and a meet help for me in the ways of her household, and also in the way of holiness. She was my companion in all my sufferings, travels, and hardships that I endured for the gospel. She departed this life April 30, 1671, in full assurance of eternal life and salvation.

Presently after I was married, I was convinced of some things about the worship of God (which I had conformed unto) to be sinful; namely, the surplice, the cross in baptism, and admitting wicked persons to the Lord's supper. Whereupon I resigned my living to the Bishop, who offered me a better living. I told him I could not conform any longer, and would do nothing but preach, which he connived at for two or three years. Shortly after, I was convinced that my ordination received from the Bishop was not right; and though I had preached for some years by virtue of that ordination, I had not received any seal from Christ of my ministry. For though many had been reformed and moralized, yet I knew not that I had been instrumental to convert any soul to God. Thereupon, I renounced that ordination, and silenced myself, resolving not to preach any more until I had a clear call and commission from Christ to preach the gospel. To that end and purpose, I gave myself to prayer, day and night, for several weeks together; and at last being at prayer in a wood at Anderby in Lincolnshire, where I had preached before, and prayed with loud cries and tears that Christ would count me worthy, and put me into the ministry, and show me how to glorify God in the ministry. Though I was much melted and enlarged in prayer at that time, yet I had no answer from the Lord. After prayer, I walked and meditated under the wood-side till sunset, and then went homeward, resolved not to preach till the Lord made my call to that great work of preaching the gospel clear to me. As I was going home, an answer to my prayers was given me in these words, "Go to Mr. Wheelwright[2], and he shall tell you, and show you how to glorify God in the ministry;" but I heard no voice, nor did I see any vision, only those words were plainly and articulately spoken into my ears and understanding. At this I was astonished and said, "Lord, let me not be deluded nor deceived." Then was brought to my mind that passage of Cornelius sending to Peter, who would tell him what he ought to do; whereupon I was fully persuaded it was an answer to my prayers from the Lord, and I was filled with such joy that I went on my way rejoicing, leaping, and praising God.

The next morning I went to seek out Mr. Wheelwright, who was a silenced minister whom I had heard of by some Christians that he had been instrumental to convert many souls. I knew him not, nor did I know where he was, yet I was resolved to find him, for I had heard that he was near Lincoln, about twenty-five miles from me, where he lived privately. As I was getting up on horseback, one of my neighbours coming by asked me where I was riding. I said I did not certainly know; I was going to Mr. Wheelwright, who was as I heard about Lincoln. "No," said he, "Mr. Wheelwright and his family came to dwell at a village which is but three miles from my house, for," said he, "I saw him come there but three nights since, with his family and household goods, in a coach and a wagon." There I rode presently, and found it so. I told Mr. Wheelwright that the night before I was praying as before, and was sent unto him by the Lord, etc. After he had asked me many things about the work of God upon my soul, and I had told him, he said I could not glorify God neither in the ministry, not in any other way or work, for I was building my soul upon a covenant of works, and was a stranger to the covenant of grace. At this I was startled, troubled, and somewhat amazed, but told him I was assured God had sent me to him, and by his mouth I should be instructed how to glorify God in the ministry of the gospel. I did earnestly entreat and beseech him to apply himself to give me his counsel and directions touching that matter.

Then Mr. Wheelwright opened to me the nature of the covenant of free grace, which I confessed to him I was a stranger

---

2. John Wheelwright was born about 1592, entered Sidney Sussex College in Cambridge in 1611. He was ordained a deacon and priest in December 1619. In April 1623 he was instituted as the vicar of Bilsby. He served as vicar for ten years at which time he was removed from his office for the charge of simony. Sometime after this he was preaching at Belleau in Lincolnshire but was eventually silenced by the Church authorities for his Puritan opinions. In 1636 he left for New England. It is likely during these years 1633–36 that Knollys came in contact with him.

to in a great measure, having been only under legal convictions and a spirit of bondage. Though I had some discoveries of my want of Christ, yet I had sought righteousness as it were by the works of the law, and got my peace by performing duties, and rested on them. Mr. Wheelwright desired me to consider what he had said to me, and to come to him two or three days after. So I left him at that time, and went home exceeding sorrowful about my soul's condition: but I gave myself to prayer, and begged of God to teach me the covenant of grace. To that end I searched the scriptures; and I heard one Mr. How[3] preach upon Gal. 2:20. "I live by the faith of the Son of God;" whereby I saw that I had lived a life of works, and not of faith. Then I began to see a necessity of believing in Christ for pardon and salvation; and hearing the minister say that Christ was the author, root, and only foundation of saving faith, and that God did give the faith of evidence, Heb. 11:1, in some new covenant promise, Gal. 3:14; and that those promises were given of God, 2 Pet. 1:4; I prayed that night, and next morning, and in the night season, that God would give me such a promise. The next day I locked myself in the church, and in the chancel, or choir, I prayed very earnestly, mourning and bemoaning myself and my soul's condition, fearing, and with great brokenness of spirit and many tears expressed my fears, that God would leave me and forsake me, and then I should utterly perish forever. At this time that promise, "I will never leave you, nor forsake you," was given me, which promise stopped me a little in prayer, and I broke forth into this kind of expostulation with God, saying, "Lord, who am I! I am a vile sinful sinner, the chief of sinners, most unworthy of pardon and salvation! How, Lord! Never leave you nor forsake you? Oh, infinite mercy! Oh free grace! Who am I? I have been a graceless soul, a formal professor, a legal performer of holy duties, and have gone about to establish mine own righteousness, which I now see is but filthy rags," etc. Then God gave me those two promises, Isaiah 43:22, 25 and Isaiah 54:9, 10; "But you have not called upon me, O Jacob, but you have been weary of me, O Israel. You have not brought me the small cattle of your burnt offerings, neither have you honoured me with your sacrifices. I have not caused you to serve with an offering, nor wearied you with incense. You have bought me no sweet cane with money, neither have you filled me with the fat of your sacrifices: but you have made me to serve with your

---

3. This is likely Samuel How who wrote *The Sufficiencie of the Spirits Teaching without Human Learning*.

sins, you have wearied me with your iniquities. I, even I, am he that blots out your transgressions for my own sake, and will not remember your sins." "For this is as the water of Noah unto me; for as I have sworn that the waters of Noah should not more go over the earth; so have I sworn that I would not be angry with you, nor rebuke you. For the mountains shall depart, and the hills be removed, but my kindness shall not depart from you, neither shall the covenant of my peace be removed, says the Lord, that has mercy on you." The application of these promises filled my soul with joy and peace in believing, so that I broke forth into praises and thanksgiving.

The next day I went again to Mr. Wheelwright, and told him what God had done for my soul. He said unto me, "Now you are somewhat prepared to preach Jesus Christ and the gospel of free grace to others, having been taught it of God, and having heard and learned Jesus Christ yourself." He advised me to wait still upon God in prayer, and Christ would appear again to me by his Holy Spirit in his word, and show me and teach me how to preach. I went home again and continued in prayer; and one day begging earnestly of God that, if he had designed me to that great work of preaching the gospel, then he would give me some testimony out of his holy word of his calling me thereunto. At this point, these words were spoken by his Spirit to my heart; "I have appeared unto you for this purpose, to make you a minister and a witness both of those things which you have seen, and of those things in the which I will appear unto you;" Acts 16:26. Whence I believed that now I had received a call and commission from my Lord Jesus Christ to preach the gospel of his free grace; and I blessed God and expected a further appearance of Jesus Christ unto me. That night in my sleep, Christ put into my mind that, the next Lord's day, I should preach on Rom. 8:1; "There is therefore now no condemnation to them which are in Christ Jesus, who walk not after the flesh, but after the Spirit;" and he dictated to me in my sleep, what doctrine I should preach from that text. The next day I went and told all this to Mr. Wheelwright, who said, "Now my beloved Brother and fellow-labourer in the gospel of the grace of God, Christ has given you authority, a call and a commission to preach: I pray you be humble and holy, and delay not to do your master's work," or words to that effect. That night in my sleep the Lord taught me more, and the third night also; and I retained it all in my memory, and wrote it down, and searched the scriptures which I received in my sleep for the confirmation of my doctrine. The next day, being the Lord's day, I preached that which I had received from the Lord, and God made it useful and powerful to conversion as appeared to me afterwards. Thus I was night by night taught of God to preach the doctrine of free grace, according to the tenor of the new and everlasting covenant, for three or four years together; whereby very many sinners were converted, and many believers were established in the faith. In three or four years space, I preached in three separate places, at Anderby, at Fulleby on the Hill, and at Wainfleet, where I was silenced, and from there removed to London, and then to New England with my wife and child.

About the year 1636, I was persecuted, and prosecuted in the High Commission Court by virtue of a warrant wherewith I was apprehended in Boston, and kept a prisoner in the man's house who served the warrant upon me; but God helped me to convince him, and he was so greatly terrified in his conscience that he set open his doors, and let me go away. Before I quitted my native country, I tarried so long in London, what when I went aboard, I had but six brass farthings left, and no silver nor gold, only my wife had five pounds which I knew not of, which she gave me when we came there. By the way, my little child died with convulsion fits, our beer and water stank, our biscuit was green, yellow, and blue, moulded and rotten, and our cheese also; so that we suffered much hardship, being twelve weeks on our passage. But God was gracious to us and led us safe through those great deeps, and before we went on shore came one and enquired for me, and told me a friend that was gone from Boston to Rhode Island had left me his house to sojourn in; to which we went and two families more with us, who went suddenly to their friends and other relations in the country. I, being poor, was necessitated to work daily with my hoe for the space of almost three weeks. The Magistrates were told by the ministers that I was an Antinomian, and desired they would not suffer me to abide in their district; but within the time limited by their law in that case, two strangers coming to Boston from Piscattuah, hearing of me by a mere accident, got me to go with them to that plantation, and to preach there, where I remained about four years. Being sent for back to England by my aged father, I returned with my wife and one child about three years old, and she was then great with another. We came safe to London on the 24th of December, 1641; in which year the massacre in Ireland broke forth, and the next year wars in England between King and Parliament. I was still poor and sojourned in a lodging till I had but sixpence left, and knew not how to provide for my wife and child. But having prayed to God, and encouraged my wife to trust in God and to remember former experiences, especially that word of promise God had given us and would perform to us, Heb. 13:5, having paid for my lodging I went out, not knowing to what place God's good hand of providence would lead me to receive something towards my present subsistence. About seven or eight doors from my lodging, a woman met me in the street, and told me she came to seek me and her husband sent her to tell me that there was a lodging provided and prepared in his house, by some Christian friends, for me and my wife. I told her my present condition, and went along with her to her house, and there she gave me twenty shillings, which Dr. Bastwick, a late sufferer, had given her for me, and some linens for my wife, which I received, and told her and her husband I would fetch my wife and child and lodge there. So I returned with great joy, and my wife was very much affected with this mercy and divine providence, being so suitable and seasonable a supply unto us. She said, "Oh dear husband, how sweet it is to live by faith, and trust God upon his bare word; let us rely upon him while we live, and trust him in all straits:" with many such like expressions. After we had returned praises to God, we went to our new lodging where we found all things necessary provided for us, and all charges paid for fifteen weeks. My wife, being bruised much on shipboard, had sore labour, and lay under great weakness above ten weeks, during which time two doctors, an apothecary and a surgeon, did daily attend her and administered unto her freely without any money. At the end of sixteen weeks, we had seven pounds that was given us by some Christian friends. I had spoken to some of those friends to get me some scholars, and I would provide me a convenient place to teach school; for I had rather work for my bread than be maintained by the charity of good Christians. One morning a friend came and told me a school-master on Great Tower Hill died last night, and said if I would come presently, I might probably get some of his scholars. So I went and got three or four scholars that day. My school was very much enlarged, and I continued there till I was chosen Master of Mary-Axe free school, to which place I carried sixty scholars from Great Tower Hill; and within one year I had above one hundred and forty scholars, and sixteen boarders.

This free school, and all the benefits thereof, I left to go into the Parliament's army. I preached freely to the common soldiers until I perceived the Commanders sought their own things more than the cause of God and his people, breaking their vows and solemn engagements. Then I left the army and came to London again. Shortly after, the Committee for plundered ministers sent their warrant to the then keeper in Ely House to apprehend me and bring me in safe custody before them; who took me out of my house, carried me to Ely House, and there kept me prisoner several days without any bail, and at last carried me before the Committee; who asked me several questions, to which I gave them sober and direct answers. Among others, the Chairman, Mr. White, asked me who gave me authority to preach. I told him the Lord Jesus Christ. Then he asked me if I were a minister. I answered, I was made a priest by the prelate of Peterborough, but I had renounced that ordination, and I did here again renounce the same. They asked me by what authority I preached in Bow Church. I told them after I had refused the desire of the then church-wardens three times, one day after another, their want of supply and earnestness prevailed with me, and I went there; they opened the pulpit door and I went up and preached upon Isaiah 58; and gave them such an account of that sermon (thirty ministers of the Assembly of the Divines, then so called, being present) that they could not gainsay, but bade me withdraw, and said nothing unto me. Nor would my gaoler take any charge of me, for the Committee had called for him and did chide him, and threaten to turn him out of his place for keeping me prisoner so many days. So I went away without any blame or paying of any fees. Not long after, I was brought before the Committee of Examinations, being accused to them that I occasioned great disturbance to ministers and people in Suffolk; which I gave so good and satisfactory an account of to them, that upon their report thereof to the House of Commons, they ordered that I might preach in any part of Suffolk when the minister of that place did not preach. This was all the satisfaction I reaped for the charge of sixty pounds which that trouble cost me, to clear my innocence, and the honour of the gospel; which expense I put upon Christ's score; for whose gospel and preaching Jesus Christ from that text, Col. 3:11, "But Christ is all, and in all" I was stoned out of the pulpit; prosecuted at a privy Sessions; fetched out of the country sixty miles up to London; and was constrained to bring up four or five witnesses of good repute and credit to prove and vindicate myself from false accusations.

    Sometime after that, I was summoned before a Committee in the chamber (called the Queen's Court) at Westminster, whereof Mr. Leigh was Chairman, for preaching without holy orders. To which I answered that I was in holy orders. Some of the Committee told the Chairman I had renounced my ordination by the Bishop. In the Committee for plundered ministers, I confessed that I did so, but that I was ordained since in a church of God, according to the order of the gospel of Christ; the manner of which I then declared to the Committee before Mr. Nye and other ministers present. At last the Committee, by their Chairman, commanded me to preach no more. I told them I would preach the gospel, both publicly and from house to house; for it was more equal to obey Christ who had commanded me than them who forbid me. So I went away, and ceased not to teach and preach Jesus Christ, and him crucified.

I was then pastor to a church which I had gathered two or three years before, in the year 1645, with whom I have walked ever since; except that I was absent from them sometimes upon just occasions and with their leave, or forced from them by violent persecution. My chief means of livelihood has been by teaching school, wherein God was pleased to make me serviceable in my generation; to communicate liberally to the poor of the church, and to strangers that stood in need; and plentifully to provide all things necessary and convenient for my wife and children through God`s blessing upon my honest labours. I received from the church always according to their ability, most of the members of the church being poor; but I coveted no man`s gold nor silver, but chose rather to labour, knowing, "It is more blessed to give than to receive." Nor did I neglect the whole of my duty as a pastor, but preached two or three times in the week, and visited the members of the church from house to house, especially when they were sick. During twenty-five years now past, the church has continued in the Apostle's doctrine, fellowship, in breaking of bread, and in prayer; without division and separation of any part or party within: though some few particular members, being led away by some error in their judgment, have forsaken the assembling of themselves with the church as the manner of some is and was in the Apostles' time.

In the year 1660, upon Venner's rising, and others with him who made an insurrection in the city of London, many other godly and peaceable persons and I were taken out of their own dwelling houses and brought to Wood-street Compter, to Newgate, and other prisons, though we were innocent, and knew not of their design. At this time, I suffered imprisonment eighteen weeks, till we were delivered by an act of pardon upon the King`s coronation unto all offenders except murderers. We were above four hundred prisoners kept all this time in Newgate, because we refused to take the oaths of allegiance and supremacy.[4] After I was set at liberty out of prison, I went to Holland and then up into Germany with my wife and two of my children, where we sojourned about two or three years. In my absence, one Colonel Legge, a Bed-chamber man, and Lieutenant of the Ordnance, charged me in the Court of Exchequer for keeping a house and ground from the King; against whom I stood suit by my Attorney. But when Col. Legge could not get my house from me by law, he and some others brought a troop of soldiers, took it by force, thrust out those persons I had left in possession, and kept possession by soldiers both of my house, garden, and goods, which had cost me above 700 pds. to purchase. This estate I bought of the Artillery Company of London, to whom I paid 300 pds. and laid out 400 pds. more in building upon the ground; the whole of which I had paid for. I had at the same time 200 pds. in Weaver's Hall, which was given away to the King, among many greater sums of other men's money. I spent above 150 pds. more in Holland and Germany; and when I had spent all that, I was forced to sell all my goods there to bring me to England again.

In this return, I met with two remarkable acts of providence towards me, my wife, and two children. I had agreed with a Skipper at Cullen in Germany to carry me and my family to Rotterdam for a sum of money, and he was to pay all the tolls and licences; which he did at two or three places until we came where we were strangers. Then he made me pay licences at two places, and at a place called Rurote upon the river Rhine, he made me pay both toll and license, and kept me there two or three days at great charges. My wife sat down very sad in a harbour or victualling-house. A gentleman came in, and observing of her, asked me what the gentlewoman ailed. I told him she was my wife, and he understanding the Latin tongue, asked me what the matter was. I told him all my case and what my troubles were. "Well," said he, "if you be a son of Abraham, God will deliver you." So he went into his chamber, and sent for the skipper and toll-masters, and caused him to produce our agreement. And understanding how he had wronged me (he being lord and chief over the toll-masters there), he commanded them to take our goods from him, and to hire us another skipper to carry us and our goods to Rotterdam. He also made the

---

4. Those who desired to hold public or military offices or places of trust were required to take the oaths of allegiance and supremacy acknowledging that the king was the supreme head of the Church of England. These regulations were laid down in the corporation Act of 1661 and the Test Act of 1673. These Acts essentially did not allow nonconformists, dissenters and Roman Catholics from taking up official positions.

skipper that had done me wrong to return me so much as I had paid for licenses all the way there.

After we were come to Rotterdam, and my wife and son and daughter were gone to England, God made two Catholics in Cullen instrumental to prevail with the Prince Dewit to send me, by a bill of exchange, 160 Rix dollars for a house that I had built in his country and could not sell. This money I received at Rotterdam, and came to my wife and children, whom I found at a friend's house in London. Again I set upon teaching school, and by God's blessing upon my honest labours, have provided things honest, necessary, and convenient for my family. To my eldest son I had given sixty pounds per annum, during his life, which he enjoyed above twenty-one years, when he died. To my next son, that lived to be married, I gave the full value of 250 pds. in money, house, school, and household goods, and left him fifty scholars in his schoolhouse. To my only daughter then living, I gave upon her marriage above 300 pds. in money, annuity, plate, linen, and household stuff, and left her husband fifty scholars in the said school-house in partnership with my said son. To my youngest son, that lived to be married, I gave more than 300 pds. sterling; besides it cost me above sixty pounds in his apprenticeship and forty pounds afterwards.

Thus my heavenly Father made up my former losses with his future blessings, even in outward substance; besides a good increase of grace and experience in the space of forty years that I and my dear faithful wife lived together. We moved several times with our whole family; once from Lincolnshire to London, and then from London to New England. We moved once from England into Wales, twice from London into Lincolnshire; once from London to Holland, and from there into Germany, then to Rotterdam, and then to London again. In these removings, I gained great experiences of God's faithfulness, goodness, and truth in his great and precious promises; and I have gained some experience of my own heart's deceitfulness, and the power of my own corruptions; the reigning power of Christ, and his captivating and subduing my sins; making conquests of the devil, world, and sin, and then giving me the victory, and causing me to triumph and to bless his most holy name. Three things made my latter sufferings very easy to be endured: 1. The former straits and hardships which I had undergone with patience. 2. The present lively acts and exercise of grace, especially faith and hope, under those latter and greater trials. 3. The light of God's countenance, and the full assurance of his love, and of eternal life. I would not lack those experiences and teaching that my soul has enjoyed, for all that ever I suffered.

My wilderness-mercies, sea-mercies, city-mercies, and prison-mercies afforded me very many and strong consolations. The spiritual sights of the glory of God, the divine sweetness of the spiritual and providential presence of my Lord Jesus Christ, and the joys and comforts of the Holy and Eternal Spirit, communicated to my soul; together with suitable and seasonable scriptures of truth; have so often, and so powerfully revived, refreshed, and strengthened my heart in the days of my pilgrimages, trials, and sufferings, that the sense, yea the life and sweetness of it, still abides upon my heart, and has engaged my soul to live by faith, to walk humbly , and to desire and endeavour to excel in holiness, to God's glory and the example of others. Though I confess many of the Lord's ministers, and some of the Lord's people, have excelled and outshined me, with whom God has not been at so much cost, nor pains, as he has been at with me. I am a very unprofitable servant, but yet by grace I am what I am.

In the beginning of my ministry, I studied in the forenoon, visited my religious acquaintances in the afternoon, and some of my natural relations. I preached constantly twice, often three times, and some Lord's days four times: at Holton at seven in the morning; at Humberstone at nine; at Scarthe at eleven; at Humberstone at three o'clock, all in the same day. I also preached every holy-day once; at every burial, poor or rich. I have most commonly preached three or four times every week, if in any measure of health for above forty years together; except now and then I got some godly person to preach for me, but rarely. When I was in prison, I did preach usually every day, if well; and God was pleased to confirm my call unto that great work 1. By the conversion of many sinners, who having declared the dealings of God with their souls, testified God did convince them, convert them, and establish many of them by my ministry through the powerful and effectual operation of his Holy Spirit and word, preached by me unto them. 2. By some healing power of God put forth upon the sick and infirm bodies of several persons, who were suddenly restored to health immediately in time of prayer with them, or by and through faith in Jesus Christ, especially in this City of London; and of the sickness called the plague, both in former years and in the year 1665. Not to me, but to God, be given glory and praise, for in his name, through faith in his name, they were healed. 3. By enabling me, standing by me, and strengthening me, by his Holy Spirit and sanctifying grace, to preach the gospel, in season and out of season, with all boldness; neither being ashamed, nor afraid to bear my testimony for Christ, his gospel, churches, ministry, worship, and ordinances, against the antichristian powers, ministers, worshippers, and traditions of the beast, the great mystical whore, and the false prophet.[5] Nor have I been terrified by the adversary, by virtue of the Acts of Parliament, touching private meetings and conventicles, commencing May 10, 1670. I was taken at a meeting in George Yard, and the then Lord Mayor committed me to the Compter in Bishopsgate for preaching there; but having favour in the eyes of the keepers, I had liberty to preach to the prisoners twice every day of the week, in the Common Hall, where most of the prisoners came and heard me; and some of them blessed God that ever I came to that prison. Soon after I was set at liberty at the Sessions in Old Bailey, God made me his prisoner, by a sharp and painful distemper in my bowels, by which he brought me near to the grave; but in time of my greatest extremity, God remembered mercy, forgave my iniquity, healed my disease, and restored my life from death. No tongue can express my pains, yet God gave me much patience, in which I possessed my soul. I had 1. A very clear discovery from the Lord of the causes why he so contended with me; one was the meritorious cause of some former visitations, and especially of this sore disease. 2. I saw the sin of my sinful nature, which was not so crucified as that it was destroyed, but I found some motions of it of late stirring in my sinful heart. The sense of this was a very sore burden and trouble to my soul in this day of my calamity, for which I mourned in secret before the Lord, and lay at the throne of grace loathing myself, and begging that God would kill that sin and destroy it, and all the rest of my sins. I received this answer: his grace was sufficient for me, he had pardoned, and he would subdue and destroy that and all other of my iniquities, according to his everlasting covenant of free grace. Satan was sometimes very busy during this time of sickness, and tempted me sorely in the night season, suggesting to me that I was but a hypocrite, that my evidences for heaven were not good. God helped me to resist him steadfastly in the faith, and he fled away. Another cause why the Lord now contended with me was for the trial and exercise of those graces which he had given me. It was the trial of my faith and the exercise of my patience, and that I might be to his praise, and an example to weak believers whose eyes were upon

---

5. He is referring to the Roman Catholic Church. For more on this see the final chapter which addresses Knollys's eschatology.

me, and were observing and hearkening how I behaved myself under all the great rebukes and chastisements of the Lord upon me. For they had heard that God had taken one grandchild away by death, and was visiting another, who was above sixteen years old, with the small-pox, and she was likely to die; and one son died and was buried during my sickness; and my eldest son was dead and buried in the country, of which I was told before I was recovered: my other son's wife had sore labour, a dead man-child, and she likely to die; and my dear loving wife then began to be sorely afflicted with a pain and swelling in her face, of which she since died.

But God did give a proportionable measure of faith and patience to me his poor unworthy servant, under all these his fatherly chastisements; he strengthened me with strength in my soul, and upheld me with the right hand of his righteousness, so that I fainted not nor was I weary, his rod and his staff did comfort me; he brought out my will unto a free submission, subjection, and resignation to his own most wise and holy will. Yea, my Father's visitations so preserved my soul that I sang and rejoiced under the sights and smiles of Christ, even while I was sighing and sorrowing for my transgressions.

Two learned, well practised, and judicious Doctors of physic had daily visited me, and consulted several days together, and I was fully persuaded that they did what they possibly could to effect a cure: and knew also that God did not succeed their honest and faithful endeavours with his blessing. Although God had given a signal and singular testimony of his special blessing by each of them unto others of their patients, at least sixteen, at the same time I resolved to take no more sick, but would apply to that holy ordinance of God appointed by Jesus Christ, the great Physician of value, in James 5:14, 15. "Is any sick among you? Let him call for the elders of the church, and let them pray over him, anointing him with oil in the name of the Lord: and the prayer of faith shall save the sick, and the Lord shall raise him up; and if he have committed sins, they shall be forgiven him" and I sent for Mr. Kiffin, and Mr. Vavsor Powell, who prayed over me, and anointed me with oil in the name of the Lord. The Lord did hear prayer, and heal me; for there were many godly ministers and gracious saints that prayed day and night for me (with submission to the will of God) that the Lord would spare my life, and make me more serviceable to his church, and to the saints, whose prayers God heard. As an answer to their prayers, I was perfectly healed, but remained weak long after. My dear wife was greatly afflicted day and night, but the Lord gave her a great measure of faith and patience even to the end. She enjoyed the light of God's countenance, had full assurance of his love, the pardon of her sins, and of eternal life; and having patiently endured six months sore pains, upon the thirtieth of the second month, called April 1671 (being the Lord's day), about four or five o'clock, slept in Jesus. I was doing my Master's work at that time in the congregation, and towards the end of my sermon had a strong impulse upon my spirit that my dear wife was departing; and in my prayer after sermon was drawn forth by faith to commend her to God that gave her to me, and blessed him for receiving her soul into Abraham's bosom, and placing her among the spirits of just men made perfect in the paradise of God.

Since the death of my wife, it has pleased God to stretch forth his hand upon my only son then living, and to afflict him with a deep consumption, occasioned as I judge by grief for his dearly loving and beloved Mother, for he drooped ever since she was first taken ill of that distemper of rheum, which fell from her head into her face, of which she died; and he has been worse and worse ever since. Having had great expenses and a great charge of dear relations, and owing some considerable debts, I was necessitated to teach school again in my old age, that I might pay my debts, succour my dear relations, and not be too great a burden to the church of God: and this I have willingly and cheerfully undertaken, that if persecution do come upon me again (which I expect and prepare for) and I shall be hauled to prison or forced to fly, it may be my mercy and comfort (as at all other times of my many removals in the days of my pilgrimage and persecutions) that no person shall have any occasion to come to me and say, "Pay me what you owe me before you go;" for I desire to owe no man anything but love, and honestly to pay every man his own: and if death seize on my body, that I may leave enough of my own behind me to pay all my debts, and a little for the relief of God's poor, and some of my poorest natural relations. I had a summoning in June last to prepare myself for the grave, by a sudden and sore fit of the wind-cholick and vomiting; and on the the 3rd of October last, 1671, I had another summons to be ready to depart this life, by another sudden, more violent tormenting fit of the wind-cholick and vomiting. I am alarmed by these awakening visitations of the Lord to prepare and be ready, that when my Lord and Master comes, or calls for me to come to him, I may be found so doing that he may say, "Well done you good and faithful servant; enter you also into the joys of your Master."

The next trial my heavenly Father saw needful for me to be exercised under was the sickness and death of my then only living son, my Isaac, my most loving and beloved son, who was translated the 15th day of November, 1671; which great trial and loss God made gain to him, and easy to me, by a manifest and powerful work of conversion, repentance, and faith upon his soul in the time of his sickness; which administered much comfort to me, so that I sorrowed not for him as one without hope, who exercised great patience under his very great pain, soreness, and burning fever, while his flesh, marrow, and moisture consumed, and acted faith and hope very lively and constantly upon Christ in that word, "And him that comes to me, I will in no wise cast out," John 6:37; very often expressing his former bondage and slavery to sin and Satan which he bewailed; and acknowledged often God's free and rich grace in giving him Christ, and pardon, and salvation now at last, which he had neglected the offers and tenders of so often. Some combats he had, but after a manifestation of Christ to his soul, he died in faith and peace.

And albeit my natural affections caused me to weep often, and the sense of God's hand and rod upon me caused me to mourn very much in secret, yet the Almighty by his rod and staff did so comfort me that I walked through this valley also of the shadow of death, without fear of evil; and was assisted, and enabled, to perform the work of my ministry in the congregation without any omission or interruption. And that very night my only son died, the Lord brought to my mind that scripture; "Feed your people with your rod," Micah 7:14: which was made a seasonable, suitable, and powerful word by the teachings of the Holy Spirit unto my soul, in my solitary condition; who thus administered food, yea, and a feast also to my soul. By this rod of God, I had served into my soul a dish of sour or bitter herbs, I mean sorrow for my sins; but I fed also on the Paschal Lamb, in whose blood I saw all my sins washed away; and the Spirit of God witnessed with my spirit that I was a child of God, and one of those children with whom God will keep covenant, and not take his love from, though he visited my transgressions with the rod, and my iniquities with stripes, Psal. 89: 28-34. This scripture was then brought again with power to my heart. The next dish of spiritual food under this rod which God brought me, or sent me by his Spirit in his word to feed upon, was full of love; then that holy scripture came to me, not in word only, but in power, in the Holy Ghost, and in much assurance; "As many as I love, I rebuke and chasten: be zealous therefore and repent. Behold,

I stand at the door and knock: if any man hear my voice, and open the door, I will come in to him, and will sup with him, and he with me," Rev. 3:19, 20. In this scripture, he showed me his face; and I saw my Father's face in that glass of the gospel, "For whom the Lord loves he chastens, and scourges every son whom he receives. If ye endure chastening, God deals with you as with sons: for what son is he whom the father chastens not?" Heb. 12:6, 7; which the Holy Spirit held forth to me by this rod, and shed abroad in my heart the love of the Father in his Son Jesus Christ. After this, the next day God gave me a dish of spiritual fruits by this rod to feed upon, served up in that holy scripture, "No chastening for the present seems to be joyous, but grievous: nevertheless, afterward it yields the peaceable fruit of righteousness, unto them which are exercised thereby." After God had thus fed me, and feasted me several days and nights together with this rod, he very graciously pronounced his blessing upon me in these words; "Blessed is the man whom you chasten, O Lord, and teach him out of your law," or word, unto which I was helped heartily to say "Amen, It is good for me that I have been afflicted," etc. After God had thus communed with me from his mercy-seat, and had instructed me, I experienced such divine loves, shinings, and perpetual sweetness, as Jonathan did when he tasted a little honey-dew on the end of the rod in his hand, and was enlightened and refreshed; so that I was enlivened or revived, fed and feasted by the rod and word, even the bond of God's everlasting covenant of free grace and love.

About four or five months after the death of my son, his wife remarried a gentleman of 300 pds. per annum, and left me engaged to receive and pay all my son's debts. To preserve his credit, and his wife's, I borrowed 200 pds. for that purpose, and suffered the loss of it, which necessitated me still to keep school. And I having a granddaughter with me three years before, she, being nineteen years old, did take the charge of my household affairs, and of my boarders, who managed all things with so much discretion that my life was very comfortable, and I had great content. In September 1672, my only daughter's husband went by her consent into the country, and left her.

Thus far was written with his own hand, and there we must be forced to break off, though abruptly; the remaining part of his life, written by himself as this was, being (as Mr. Kiffin mentions in his preface) unhappily lost; which, because it is impossible to be supplied by any hand so particularly as his own, must be done in general, by letting the Christian reader know that this holy man's life was all of a piece, and that he maintained his zeal, fidelity, and integrity in the latter part of it as well as in the former, even to the end of it. He was not very long sick; not keeping his chamber above five weeks, nor his bed above ten days. All the time of his sickness, he behaved himself with extraordinary patience and resignation to the divine will, longing to be dissolved and to be with Christ—not so much to be freed from pain and trouble, as from sinning, which he expressed to one near him, with a more than ordinary transport of joy. A little before his death, he wrote the following epistle, which he left as his last legacy to the church.

Mr. Knollys's
Last Legacy to the Church.
Written a little before his death.

To the church of which I am Pastor: grace, love, and peace by Jesus Christ our Lord and Saviour, Amen.

Holy Brethren, partakers of the heavenly calling, I not being able to preach any more unto you, do take liberty by writing to give you this as my last counsel; and I hope the whole church will seriously consider what I have written, as the last words of your very aged Pastor, whose departure, as I hope, is at hand.

First of all, I do humbly beseech my reverend and beloved brother Steed[6], for Christ's sake, that the fervent love to the church, and the watchful care over the particular members of it, expressed and published in his little epistle touching singing, may be revived; and also that the brotherly love of the ministering brethren, and likewise of all my beloved brethren who are helps in government, many be stirred up to help, to assist, to provoke the rest unto good works, Gal. 4:18.

Now I do unfeignedly, and without vain boasting, commend many of you, my beloved brethren and sisters, for continuing in the Apostle's doctrine and fellowship, in breaking of bread, and in prayer (but as for the rest, who forsake the assembling of themselves with the church on the Lord's day, I commend them not), especially not only in this time of liberty, but when it was a time of violent persecution, when I was shut up for a year and four months (blessed be God for prison-mercies) in New Prison. And having mentioned that time of persecution, can I pass it by without commending the constant assembling of our brethren and sisters all that time, every Lord's day, to worship God? And may I not with great comfort commend the labour of love of our ministered brethren in the work and doctrine of the gospel, without ceasing, (as you well know) and among whom they still labour and faint not? And now some of our younger brethren begin to improve their gifts and talents for the glory of God, and the education of the church, whom I desire may be encouraged.

Another thing very commendable in this church is the charity which they have added to their brotherly kindness, 2 Pet. 1:7. It was great brotherly kindness which was manifested

---

6. Robert Steed co-pastored with Knollys at the Broken Wharf church from 1689 and then took over as pastor when Knollys died in 1691.

to the church by those brethren who looked out our Meeting House, and prepared it for us as it now is; and unto this, many of our brethren and sisters have added their charity, in a free and very liberal collection and contribution, given into the Trustees of the fund: and I hope they will be ready to do the like again, when the like necessities call for it. Read I pray you the eighth and ninth chapters of the second Epistle unto the church of Corinth; all this and much more are the riches of grace, which God has freely given by our Lord Jesus Christ unto this church, for his own glory.

Nevertheless, I must in love and faithfulness to your precious and gracious souls, holy and beloved, tell you of some things, not to shame you (for I myself am found guilty as well as you and more than some of you), but to warn you and to counsel you, as a father does his children; and they are these.

First, that several of us are fallen in some degree from our first love, cooled in our spiritual affections to Jesus Christ, and to the saints. Must not you and I confess that it is not with us now as it was in the day of our first espousals? God the Father, the Word, and the Holy Spirit remember it, Jerem. 2:1, 2; and we should remember from whence we are fallen, and should say, "I will go and return to my first husband, for then was it better with me than now," Hos. 2:7: Rev 2:4, 5.

Now the first part of my counsel, which I desire to take and receive from Christ and give unto you, my dearly beloved brethren and sisters, who are convinced and have confessed it before the Lord on several days of fasting and prayer, is this—

First, I do counsel you to repent, Rev. 2:5; and I must tell you, beloved, that our assembling once in four weeks, and spending four hours, from eleven to three, in praying and preaching as we have often done, is not such a fast as will make our voice to be heard on high, Isaiah 58:3,4. Several things are essentially necessary to evangelical repentance, that it may be acceptable unto God by Jesus Christ. Namely, godly sorrow, which works repentance never to be repented of, 2 Cor. 7:9, 10. A broken, contrite spirit. Read these Scriptures, "The sacrifices of God are a broken spirit; a broken and a contrite heart, O God, you will not despise." Psal. 51:17: "Be afflicted, and mourn, and weep: let your laughter be turned to mourning, and your joy to heaviness. Humble yourselves in the sight of the Lord, and he shall life you up," James 4:9, 10. "But to this man will I look, even to him that is poor, and of a contrite spirit, and trembles at my word," Isaiah 66:2. "For thus says the high and lofty One that inhabits eternity, whose name is Holy, I dwell in the high and holy place; with him also that is of a contrite and humble spirit, to revive the spirit of the humble, and to revive the heart of the contrite ones," Isaiah 57:15. "And I will pour upon the house of David, and upon the inhabitants of Jerusalem, the spirit of grace, and of supplications, and they shall look upon me whom they have pierced, and they shall mourn for him, as one mourns for his only son, and shall be in bitterness for him, as one that is in bitterness for his first-born. In that day shall there be a great mourning in Jerusalem, as the mourning of Hadadrimmon in the valley of Megiddon," Zech. 12:10, 11. Alas, where are our tears of godly sorrow, our broken hearts, and our afflicted souls? Reformation after humiliation? "Repent and do your first works," Rev. 2:5. O holy brethren, let us do so, let you and I beg grace, that we may both mourn and turn from all our sins to the Lord, with all our hearts.

We have cause to repent of our formality and Laodicean lukewarmness, especially for want of zeal for the house of God, Psal. 69:9; "For the zeal of your house has eaten me up." "As many as I love, I rebuke and chasten: be zealous therefore and repent," Rev. 3:19; John 2:17.

Secondly, I counsel you to be zealous; zeal is a fervent and constant affection of a gracious soul in a good thing, managed with discretion, Gal. 4:18. If our zeal be not fixed upon a right object, and good matter, it may be hot and great, but it cannot be good. Compare the zeal of Paul, Phil. 3:6; with the zeal of Epaphras, Col. 4:12, 13.

To guide our zeal aright, two things especially ought to accompany it.

First, "the light of knowledge:"Brethren, my heart's desire and pray to God for Israel is, that they might be saved. For I bear them record, that they have a zeal of God, but not according to knowledge. For they, being ignorant of God's righteousness, and going about to establish their own righteousness, have not submitted themselves unto the righteousness of God." Read the words again and again, and as often as you read this paper. Many professors of the law then were very zealous of establishing their own legal righteousness; and many professors of the gospel now are as zealous to establish their own legal righteousness, and not Christ's. Oh! say some, if I could pray so, mourn so as others do; if I were so holy and so humble, etc., then I would believe. Oh! say others, if I could get power over my corruptions, and strength against Satan's temptations, and victory over the allurements of this present evil world, then I would believe; but I have a heart so full of vile affections, vain thoughts, and doubts, that I cannot believe. Consider, are praying, mourning, humbling our souls, gospel duties? Even so is believing a gospel duty, which God commands; "And this is his commandment, that we should believe on the name of his Son Jesus Christ;" I John 3:23; and he threatens to damn those that hear the gospel preached, and will not believe, Mark 16:16.

Secondly, the aim and end of our zeal must always be the glory of God, and guided as I said by discretion, wise as well as warm; greatest zeal in greatest matters, and lesser zeal in lesser matters. Compare Gal. 5:11, 13 with 1 Cor. 11:13-16 and Prov. 19:11.

My counsel also is, and I humbly beseech our honoured and beloved Elder, and entreat our ministering brethren who are helps in government, to join together to set in order these things. I mean no other things than those holy administrations which Christ, his Apostles, and Disciples, practised in the beginning. Search these scriptures, I Pet. 2:21; Phil 3:17; Luke 14:16-22; Acts 28:23, 24, 28-31; I Cor. 14:13, 23, 24, 25, 29; 1 Tim. 4:13; Col. 4:16; 1 Thess. 5:27; Rev. 1:3. Consider, holy brethren, that as reading and expounding are two different administrations, so are prophesying and preaching, yet both gospel ordinances, Rom 12:6, 7.

Fourthly, and lastly, my counsel to the church is that you will look out a Minister of Jesus Christ, whom he has in some competent measure qualified with such ministerial gifts and graces, as may make him worthy of so great honour as is due to a Pastor, and Elder of the church of God, yea, of double honour, I Tim. 5:17; both of maintenance and obedience, Heb. 13:17.

And now my dearly beloved brethren and sisters, I commit you all to the word of his grace which is able to build you up, and to give you an inheritance among them which are sanctified. So I remain, while in this tabernacle,

Your Brother in the Lord,

Hanserd Knollys.

2

Christ Exalted

Introduction to Christ Exalted

It appears that Knollys came to accept believer's baptism sometime in the year 1643 while he was a member of Henry Jessey's separatist congregation in London. In 1644 he left the church to begin a new work based on his new found baptist principles at Great St. Helens in London. It was during this time in early 1645 that Knollys was found preaching the gospel in Suffolk in at least two places, Debenham and Stradbrook. On February 13 he preached in the town of Stradbrooke, and the next day ten miles down the road at Debenham. In the initial publication of *Christ Exalted* the book contained first, the sermon he preached at Debenham on Colossians 3:11, and then the sermon he preached at Stadbrooke on Ephesians 1:4. The title page read:

Christ Exalted

in

A SERMON

Begun to be preached at Debenham in Suffolk upon the 14th day of February last upon Colossians 3:11

by Hanserd Knollys

Who was stoned out of the pulpit (as he was preaching by a company of rude fellows, and poor women of that town; who were sent for, called together, and set on by a Malignant High-Constable, who lives in the same town

Also,

ANOTHER SERMON

Preached at Stradbrooke in Suffolk, the 13th day of February last, concerning sanctification; Eph 1:4

It is uncertain why Knollys chose to add the sermon from Stradbrooke to this pamphlet as it was due to his sermon on Colossians 3:11 in Debenham that he encountered trouble. It is quite probable that Knollys's problems began in Stradbrooke with his message preached on Ephesians 1:4. We do know that in the second edition of *Christ Exalted*, published a year later, Knollys states that he "had the meeting house doors shut against him, and was stoned out of the pulpit," for the content of three sermons which he put together in this edition. Why he added the sermon on Ephesians 1:4 to the first edition and then added the third sermon on Luke 19:10 to the second edition is unknown. It is assumed that he preached all three of these sermons in these two towns. But in his defence against the charges he, at first, only published two of the sermons.

It was for his doctrine found in these three sermons that he was not permitted to preach in meeting houses and then eventually stoned. Exactly what it was that offended the townspeople is unknown.[1] The basic message of these sermons is that Christ is exalted in the salvation of sinful humans, that Christ has come to save poor wretched sinners, and that those who are saved are to be a holy people. It has been suggested by Simon Woodman in his essay on this event that "this 'doctrine' thus posed a direct challenge to the prevailing Anglican understanding of a church comprised of all those in a parish who had been baptised in the church from infancy. The inference being from Knollys" 'doctrine" is that infant baptism did not make one saved and that living within the perish did not make one part of God's holy people."[2]

---

1. Regarding this incident Knollys simply states in his autobiography, "I was brought before the Committee of Examinations, being accused to them that I occasioned great disturbance to ministers and people in Suffolk; which I gave so good and satisfactory an account of to them, that upon their report thereof to the House of Commons, they ordered that I might preach in any part of Suffolk when the minister of that place did not preach. This was all the satisfaction I reaped for the charge of sixty pounds which that trouble cost me, to clear my innocence, and the honour of the gospel; which expense I put upon Christ's score; for whose gospel and preaching Jesus Christ from that text, Col. 3:11, 'But Christ is all, and in all' I was stoned out of the pulpit; prosecuted at a privy Sessions; fetched out of the country sixty miles up to London; and was constrained to bring up four or five witnesses of good repute and credit to prove and vindicate myself from false accusations" (Knollys, *Life and Death*, 32–33).

2. Woodman, "Stoned in the Pulpit," 327–28.

This is quite plausible. He goes on to suggest, following the research of Muriel James, that Knollys could have angered some Presbyterians in East Anglia a month earlier, when he published a letter "complaining about their opposition to the toleration of dissenting preachers."[3] In addition, James suggests that Knollys's troubles while in America in 1638 might have been used against him while in Debenham. The governor of Massachusetts, John Winthrop, had family in Suffolk who heard of the troubles and therefore opposed this troublemaker, Knollys.[4] These are all good suggests but we can't be certain of any of them.

As Woodman has also suggested we mustn't forget that during this time Baptists were associated with Anabaptism on the Continent. As I have shown in my earlier work on Knollys, to be associated with Continental Anabaptism was to be considered a pariah and so quite dangerous to the church and state.[5]

Whatever the specific reason for Knollys's stoning, he was to appear before the Committee of Examinations that was formed by the Presbyterian controlled Parliament. They were particularly bent on persecuting Baptists who they feared were Anabaptists on English soil. In preparation for this meeting Knollys published this first edition of his sermons in 1645 which would clearly demonstrate to the committee his orthodoxy.

In the following year Knollys having been exonerated by the committee publish a second edition. In this edition the only difference from the previous one was the title page along with an additional sermon sandwiched between the two original sermons. This sermon was on Luke 19:10 where Jesus proclaims, "For the Son of Man has come to seek and to save that which was lost." The title page for this sermon reads quite differently from the 1645 edition:

CHRIST EXALTED: A LOST SINNER

Sought and saved by Christ, God's people are a holy people.

Being the sum of diverse sermons preached in Suffolk

By Hanserd Knollys

Who, for this doctrine, had the meeting house doors shut against him, and was stoned out of the pulpit (as he was preaching) by a rude multitude who were gathered together, and set on by a

---

3. Woodman, "Stoned in the Pulpit, 328.
4. Woodman, "Stoned in the Pulpit, 328; James, *Religious Liberty on Trial*, 141–42.
5. Howson, *Erroneous and Schismatical Opinions*, 194–242.

> malignant high-constable, which has been proven by diverse witnesses of good reputation before the Honourable Committee of Examination at London.

Knollys, having been exonerated from the charges before the Parliamentary Committee, published this second edition of *Christ Exalted*. It is this edition that is printed in this volume. I have provided an outline for each of the sermons so the reader can more easily follow Knollys's thought. Each of the sermons expounds on a certain doctrine drawn from a Scripture text, and follows the puritan pattern of briefly explaining the text of Scripture, stating and elaborating on the doctrine, and concluding with application, defined in the sermons as "Use".

The first sermon which was preached at Debenham on February 14, 1645 expounded the text of Colossians 3.11, that "Christ is all, and in all." The doctrine of his sermon is to show that Christ is all and in all in the new regenerate man. He does this by explaining first who is the new man and then how Christ is all in all in the new man. He has a lengthy application primarily focused on exhorting believers to prize Christ. He closes the sermon with an exhortation to believers and unbelievers: to believers he exhorts them to let Christ be all in all in their justification, their gifts and graces of sanctification, and in all their affections, words and actions. To the unbelievers he calls them to seek Christ for the new man.[6]

In the second sermon, entitled, "The Chief publican's conversion or a sinner sought and saved by Christ" is based on Luke 19:10 where Jesus encounters the tax collector Zacchaeus who receives Jesus into his home, and more importantly the salvation that he offers him. After briefly explaining the text he states that his doctrine drawn from it is "the man Christ Jesus must seek and save lost sinners." He expands on this doctrine by showing who the man Christ Jesus is, how he saves sinners, what he saves them from, and lastly why he saves sinners. The exhortation is significant but much shorter than in the first sermon. Here he focuses primarily on those who profess faith in Christ with concern that they are truly converted, and on those who are sinners that they can be saved by believing in Christ.

The third sermon in this collection is the one that he preached in Stradbrooke on February 13, 1645 on Ephesians 1:4, entitled, "That we should be

---

6. As I have argued in my book *Erroneous and Schismatical Opinions*, Knollys shows himself to be a high Calvinist in regards to the salvation of the sinner which is similar to the theological position of John Owen (138–158). High Calvinists believed that salvation was totally of God, only God could draw a sinner to himself and grant him faith to believe but they also believed that the unbeliever was responsible and accountable for their sin and response to the gospel. Therefore, the gospel was to be preached to sinners, and sinners were to be called to seek Christ for salvation.

holy." As per the other sermons he briefly explains verses 1–4 and then puts for the resulting doctrine as, 'God will have his people to be a holy people.' He first, gives other scriptural support for this doctrine, citing several New Testament texts, and then gives the reasons that God's people should be holy. This sermon is primarily taken up with application. He shows how God makes us holy, that is, by working a real change in the whole person which occurs through his Word by His Spirit; and so, on this basis, we can determine who are only legal, formal or carnal professors of faith. And by this knowledge the true believer should be encouraged when under persecution to know that God has chosen them to be holy and will faithfully complete the work in them. He closes with an exhortation to believers to be holy at all times, in all relations and in every condition.[7]

CHRIST EXALTED: A LOST SINNER
Sought and saved by Christ, God's people are a holy people.
Being the sum of diverse sermons preached in Suffolk

By Hanserd Knollys

Who, for this doctrine, had the meeting house doors shut
against him, and was stoned out of the pulpit (as he was
preaching) by a rude multitude who were gathered together,
and set on by a malignant high-constable, which has been
proven by diverse witnesses of good reputation before the
Honourable Committee of Examination at London.

Gal. 4:16.
"Have I therefore become your enemy, because
I tell you the truth?"

Acts 21:30
"And they took Paul and drew him out of the temple,
and immediately the doors were shut."

John 10:32
"For which of these works do you stone me?"

1 Pet. 4:13

---

7. These last two sermons show that Knollys, though accused of Antinomianism, certainly believed that the Christian is bound to the law of Christ and is to live a holy life. See my book *Erroneous and Schismatical Opinions*, 79-132.

"But rejoice, in as much as you are partakers of Christ's suffering."

London. Printed by Jane Coe according to Order 1645.

* * *

Outline of Christ is all and in all

Colossians 3:11

1. Doctrine—Christ is all and in all in the new man
   a) Who is meant by the new man? A true believer
   b) How is Christ all in all in the new man?
      1) He is the foundation of all
      2) Christ communicates all unto the new man
         i) Christ is our life
         ii) Christ is the true light of every believer
         iii) Christ is the Bread of life to believers
      3) That He has the preeminence in the new man
         i) As the author of all
         ii) As the preserver of all
         iii) As the finisher of all
2. Application (Use)
   a) Every true believer therefore ought to prize Christ
      1) What should be our motivation to prize Christ?
         i) Christ's worth in the invaluable preciousness of his blood, the unsearchable riches of his grace and the glorious liberties of His Spirit
         ii) The great need we have of Christ
   b) Everyone therefore ought to examine themselves whether Christ be in them
   c) Let it serve as encouragement to every true believer that Christ is ours
   d) Exhortation to all hearers
      1) Believers—Let Christ be all in all
         i) In your justification
         ii) In the gifts of the Spirit and graces of sanctification
         iii) In all your affections, words and actions
      2) Unbelievers—Seek Christ

To the Honourable Committee of Examinations:
Grace and peace from God, through Christ.

Honourable,

It may be judged an act of great boldness in me (who am under the examination of this Honourable Committee) to dedicate my poor labours at Debenham and Stradbrook to your patronage; especially to publish them to the world, had not the hard reports of some persons (too much credited by many) constrained me to vindicate first the truth, and in the next place to give satisfaction to the many who have heard those reports. I should not have been so bold. The consciousness of my own inability and the knowledge of the profitable labors of many, both learned and godly, has to this time, and still has justly, hindered me from publishing anything by print to the view of the world. Therefore, I (being enforced to print my sermons) present them to your honours; wherein you have the sum and substance of all that I preached in Suffolk (as many witnesses have testified). For my main endeavour there was to exalt Christ and to press my hearers to sanctification in heart and life. And if the Lord shall please to make my poor labours a blessing to any, he will get glory, and I have my reward with him. However, I humbly submit both myself and my book to the examination and determination of this Honourable Committee.

Your Honours, to serve you in the Lord,

Hanserd Knollys.

COLOSSIANS 3:11
"Christ is all, and in all."

The Apostle Paul, who was a chosen vessel unto the Lord to bear his Name before the Gentiles, Acts 9:15, wrote this epistle to the saints and faithful brethren in Christ who were at Colosse; Chap. 1, verse. 2. And as the ensign-bearer of His glorious Name, displayed the magnificence and transcendent excellence of Christ in the words of the text "Christ is all, and in all." And that he might lift up Christ's all-sufficiency, he nullifies all other excellencies whatsoever, chap. 3, verse 11, where he gives the Colossians to understand that the advantage of a Jew above a Gentile, the dignity of a Scythian above a Barbarian, or the immunities of a freeman above a bond slave, however esteemed amongst men, are nothing without Christ: "Who is all, and in all." These words have their dependence upon the exhortation unto mortification, chap. 3, verse 5, which exhortation the Apostle pressed upon the Colossians by telling them, in verses 9, 10, they had put off the old man, with his deeds, and had put on the new man, etc. Where (that is) in which state of regeneration, there is neither Greek, nor Jew, etc., but "Christ is all, and in all." The lesson to be learned hence, is this; that is,

Doctrine. "Christ is all and in all, in the new man."

Two things need some explanation in this doctrine; namely, first, who is here meant by the new man? And secondly, "how Christ is all, and in all, in the new man."

By the new man here, we are to understand (as was intended by the Apostle) a true believer or a faithful brother in Christ, one sanctified in Christ Jesus, called a saint; who is redeemed in the spirit of his mind, and has put on the new man, Ephes. 4:23, 24. Which is done when, by the mighty operation of the Holy Spirit, in the promises given unto us, we are made partakers of the divine nature, 2 Pet. 1:3, 4. *Non per particpationem Essentia, sed per commincationem Spiritus*, and *gratia ejus*.[8] Gal. 4:6; Ephes. 4:6. Thus, being by the Spirit and faith united with Christ, we are made a new creature, or creation, 2 Cor. 5:17, have a new heart, Ezek. 36:26, 27, and walk in newness of life, Rom. 6:4. And such may be said to have put on the new man, the sum then is this; "Christ is all, and in all, in every true believer, in every justified-sanctified person, who has a new heart, and walks in newness of life."

Touching the second particular, that is, how Christ is all and in all in the new man. The Lord Jesus Christ (who is all in himself, for in him dwells all the fullness of the Godhead bodily, Col. 2:9, which was the pleasure of God, that in all things he might have the pre-eminence, Col. 1:18, 19) is all and in all in the new man.

First, fundamentally, I mean Christ is the foundation of all, 1 Cor. 3:11. For no other foundation can no man lay then that is laid, which is Jesus Christ. I say Christ is the foundation of all that faith, repentance, love, and other graces, gifts, and fruits of the Spirit, which are in every true believer: he is a living foundation full of grace, and from his fullness have we all received grace for grace, John 1:14, 16.

Secondly, communicatively, I mean Christ does communicate all unto the new man; that is, life, light, grace, and glory,

---

8. Not by participation in God's essence but by communication of the Spirit and his grace.

etc. We have nothing but what we have received, and we have received all from his fullness, Ephes. 4:7, John 1:16. The titles given to Christ in the scripture of truth will make this appear more fully, namely, that Christ is all in the new man, or in every true believer. I shall instance some.

First, *Christ is our life*, Col. 3:4. Christ is the life of a believer, even eternal life, 1 John 5:11, 12. That is to say, the everlasting spiritual well-being of a believer is by union and communion with Jesus Christ, in whom he lives a life of grace here, and with whom he shall live a life of glory hereafter. Yes, all those spiritual breathings of the hunger-thirsting soul, after the enjoyment of God in any of his holy ordinances, are from Christ; and from him are all those quickening, and all that life we have in prayer, preaching, conference, and other spiritual duties. In a word, the Spirit of life himself, who so sweetly refreshes the weary soul, comforts the sorrowful heart, and quickens the sanctified affections, is from Christ; and he is called the Spirit of the Son, Gal. 4:6, whom God sends forth into the hearts of his children.

Secondly, Christ is the true light of every believer or in the new man. That was the true light, John 1:9, even Jesus Christ, who enlightens the eyes of our understanding that we may know what is the hope of his calling, and what is the riches of the glory of his inheritance in the saints, and what is the exceeding greatness of his power toward us who believe, Ephes. 1:17, 18, 19. And though the hearts of men and women be very dark, yet God who commanded the light to shine out of darkness has shined in our hearts (who are believers) to give light of the knowledge of the glory of God in the face of Jesus Christ, 2 Cor. 4:6. And the Apostle tells the sanctified Ephesians that they were sometimes darkness, but now they are light in the Lord, Ephes. 5:8. And indeed, all that heavenly knowledge and spiritual understanding, which believers have in the mystery of the gospel, they had it from Christ; in whom are hidden all the treasures of wisdom and knowledge, Col. 2:2, 3.

Thirdly, Christ is the bread of life to believers, John 6:35, 48, 51. He is the spiritual meat and drink of our souls who believe in him. They that eat him shall live by him, John 6:55, 57. All that spiritual nourishment and soul-refreshment, which believers have in promises, duties, ordinances, etc., is from Christ, whose flesh is meat indeed, and his blood is drink indeed, communicated by his Holy Spirit unto his people in those duties, promise, ordinances, etc. Christ is milk and wine, to be had without money, Isa. 55:1, that will quench the thirst of the newborn babes in Christ, which so much desire the sincere milk of the Word that they may grow thereby, 1 Pet. 2:2, 3, and that will make the mournful spirit of a doubting or backsliding believer to have a cheerful countenance when his broken heart is cheered and warmed, yes melted and comforted with the blood of Christ his Redeemer. Christ is the water of life, a pure river of living water clear as crystal flows from this fountain in the hearts of believers, Rev. 22:1, 17, John 7:37, 38, and John 4:10, 12, 14. This will satisfy the thirsty soul, as Christ promised, Matth. 5:7, 11. Therefore, he cried, "If any man thirst, let him come to me and drink." Christ is the tree of life, which bears twelve manner of fruits and yields her fruit every month, whose leaves are for the healing of the nations, Rev. 22:2. Christ is said to make a feast of wine and fat things full of marrow, Isa. 25:6, and he thus speaks to believers, "Eat, O friends, drink, yes, drink abundantly, O my beloved:" Cant. 5:1. I might be exceeding large in particularizing many of his other titles as, namely, Christ is a believer's justification, sanctification, redemption, 1 Cor. 1:30. He is also our peace, Ephes. 2:14, our righteousness, Jer. 13:6, our advocate with the Father, 1 John 2:1, 2, our king, high-priest, and prophet; our father, husband, brother, our all. Thus it may appear that Christ is all in the new man.

But how is Christ all in all, in the new man? I conceive it is spoken by way of pre-eminence, as it is expressed, Col. 1:18, 19. That is, in all which is in the new man, or in a believer, Christ ought to have the pre-eminence.

First, as he is the author of all. For instance, that precious faith of God's elect, which is in the new man, is an excellent grace, but yet Christ must have the pre-eminence above that faith, because he is the author of it, Heb. 12:2, and so above all other graces, gifts, and fruits of the Spirit.

Secondly, as he is the preserver of all in the new man, every believer is called and sanctified by God the Father and preserved in Jesus Christ, Jude 1. And the believer is not only preserved in the state of grace by Christ, but the grace of God wrought in him, that is, faith, etc., is by Christ preserved also, namely, by the intercession of Christ. "I have prayed for you that your faith fail not."

Thirdly, as he is the finisher, who strengthens, establishes, and perfects all in the new man, Christ is not only the author, but the finisher of our faith, Heb. 12:2. He is the Alpha and Omega, the beginning and the ending, of all those graces, gifts, and fruits of the Spirit, which are in the new man. Rev. 1:8. Thus, Christ is all and in all, in the new man. He is the author, preserver, and finisher of all; He purchased all, He is the donor of all, He is the beauty of all, the sum of all, the perfection of all in the new man.

Reason: This was the good pleasure of the Father's will, that all fullness, all sufficiency, all spiritualness, should dwell in Christ, and should by Christ be communicated to his people, that in all things Christ might have the pre-eminence, Col. 1:18, 19. And thus God will have it done to the man Christ Jesus, whom he delighted to honour, for the service Christ did unto his Father in the redemption of his people. Therefore, he gave him a name above every name, "Christ is all, and in all." Which honour and dignity, Christ will, at the last day, prostrate at the feet of his Father that God may be "all in all," 1 Cor. 15:28. Moreover, this being the design of God, that Christ should communicate all grace, gifts, etc., unto his people, it was requisite that all fullness should be in Christ. And so we read John 1:14, 16. Yes, the great necessity of the Lord's redeemed ones to have a constant supply of grace and spiritual gifts, also a continual growth of the fruits of the Spirit, requires this all-fullness to be in Christ.

Use 1: Seeing "Christ is all and in all" in the new man; let us hence be instructed, first, to prize Christ highly, to set a high esteem upon Christ, to let him have the pre-eminence, who is "all in all." It is that which the prophet complained of, Isa. 53:3. He, that is Christ, was despised, and rejected of men, and we esteemed him not. We are apt to slight Christ, and to disesteem him, because we discern not that beauty, excellency, riches, and glory, which is in Himself. We are ignorant of the worth of Christ, and know not our need of him, and therefore we do not so prize him as we ought. These two considerations I desire to propound as motives to prize Christ. First, Christ his worth, which I may hint unto you in three particulars. That is,

[First], The invaluable preciousness of his blood, which has in it a cleansing virtue, 1 John 1:7, 9. "And the blood of Jesus Christ his Son, cleanses us from all sin"; therefore, we are said to be justified by his blood, Rom. 5:9. Let me ask you, who now believe, how did you esteem of this precious blood of Christ? When you were sighing out your mournful requests to God in secret corners, for one drop of Christ's blood, one dram of the grace of God, and faith of God his elect, one word of promise, one smile of a reconciled Father, or one beam of the light of God's countenance, did you not prize the blood of Christ above all corruptible things as silver, gold, honour, riches, pleasure, etc.? Did you not esteem the least drop of it more precious than all creature-comforts whatsoever, as friends, liberties, and life? Again, the precious blood of Christ has a purging quality, Heb. 9:14. The blood of Christ shall purge your consciences from dead works to serve the living God. Sin does both contract guiltiness and pollution, and therefore the blood of Christ does both cleanse and purge, pardon, and purify. Therefore we are also said to be sanctified by the blood of Christ, Heb. 13:12. Wherefore Jesus also, that he might sanctify the people with his own blood, suffered without the gate. Oh beloved, what can be esteemed so precious to a gracious heart as this blood of Christ, which washes away all those defilements and uncleanness, which through our corruptions cleave unto us, even in our best actions and holy duties. Such of you (as have many times groaned in prayer to God under the feeling, sense, and sight of any corruption) know by experience what high esteem you have had of the blood of Christ to save you from your uncleanness.

Secondly, the unsearchable riches of his grace, Ephes. 3:8. To me who am less than the least of all saints, is this grace given, that I should preach among the Gentiles the unsearchable riches of Christ. Christ's riches are of such a height, depth, length, and breadth that passes knowledge: yes, thus much is spoken of the love of Christ, Ephes. 3:18, 19. Also faith in Christ is called precious faith, 2 Pet. 1:1. To them that have obtained the like precious faith with us, through the righteousness of God and our Saviour Jesus Christ; yes, all the graces of Christ are the riches of the poor saints, James 2:5. God has chosen the poor of the world, rich in grace, etc. Tell me, beloved, how did you esteem the riches of Christ when you, being poor in spirit, mourned for Christ and his grace, when you discerned faith, love, humility, etc., in others of the children of God? Did you prize it highly in them? Did you not account them happy, rich, and blessed whom Christ had enriched with those jewels and adorned with such graces? Ah, how much more should you now prize CHRIST, in whom is all fullness of these unsearchable riches, and especially considering that, from his fullness, you have received grace for grace, John 1:14, 16.

Thirdly, the glorious liberties of His Spirit: "for where the Spirit of the Lord is, there is liberty," 2 Cor. 3:17. Not any carnal liberty to sin and so fulfil the lust of the flesh, Gal. 5:13, but spiritual liberty and freedom from sin. I mean not a perfect and total freedom from all sin, as if the people of God could never sin after conversion. For "if we say that we have no sin, we deceive ourselves, and the truth is not in us," 1 John 1:8, 10. But I mean a freedom, first, from the guilt of sin, Rom. 8:33. And the

Apostle said, Col. 2:13, that "he has forgiven us all trespasses." Secondly, from the pollution or filth of sin, Zech. 13:1, a fountain set open to believers for sin and for uncleanness. And Ezek. 36:25, 29: God promised they shall be clean, and he will save them from all their uncleannesses. Thirdly, from the reigning power of sin, Rom. 6:14. "Sin shall not have dominion over you, under grace." Fourthly, from the punishment due for sin, which is the curse of the law, Gal. 3:13, "or condemnation," Rom. 8:1, "or any other satisfactory punishment."

[Second motive to prize Christ]. The great need you have of Christ may move you to prize him and set a high esteem of him. Christ is the only thing necessary, and therefore the titles given him in the scripture are such as declare his usefulness to believers, for he is our life, our light, our bread, water, milk, wine. His flesh our meat indeed, His blood our drink indeed; He is our father, our husband, our brother, our friend, our king, priest, and prophet. He is our justification, sanctification, and redemption; He is our peace, our all. We can have no access to God but by his mediation, no acceptance with God without his intercession, Rev. 8:3, 4. We cannot resist the next temptation, neither can we overcome the next corruption, nor shall we be able to suffer with patience the next persecution, or endure any tribulation, unless we have renewed strength from Christ. Believers have received that grace they have from Christ, John 1:16. And they cannot have increase of grace but by Christ, John 15:1, 2. "Lord, increase our faith," said the disciples, neither can they persevere in grace unless they be preserved in Christ, Jude 1. To conclude, we are nothing, have nothing, can do nothing without Christ, John 15:5. "Without me, you can do nothing"; that is to say, you cannot in your own strength nor in the strength of any grace received, do anything to please God or to glorify God, without Christ; "Unless you abide in me", and have renewed ability and strength from me, "you can do nothing" that God my Father will own or crown with acceptance or reward: But yet we, who are believers, have all and abound, Phil. 4:18. We can do all things through Christ that strengthens us, Phil. 4:13, we can suffer the loss of all, Phil. 3:7, 8, 9, yes, and conquer all; no, be more than conquerors through Christ, Rom. 8:35, 36, 37, 38, 39. Oh, consider your need of Christ and learn to prize him, let him be exalted highest in your hearts as the pearl of greatest worth, as the one thing necessary which you most of all need, let him be all in all in your communication and conversation.

Use 2: Seeing Christ is all and in all in the new man, let everyone examine whether Christ be in him, 2 Cor. 13:5. Examine yourselves, know you not that Christ is in you, etc. This nearly concerns you, beloved, for if you have Christ, you have all. Christ is all, but if you lose him, you lose all. You will lose your hopes, comforts, and all your duties, yes, you will lose God, heaven, and soul, and all. It matters not what you have if you want Christ: no gifts, duties, reformations, qualifications, or other things whatsoever will make you happy without Christ; and if you enjoy Christ, it is not material whatever you want, "for my God" (says the Apostle) "shall supply all your needs, according to his riches in glory by Christ Jesus," Phil. 4:19. Therefore, make sure that Christ is yours. Some would ask this question, "How shall I so examine that I may know assuredly that I have Christ?" I answer: you must bring your hearts to the touchstone of the Word of God and cast them into the balance of the sanctuary and weigh them there. And to this purpose, I shall propound one scripture of truth for your examination and trial, that is, 2 Cor. 5:17, "If any man be in Christ, he is a new creature, or creation." That is to say, he is newborn, born again, or born of God, John 1:12, 13. But as many as received him, etc., which were born of God. And our Saviour urged the necessity of this new birth, John 3:3, 5, 7, 8. Except a man be born again, he cannot see the Kingdom of God; he cannot enter into the Kingdom of God, verse 5. Now everyone who is a new creature in Christ, all things are become new in him or all things are made new [as in the Greek]. That is, first, he is made a new man, Ephes. 4:21, 22, 23, 24; Col. 3:10, 11, and has put on the new man where Christ is all and in all. Secondly, he has a new heart, Ezek. 36:26. "A new heart also will I give you," etc. That is a new will, and new affections, yes, and "a new spirit will I put within you," verse 26. That is (Ephes. 4:23) to be renewed in the spirit of our mind, that is, a new judgement or spiritual understanding in the knowledge of God's will, Col. 1:9. Thirdly, he walks in newness of life: Rom. 6:4. Even so, we also should walk in newness of life. That is, the conversation of a new-creature should be seen as becomes the gospel: Phil. 1:27. That is, humble, harmless, and holy: 1 Pet. 1:15, 16. And thus God has promised in the everlasting covenant of grace that all and every one of his people shall walk: Ezek. 36:27. "And I will put my Spirit within you, and cause you to walk in my statutes," etc. Examine yourselves, are you a new creature? Such of you as have not put off the old man, but still have your old hearts, and your old sins, and walk in your old ways, and fulfill the old lusts of your sinful natures are not a new creature, you are not in Christ, nor Christ in you.

But some may thus say within themselves, "I hope my soul is in a better condition, I am not so wicked and carnal as some others are, neither am I so vile a sinner as I have been formerly; but I am somewhat reformed, and have forsaken my sinful courses, and begin to delight to hear sermons, and I pray with my family." To this I would answer: although your condition be not so desperate as others, who have lived long under ordinary means of grace, and yet are not at all wrought upon, I must tell you that professors may (through strong convictions, horror of consequence, and fears of hell) leave the act of some sins and may customarily perform some religious duties and yet be not regenerated. Professors may have leaves like the unfruitful fig-tree, and lamps like the five foolish virgins: they may seem to be religious, and have a form of godliness, and not be a new creature or creation. I might instance many such in the scriptures. Herod, Mark 6:20. He heard John gladly, and did many things. Saul, 1 Sam. 10:6, 9 was turned into another man, had another heart, yet unconverted. So you may be another man, and not a new man; may have another heart, but not a new heart.

But I speak not this to add sorrow to the afflicted, nor to break the bruised, for though some may deceive themselves in this; yet such of you as are born again or born of God, though but new-born babes, who have put on the new man, have a new heart, and walk in newness of life are in Christ, and Christ in you.

Use 3. Seeing "Christ is all, and in all in the new man;" let it serve for the consolation of every true believer, Christ is yours, and all things are yours: 1 Cor. 3:21, 22, 23. All are yours, and you are Christ's, and Christ is God's. Christ is your life, your light, your food, your all, and by union with Christ, you are one in God, John 17:21. God is your God and Father, John 20:17. All that is Christ's is yours, his wisdom, righteousness, sanctification, faith, love, humility, etc. All in all fullness was in him, and dwells in him for his people to communicate to them, Ephes. 4:7. Are you full of spiritual wants? You may have supply from the fullness of spirituals in Christ. Do you want wisdom, faith, love, etc.? Whatever you want, go to Christ for that grace; there is enough in Christ to satisfy the most hunger-thirsting souls in spiritual things, Ephes. 1:3. God has blessed us with all spiritual blessings in heavenly things in Christ; in whom are hid all the treasures of wisdom and knowledge: Col. 2:3. Do you want power against corruption? Go to Christ for strength, His grace is sufficient for you, 2 Cor. 12:8, 9. There is an all-sufficiency in Christ, "Christ is all," says the text, therefore, the Apostle having Christ, said, "I have all, I can do all through Christ," Phil. 4:13, 18. And know for your further consolation that Christ is in all in the new man or in every true believer.

He is in you, Col. 1:2. Christ in you, the hope of glory. Christ lives in me says the Apostle, Gal. 2:20. Christ is and lives in a true believer by participation of his divine nature, 2 Pet. 1:3, 4. By inchoation of his Holy Spirit, Gal. 4:6, and by communication of his saving grace, Ephes. 3:17 and 47, Christ is in your hearts, in your gifts, in your graces, in your duties, in all, by whom you find acceptance of your persons, and services with God your heavenly Father, Ephes. 1:6. Christ is with you, and in you, in all conditions, in all relations, in all afflictions, Isa. 63:8, 9. And to conclude this use, know for your increase of joy that Christ, "who is all, and in all in you," will abide in you forever. Nothing shall be able to separate Christ and your souls, Rom. 8:35, 38, 39. Christ is the strength of your heart, and your portion forever, Psal. 73:26.

Use 4: Seeing "Christ is all and in all in the new man," suffer a word of exhortation, which will concern everyone present to hearken to, namely, both such as are in Christ, and out of Christ, and I am sure every one of you are in one of these two states, either you are in Christ or without Christ. The first branch of the exhortation shall be to you who are believers and sanctified in Christ Jesus, called saints. Seeing "Christ is all, in all," let him be all in all in your justification. Take you heed you bring not any righteousness of your own, nor any grace or works of his in you, to join with Christ and his righteousness in point of justification: Phil. 3:9. This glory Christ will not give to another, He is our justification or righteousness, 1 Cor. 1:30, 31. Christ will not permit any coadjutor, concause, or cooperator whatsoever in the justification of sinners.

Consider this, you who will not believe, unless you could see yourselves so holy, so humble except you can first have such a sin subdued. You will not believe any of your sins are pardoned until you find and feel in yourselves a soft heart, a broken heart, a praying spirit, a mourning spirit, and you cry out you are not justified. "Oh," say you, "If I could pray, mourn for sin, profit by the means, as such and such do, then I would believe; but alas, I have a hard heart, a blind mind, a perverse will, carnal affections, etc. I cannot, dare not, I will not believe that my sins are forgiven." Thus most professors would bring in (if not their own righteousness) some grace or work of God in them to join with Christ in their justification, not considering that God justifies the ungodly, Rom. 4:5, and that Christ is all, and in all, in the justification of sinners.

Secondly, let Christ be all, in all in the gifts of the Spirit, and graces of sanctification; for, as you heard, he is the author, the preserver, and the finisher of them all. Therefore, let him have the pre-eminence above all, set a high esteem of every gift and grace of God, account a little grace better than all the riches, honours, pleasures, and creature-comforts of this world. But you ought to prize Christ far above all his own gifts and graces in us, for he is the life of them all, the marrow and substance of them all. What is all knowledge, unless you know God in Christ? 1 Cor. 13:2: nothing. What is all faith, except Christ be the object of it? 1 Cor. 13:3: nothing. Patience, temperance, and all other virtues, what are they but either natural qualities or moral habits unless Christ be the root of them. Nature education and acquired gifts of art may produce the like, yes the same, in heathens. But Christ is the lustre and beauty of each spiritual gift and grace: that influence believers receive from Christ and those rays that come from this Sun of Righteousness upon their graces, makes them shining saints, beautiful, and all glorious within. Hear this, you poor in spirit, you new-borne babes in Christ who have the persons of believers (especially preachers) in admiration, and set them up on high in your hearts, and extol them with your tongues; because you discern so much humility, love, patience, faith, and other gifts of the Spirit, and graces of sanctification in them. Should you not rather admire Christ, exalt Christ, and extol him, who is the purchaser, the owner, the donor, and the author of all these spiritual gifts and graces, for we have nothing but what we have received, by his grace we are what we are, and all the grace we have, from his fullness we received it, John 1:16. Therefore, let him receive the glory of all, and let him have the pre-eminence in all, for he is all in all.

Thirdly, let Christ be all, in all your affections, words, and actions. Set your affections on Christ. Oh, let the discoveries of that superlative excellency, and glorious beauty of Christ, which are made out to your soul by the Spirit and Word of God, draw you to set your affections on him, Col.1:1, 2. Love everyone and everything that God has put the name of Christ upon, for his sake, but chiefly set your affectionate love upon himself: love Christ in his saints, love Christ in his messengers, in his ordinances, and this will quicken your desires to enjoy more of Christ. More of Christ in his saints, ministers, ordinances, and in your own hearts. Oh, let Christ be chief in your affections! He is altogether lovely, Cant. 5:16. Let him have your dearest love; he is the well beloved of his Father and yours, 2 Pet. 1:17. Let him be your well beloved. Christ bears you in his arms, everlasting arms of mercy, yes in his bosom Isa. 40:11 & 63:9. Do you bear him in your heart and let Christ be exalted highest there? Again, let the absence of Christ be the chief occasion of your sorrow and mourning, Matth. 9:15. Cry after him, enquire for him, give him no rest until he return: this was the practice of the spouse, Cant 3:1, 2, 3, 4 & Cant. 5:4, 6, 8. "Oh how was her affections set upon her beloved! Tell him I am sick of love," Cant. 5:8. Though there be many other just occasions for mourning to the saints, yet this is the chief. If a loving wife cannot think of the departure of her dear husband without sorrow, how much more sorrowful will a gracious heart be in the absence of Christ? Mary, who wept and being asked the reasons by the angel, answered: "Because they have taken away my Lord," etc., John 20:11, 13, 15, 16. And as Christ should be in all your affections, so let him be in your words and actions: speak for him, do for him, suffer for him, let him be the matter of your communications and conferences, that you may minister grace to the hearers: whatever you do in word or deed, let all be done to the honour of Christ; for he who honours the Son, honours the Father also.

The other branch of the exhortation is to such as are in their natural condition, without Christ. Seeing Christ is all and in all, be exhorted to seek Christ. Paul, preaching on the Mars-hill to the Athenians, tells them, God made of one blood all nations of men that they should seek the Lord, Acts 17:22, 26, 27, and there be many exhortations in holy scripture to this purpose, as Isa. 55:6, 7, "Seek you the Lord while he may be found, etc. Let the wicked forsake his way, and the unrighteous man his thoughts, and let him return unto the Lord, etc." The Apostle Peter, in his speech to Simon Magus, Acts 8:20, 21, 22, 23, told him his heart was not right in the sight of God, that he was in the "gall of bitterness, and in the bond of iniquity." And he exhorted him to repent and pray to God, verse 22. Not that any man in his natural condition can, of himself, come to Christ, desire him, or seek to enjoy him, for none can come to except the Father draw him, John 6:44. It is God that works in us to will and to do according to his good pleasure, Phil. 2:13. So then, says the Apostle, it is not of him that wills, nor of him that runs, but of God that shows mercy; only know this, God, requiring poor sinners to use the means he has appointed, is pleased to make that means effectual for their conversion and salvation. For if God has purposed to show mercy and confer his grace upon your souls, he will cause you to seek him, Ezek. 36:26, 27, 37. "A new heart will I give you, and I will put my Spirit within you, and cause you to walk in my statutes." "Thus says the Lord God, 'I will yet for this be enquired of by the house of Israel to do it for them,'" verse 37. God's gracious and free promises do not exclude the means he has appointed to attain the mercies in them promised. It pleased him to tie his creatures to the use of means when he affords it them, though he will sometimes work without it. Now the ordinary means which God has in his infinite wisdom appointed to convert sinners, and also to build them up in Christ, is the Word preached, Rom. 10:8, 17. This word of the gospel God will have preached to every creature in all parts of the world, Mark 10:15. None are exempted or prohibited from hearing the gospel preached, but everyone that has an ear is required to hear, Rev. 2:7. And let such as neglect the hearing of the word of God (preached by such as are called and sent of Christ) consider what the Lord says, Prov. 1, from the 20th verse to the 32nd verse. But although some of you see it is that which you ought to do and that you had need to do, that is, to seek the Lord; assenting to what you heard in the first use of the doctrine, that there is much worth, beauty, and excellency in Christ, and that poor lost undone sinners stand in need of him: Notwithstanding how to obtain Christ, you know not as yet. Let me tell you, God offers you Christ upon gospel-terms, which are these three.

First, God, in the dispensation of the gospel, propounds Christ to lost sinners, as the only necessary and all sufficient means of salvation: Christ is the only necessary means of salvation, Acts 4:12. Neither is there salvation in any other. And Christ is the all-sufficient means of salvation, so that we need none but him; Heb. 7:25. He is able to save them to the utmost, etc.

Secondly, God does offer Christ to lost sinners without respect to price or person. He invites them that have no money, to come, and buy wine and milk (that is to say, Christ) without price, Isa 55:1. And anyone that will is invited to take Christ freely, Rev. 22:17. And whoever will, let him take the water of life (that is Christ) freely.

Thirdly, God requires that those who do receive him shall depart from iniquity, 2 Tim. 2:19. Live soberly, righteously, and godly in this present world, Titus 2:11, 12, 13, 14, 15. And that they shall sell all, lose all, and have all for the sake of Christ, and take up the cross and follow him.

You will say to me, "Alas, here is my misery, that is, although God propound Christ upon good terms to poor sinners, to me among others, I have no power of myself to receive Christ, to believe in him, and accept of him." True, it is not (as I said) in him, that wills, nor him that runs, but in God, who shows mercy, Rom. 9:16. It is the exceeding greatness of his power towards us who believe, which must be put forth in your hearts to make you believe also, according to the working of his mighty power which he wrought in Christ when he raised him from the dead, Ephes. 1:19, 20. And you ought to wait on God in the diligent use of means until the day of his power come upon you, and then you shall be a willing, a believing people: Psal. 110:3. I may exhort you to repent of your wickedness, profaneness, etc. as Peter did: Acts 8:22. But God must give you repentance unto life, Acts 11:18. It is my duty to preach the gospel to you, and to exhort you to seek Christ, Acts 17:22, 27, but it is the mere mercy and free grace of God to drive you to Christ, which nothing but his everlasting love can move him to do, Jer. 31:3. You ought to see, and wait, ask, and use all the means which God has appointed, and afforded you, both secret, private, and public, Rev. 2:29. But God must make the means effectual, Acts 16:14. And therefore, I must say, it is not in me, I cannot draw you to Christ: that is the Father's work, John 6:44. But having exhorted you to seek him in the use of means, there I must leave you to wait on God for the moving of his Holy Spirit where you must lie and continue like the poor impotent man at the pool of Bethesda for healing: And though as he did, so you may see many a lame, blind, deaf, dumb, naked-leprous soul get healing and go away rejoicing and praising God, and you remain still so impotent that you cannot get into the fountain, set open for sin and for uncleanness, nor have any that can help you in that you may be cured; yet be not disheartened, as Christ came suddenly and unexpectedly, and healed the impotent man after long waiting, so Christ will come according to his promise to you souls that seek him, Mal. 3:1. "'The Lord whom you seek shall come, shall suddenly come,' says the Lord of Hosts."

> For the Son of Man is come to seek
> and to save that which is lost
>
> Luke 19:10

Doctrine—the Man Christ Jesus must seek and save lost sinners

1. Three things from the text
   a) Who is the man Christ Jesus?
      1) He is God
      2) He is mediator between God and man
      3) He is the great prophet and King of his people
   b) How does he seek lost sinners?
      1) By drawing the sinner to Himself through His word and Spirit
         i) By convincing/convicting him of sin, righteousness and judgement
         ii) By enlightening Him to know what is the hope of his calling, etc
            a) To see that Jesus Christ is the Saviour
            b) To see that He came into this world to save sinners
            c) To see that whoever believes in Him shall be saved
         iii) By converting him
   c) Christ does save sinners
      1) He saves them from sin
         i) From the guilt or imputation of sin
         ii) From the filth or pollution of sin
         iii) From the power or dominion of sin
         iv) From the curse or punishment of sin
      2) He saves them from the law
      3) He saves them from the schoolmastership of the law
      4) He saves them from the Old Covenant of the Law
      5) He saves them from Hell and from Satan's deluding temptations and allurements
   d) Why does Christ save sinners?

1) Because the Father sent him from heaven to finish the work of redemption

2) Because the Father promised in his everlasting covenant to save all of His people

3) Because the Father will not have any of those that he has given to Christ, perish

2. Application

   a) Use it to help professors to see that salvation is not in their religious activities

   b) Use it to see that sinners see that they are truly sinners before God and so lost

   c) Use it as encouragement for believers that Christ has saved them and can save others

   d) Use it to exhort sinners who see their need of salvation that they can be saved by believing

Luke 19:10

*For the Son of Man is come to seek and
to save that which was lost.*

The chief publican's conversion;

or

A lost sinner sought and saved by CHRIST.

The Lord Jesus Christ, whom the Father has sanctified and sent into the world, John 10:36, came to save sinners, 1 Tim. 1:15. And being sent to the lost sheep of the house of Israel, Matth. 15:24, found Zacchaeus a Son of Abraham, Luke 19:9, in his blood: that is, in his natural estate. A lost sinner, for this Zacchaeus was . . . the prince of the publicans, or chief among the publicans, verse 2, . . . and a sinner . . . so that he was known of all to be a sinner, verse 7. To whom Christ said, "Zacchaeus, today I must abide at your house," and Zacchaeus received him joyfully, that is, both into his house and into his heart, verses 5, 6, 8, 9. Now when the Pharisaical Jews saw Jesus ... to lodge or make his abode at the publican's house, they all murmured, saying that he was gone to be a guest (or as it is in the Greek . . . ,[)] with a man that is a sinner. Whereupon our Saviour gave them to understand that this was the business for which he came into the world: namely, to call sinners, Matth. 9:13. This was the great design of God the Father in sending his Son Jesus Christ, that is, to save lost sinners, Matth. 18:11. And this was the very cause why he would be Zacchaeus' guest because Zacchaeus was a sinner, a lost sinner. For the Son of Man is come to seek and save that which is lost. So that the words of the text contain in them a reason why Christ would be Zacchaeus' guest, and implicitly an answer to their objection, who murmured at it: as may appear in the like case, Mark 2:15, 16, 17. In the text, consider these three things: first, a Saviour, the man Christ Jesus, 1 Tim. 2:5, the Son of Man. Secondly, the work he came about, and that is two-fold: to seek and to save. Thirdly, the persons whom Christ came to seek and save, that is, lost sinners. The doctrine which arises clearly from the words is this.

Doctrine. The man Christ Jesus must seek and save lost sinners.

This was his errand from heaven, the work he came to do, and this he must accomplish as the scriptures declare, John 6:38, 39. For explanation of the doctrine, three things must be opened and proved by the word of truth. That is; first, who the man Christ Jesus is. Secondly, how he seeks lost sinners? And thirdly, what he saves them from?

Touching the first query; the scriptures do declare that the man Christ Jesus is "God with us," Matth. 1:23. This was long since foretold by the prophet, Isa. 7:14. "Behold a virgin shall conceive and bear a son, and shall call his name IMMANUEL, (*nobiscum Deus*)[9] God with us." This is a great mystery says the Apostle, 1 Tim. 3:16, God manifested in the flesh. He is also called "the WORD of God," Rev. 19:13, "And the Word was God," John 1:1, and man, "The WORD was made flesh," John 1:14. "The only begotten of the Father, called the Son of God," John 3:16, and Luke 1:35. "Equal with God," Phil. 2:6. "And one with the Father and the Holy Spirit," 1 John 5:7. Which oneness is a mystery, Col. 2:2. The hypostatical union of the divine and human nature is a great mystery, 1 Tim. 3:16. "Oh, the depth of the riches, both of the wisdom and knowledge of God," Rom. 11:33. Furthermore, the scriptures of truth do declare touching the Lord Jesus Christ, who is God-man, that he is mediator between God and man, 1 Tim. 2:5. By whom and in whom God is reconciled to man, and man is reconciled to God. Therefore, Christ took upon him the seed of Abraham, that he might be a merciful and faithful high priest in things pertaining to God, to

---

9. God with us.

make reconciliation for the sins of the people, Heb. 2:16, 17 and Col. 1:21, and he is therefore called the mediator of the new covenant, Heb. 12:24. The better covenant, which was established upon better promises, Heb. 8:6. And for this cause, he is the mediator of the New Testament, or covenant, that by the means of death for the redemption of the transgressions under the first testament, or covenant, they which are called might receive the promise of eternal inheritance, Heb. 9:15. The man Christ Jesus is also the great prophet and king of his people, Acts 3:22, 23, and 5:31, 32, the head and saviour of his church, Ephes. 5:23. And this Son of Man came to seek and to save lost sinners.

Touching the second query:

The scriptures do witness that (Christ seeking his lost sheep) finds them in their blood, polluted, corrupted, filthy, naked, and loathsome, Ezek. 16:3, 4, 5, 6. But the poor sinner knows not that he is wretched, and miserable and poor, and blind and naked, Rev. 3:17, until the Lord by his Holy Spirit and Word convinces him and enlightens his understanding.

Now the Lord, seeing the poor sinner polluted in his own blood, that is, in his natural estate of sinful corruption, and looking upon him with an eye of compassion (for his time is the time of love), he draws him with his everlasting loving-kindness, Jer. 31:3. Without which powerful drawing no sinner can come to Christ, John 6:44. The means by which the lost sinner is drawn to Christ is the Spirit and Word of God, whereby he is convinced, enlightened, and converted.

First, God does by his Spirit and Word convince the soul of sin, righteousness, and judgement, John 16:8.

First, of sin, that is, sins not only against the law, such as drunkenness, uncleanness, covetousness, etc., but also sins against the gospel, because they believe not in Christ, verse 9. That you may perceive what it is to be convinced of sin, because they believe not in Christ, John 16:8, 9. That is, the Spirit of God in the Word, and by the Word, convinces the sinner; first, that he has no saving, justifying faith, Heb. 3:24, 4:2, which is the precious faith of God's elect. Secondly, that without this faith, he cannot please God, Heb. 11:6. Unless he believes in Jesus Christ, he shall perish. And thirdly, that it is not in his own power to believe, but the exceeding greatness of God's power is put forth in them that believe, Ephes. 1:19, 20. And this almighty power must be given to enable the soul to believe. Now this is not a general conviction, that all men are sinners, and consequently you are a sinner as well as others; but it is a particular convincement with divine light and power, which causes the soul to understand and believe that he is indeed a sinner, a miserable sinner, a lost sinner, for it is the Spirit in the word that does thus convince the soul of sin. The effect of this conviction usually is much trouble of conscience, fear of hell, and sensible apprehensions of the wrath of God and such like; for the poor sinner now sees, and feels, that it is an evil thing and a bitter thing to sin against God. He has caused the arrows of his quiver to enter into his veins, Lam. 3:1, 13. This arrow of the Almighty is sharp in the heart of the King's (that is Christ's) enemies, Psal. 45:5. It pricks the sinner in the heart, Acts 2:37. And causes him to cry out, "What shall I do?" Acts 16:30. "What shall I do to be saved?" Now this sinner is bidden: believe in the Lord Jesus Christ, Acts 16:31. But, alas, he cannot believe: "Ah, no, no," says the poor sinner, "I am a sinful wretch, a vile abominable sinner; I have been a blasphemer of the name of God, a persecutor of the people of God, a despiser of the word and ministers of God, disobedient to parents, etc. There is no hope for me; I shall perish, I shall perish everlastingly; I am undone, I am lost forever, I cannot believe I have an unbelieving heart, and this, my sin of unbelief added to all my other sins, fills up the measure of my iniquities."

[Second] The Spirit does also convince the soul of righteousness, John 16:10. That is to say, first, that he is not righteous, but a sinner, Rom. 3:9, 10. Secondly, that his own righteousness, which he has gone about to establish, is as filthy rags, Isa. 64:6. And thirdly, that Christ is the end of the law for righteousness to everyone that believes, Rom. 10:3, 4. Fourthly, that this righteousness of Christ must be imputed to him to justification of life, Rom. 5:18, 19. And thus the sinner is taken off from trusting to himself, to the law, or to his performances any longer, now he dares not rest upon his duties, gifts, reformation, humiliation, or any work of God in his soul for life or salvation. Now his prayers, his mourning, his exact walking, nor his universal obedience, cannot mediate for him, nor be his Saviour. It is not his inherent qualifications, but the righteousness of Christ, whereby he must be justified before God. And yet notwithstanding, he is not taken quite off from duties but from resting in them and trusting upon them. The poor sinner prays still, reads the scriptures, hears the Word, is both constant and conscionable in the performance of holy duties, but now he cannot (as formerly he did) raise his hopes of salvation, gather his comforts in promises, nor conclude his assurance of eternal life from his duties done, because he knows not whether Christ be his or not, and whether or not he performs those duties from the Spirit of life in Christ.

[Third], The Spirit does likewise convince the sinner of judgement, 1 John 16:11, that is to say, first that there is a day of judgement 2 Pet. 2:9. Secondly, that all men shall stand before the judgement seat of Christ, and then everyone shall give an account of himself to God, Rom. 14:10, 11, 12. Thirdly, that then God will render to everyone according to his deeds, Rom. 2, 5, 6, 7, 8, 9. Fourthly, that it will be a terrible day, a day of dread and horror to devils and wicked men, Mal. 4:2, 5. And for a poor soul to stand naked without Christ's righteousness at that day is a fearful thing.

Consider poor sinners what a sad day those poor creatures had who were running to Christ from between Sodom and Gomorrah when the Lord rained fire and brimstone upon them; But this great and dreadful day of the Lord will be 10, 000 times more terrible when the Lord shall say to those who are without Christ, "Go you cursed into everlasting fire prepared for the Devil and his angels. Hear you that are a far off what I have done (says the Lord), and you that are near acknowledge my might." Sinners in Zion are afraid; fearfulness has surprised the hearts of hypocrites, who among us shall dwell with the devouring fire? Who shall dwell with everlasting burnings? Isa. 33:12, 13, 14, 18.

Now the sinner's heart begins again to meditate terror; for by this powerful conviction of the Spirit and Word of God, the sinner is brought to a sensible apprehension of his natural condition, and now he apprehends himself in a miserable estate, yes, and sees himself a lost sinner, and is ready to conclude against his soul that there is no hope for him. He formerly had some hopes, some comforts, some confidence of his own salvation, but they were all false, being built upon the sand of his duties, humiliations, and legal performances: "Alas, alas," (says the poor sinner) "I have kindled a fire, and compassed myself about with sparks, and did walk in the light of my fire, and in the sparks that I have kindled. And this now I have received at the hand of God, to lie down in sorrow," Isa. 50:11. Here the soul has his burden, which is too heavy for him to bear. And under the feeling sense and sight of his own sinful lost condition, he gets into a corner alone, where no eye can see, and no ear can hear him, and cries mightily to God with prayers and tears, spreading his miserable estate before the Lord, begs sin-pardoning mercy, and heart-changing grace, power against corruption, and patience to wait on God, and to seek him that hides his face for a little moment. Then, to some experienced preacher or believer, this poor sinner gets to enquire after the way to heaven; to whom he declares his miserable condition and asks what he shall do to be saved, and being exhorted to believe, cries out, "Oh! I cannot believe, I dare not believe," and then propounds all his objections against believing. This is (I conceive) the work of thorough conviction by the Spirit.

Secondly[after convicting of sin, righteousness and judgement], God does, by his Spirit and Word, enlighten the soul to know what is the hope of his calling, and what are the riches of the glory of his inheritance in the saints, and what is the exceeding greatness of his power towards them that believe, Ephes. 1:18, 19, 20. The Lord, having convinced the sinner of his lost estate and sinful condition by nature, does by his Spirit and Word enlighten his understanding to see and know;

First, that there is a Saviour, that is, Jesus Christ, Matth. 1:21. "You shall call his name Jesus, for he shall save his people from their sins," and Acts 5:31, "Him has God exalted to be a prince and a Saviour to give repentance to Israel and forgiveness of sins."

Secondly, that this Saviour Christ Jesus came into the world, to this very end, to save sinners, 1 Tim. 1:15. "This is a faithful saying, and worthy of all acceptation, that Christ Jesus came into the world to save sinners," and Matth. 18:11, "For the Son of Man is come to save that which was lost."

Thirdly, "that whoever shall believe in this Jesus Christ shall be saved," Mark 16:15, 16. "Preach the gospel to the whole creation." "He that believes and is baptised shall be saved," and John 3:16, "Whosoever believes in him shall not perish but have eternal life." Now as God gives the sinner a spiritual understanding to see and know this, so the Lord brings over his heart, and causes him to assent unto all this as the truth, and to believe it to be the will of the Father, that everyone that believes in his Son Jesus Christ shall be saved. "And if I could believe in him" (says the poor lost sinner), "I should be saved by him, but alas here is my misery, I cannot believe: This is the condemnation to my poor soul, my unbelief: I must needs justify God; He is just in all his ways, he has done right, but I do wickedly; I cannot believe." Oh beloved! The poor lost sinner now can tell you it is not an easy matter to believe in Jesus Christ: no, no, it is a difficult a thing to believe, as it is to keep all the commandments. The poor sinner could do something touching the commandments, but he cannot tell how to do anything about believing. He knows not how to begin to believe. "Nay," says the sinner, "I now know by experience, nothing but an Almighty power of God, who raised Christ from the dead, can enable me to believe, and this day of his power I must wait for." Thus the Lord leads the soul by a way that he knows not, Isa. 42:16. "I will bring the blind by a way they know not, I will lead them in paths that they have not known; I will make darkness light before them." And thus the poor sinner is enlightened to see the hope of his calling. "Well," says the poor soul, "I have some secret hopes that God will show me mercy and will give me Christ, and forgive my sins according to the riches of his grace." For the Lord waits to be gracious, and will be exalted that he may show mercy unto sinners, Isa. 30:18.

Thirdly [after convicting and enlightening the sinner], God does by his Spirit and word convert the sinner, that is to say, changes him into the image of his Son Jesus Christ, 2 Cor. 3:18. But we all with open face, beholding as in a glass the glory of the Lord, are changed into the same image, etc. Let me open this scripture a little to you that so you may understand the work of conversion. But we all, that is, who are converted or turned to the Lord, as in verse 16, with open face, *revelata facie*, with unveiled face, that is to say, the eyes of the understanding being enlightened, Ephes. 1:18. Beholding as in a glass the glory of the Lord: that is, looking upon that object of faith Jesus Christ, who is the glory of the Father, John 1:14. Yes, the brightness of his glory, and the express image, Heb. 1:3, set forth in the word of the gospel preached, as in a glass (James 1:23, 24, 25) to be looked unto for salvation, Isa. 45:22. We are changed into the same image, that is to say, we are converted, made a new creature, regenerated, made a new man, and renewed into the likeness of Jesus Christ or conformed to the image of his Son, Rom. 8:29, 2 Cor. 5:22, Ephes. 4:23, 24. And this change is wrought by the Spirit of God, 2 Cor. 3:18. And that thus the Lord having propounded or offered Jesus Christ to lost sinners, outwardly and in general by the word, and inwardly and particular to this or that lost sinner by the Spirit, accompanying that word of the gospel with divine light and power to the heart of the sinner, does enable the poor soul so to assent unto what is propounded; as to receive what is thereby offered. Namely Jesus Christ, and by faith to rest on him for wisdom, righteousness, sanctification, and redemption: which Christ being given to the sinner, of the Father, is of God made all this to him; as we read in 1 Cor. 1:30. And now the sinner is drawn to Christ, and is sought and saved by Christ.

Touching the third query, the scriptures of truth do testify that Jesus Christ, having sought lost sinners, does save them.

First, Christ does save them from sin, Matth. 1:21.

That is to say, first, from the guilt or imputation of sin. For all have sinned (says the Apostle) and all the world is become guilty before God, Rom. 3:9, 19, 23. Now Jesus Christ does save them from this guiltiness by being made of God their righteousness, in point of justification, and therefore the same Apostle says, Rom. 3:24, that those who before were proved to be sinners and were become guilty before God are now justified freely from his grace through the redemption that is in Jesus Christ, whom God has set forth to be a propitiation through faith in his blood to declare his righteousness for the remission of sins that are past, through the forbearance of God, that he might be just, and the justifier of him which believes in Jesus, Rom. 3:25, 26. At this, the Apostle triumphs, Rom. 8:33. Who shall lay anything to the charge of God's elect? It is God that justifies. And therefore God has freely promised in the everlasting covenant of his rich grace, Heb. 2:12, to remember their sins no more. David describes the blessedness of the man unto whom God imputes righteousness without works; saying, "Blessed is the man to whom the Lord will not impute sin," Rom. 4:6, 7, 8.

Secondly, from the filth or pollution of sin.

For sin contracts filthiness, and defiles the sinner, Matth. 15:18, 19, 20, and Ezekiel 16:6, 22. Now Jesus Christ does save them from this pollution and defilement by being made of God their sanctification, 1 Cor. 1:30, and therefore, although the saints have sin, and do sin, 1 John 1:8, 10, yet the blood of Christ, which is the fountain set open for sin and for uncleanness, Zech. 13:1, does cleanse them from all sin, 1 John 1:7, 9. And being so sanctified and cleansed, they are presented by Christ to the Father, holy and unblameable and unreprovable in his sight, Col. 1:22. Not having spot nor wrinkle nor any such thing, Ephes. 5:26, 27. For both he that sanctifies, and they who are sanctified, are all of one, Heb. 1:11. And by one offering, he has perfected for ever them that are sanctified, Heb. 10:14, according to the request of the Apostle Paul, 1 Thes. 5:23. Now the very God of peace sanctify you wholly, etc.

Thirdly, from the power or dominion of sin; for sin has a domineering power in the hearts of natural men, Col. 1:13. It's called the power of darkness, and Rom. 8:2, "the law of the Spirit of life in Christ Jesus has made me free from that law of sin," etc. Sin has the force of a law upon a carnal heart. Let a man or a woman, who are in the state of natural corruption, resolve to forsake their sinful ways. Let them purpose in themselves, and promise to their friends, to leave such a sinful course. They shall still be overpowered by their lusts to commit those very sins, and be overcome, and be held under the power of them. And although some, yes, diverse of their companions in sin, be justified and sanctified and escape these pollutions of the world through the knowledge of Christ and by the power of his free grace, yet they shall still live in their lusts and commit their wickednesses, Dan. 12:10. Many shall be purified and made white, and tried, but the wicked shall do wickedly. Now Jesus Christ does save them from this lordly power of sin by fellowship with him in his death, Rom. 6:6. Knowing this, that our old man is crucified with him, that the body of sin might be destroyed, that thenceforth we should not serve sin. And therefore, although the saints do sometimes that which they allow not, that which they would not, nay that which they hate; and on the contrary, the good that they would that they do not: and find a law that when they would do good, evil is present with them, and see a law in their members bringing them into captivity to the law of sin, which sin is in their members, Rom. 7:15, 19, 21, 23. Yet there is not one sin which has dominion over them, Rom. 6:14, 15, 17, 22. They are not now the servants of sin, sin is not their Lord and King; but they are freed from it in this regard also, Rom. 6:18. So that though sin may tyrannise and carry them captive sometimes, yet, says the Apostle, sin shall not have dominion over them who are under grace.

Fourthly, from the curse, or punishment of sin; for sin merited the curse of the law, and the wages of sin is death, Rom. 6:23. Now Christ does redeem his people from the curse of the law by being made a curse for them, Gal. 3:13. Thus faith looks at Christ as a Saviour made sin, made a curse, and crucified to redeem his elect from the curse due to sin. What punishment the law and justice of God could exact or require of sinners, the Lord Jesus Christ has suffered, and he has fully satisfied his Father's justice for all the sins of all his people. Christ is therefore called our surety, Heb. 7:22. And although God does rebuke and chastise his people for sin, Psal. 39:11, it is not in wrath for satisfaction, but in love for amendment, Rev. 3:19.

Secondly, [not only does He save them from sin but] Christ having sought lost sinners saves them from the law. For you must understand that sinners were under the law until Christ redeemed them, Gal. 4:5. But now we are delivered from the law that we should serve in newness of spirit and not in the oldness of the letter, Rom. 7:6.

First, from all the ceremonies or elements of the law, Gal. 4:3, that is, the observation of days and months and times and years, verse 10. Christ, by his coming in the flesh, abolished the law of commandments contained in ordinances, Ephes. 2:15. Blotting out the handwriting of ordinances that was against us and contrary to us, and took it out of the way, Col. 2:14. Therefore, the Apostle tells the Galatians that, if they be circumcised, Christ shall profit them nothing, Gal. 5:1, 2, 3.

Secondly, from under the penalties and curse of the law. For it is written, "Cursed is every one that continues not in all things, which are written in the book of the law to do them," Gal. 3:10. Now from this penalty and curse Christ, frees his, whom he has sought and saved, Gal. 3:13. Christ has redeemed us from the curse of the law, etc. Therefore, sinners are said to be saved from wrath through him, Rom. 5:8, 9.

Thirdly, from the schoolmastership of the law. For the law was our schoolmaster until Christ, but after faith is come, we are no longer under a schoolmaster, Gal. 3:24, 25. Now the office of a schoolmaster is to teach or instruct the ignorant. To teach is the main or essential part of a schoolmaster, and to correct is but accidental. One may be a good schoolmaster and never correct a scholar with stripes. And therefore we are thus to understand this scripture, we, who are believers, are not longer under the tutorage or government of the law, as we were in our non-age (which is the very truth which the Apostle labors to clear up to the understanding of the Galatians, chapter 3:24, 25 and 4:1, 2, 3, 4, 5). But we have a new schoolmaster, that is, Jesus Christ, Ephes. 4:20, 21. If so be you have heard him, and have been taught by him, as the truth is in Jesus. Now the difference between these two schoolmasters, the law and Christ, is this, Moses in the law commands his disciples to do this and forbear that, but gives no power, nor communicates no skill to perform any thing. Christ commands his disciples to do the same moral duties and to forbear the same evils, and with his command, he gives power and wisdom. For he works in us both to will and to do according to his good pleasure, Phil. 2:12, 13. Thus Christ, having freed us from under the tutorage of the law, takes us under his own tuition and teaches us to yield obedience of faith to his Father's will, and to serve him in newness of spirit and not in the oldness of the letter.

Fourthly, from the old covenant of the law, for the Ten Commandments are called a covenant, Deut. 4:13, Exod. 34:28. And the Apostle, in his Epistle to the Hebrews, calls it an old, faulty, vanishing covenant, Heb. 8:7, 9, 13, opposing against it that new perfect and everlasting covenant of the gospel. You know the zealous Jews sought righteousness and life by the works of the law, Rom. 9:31, 32. That is to say, they did think (as many of the professors of our times do) to be saved by keeping the Ten Commandments, Luke 18:18, 20, 21, 22. And Paul bears them record that they were zealous, but it was not according to knowledge. For they, being ignorant of God's righteousness, were about to establish their own righteousness and the Apostle on this matter tells them that Christ is the end of the law for righteousness to everyone that believes, Rom. 10:2, 3, 4, 5. And therefore we may use great plainness of speech and safely conclude that the administration of the law (written and engraved in stones, even the Ten Commandments as they were, that first, old, faulty and vanishing covenant) is now done away and abolished; And yet we do not hereby make void the law, but establish it, Rom. 3:31. For we say that we ought to yield obedience of faith, in newness of spirit, and so fulfill the royal law according to the scripture, James 2:8. You do well, says the Apostle, so speak you and so do, as they that shall be judged by the perfect law of liberty, James 2:12. Neither are we without law to God, but under the law to Christ, 1 Cor. 9:21. For though we be delivered from the law (which was our old husband) that being dead in which we were held, yet we serve God in newness of spirit and not in the oldness of the letter, Rom. 7:4, 6. The grace of God which has appeared brings us this salvation and teaches us to deny ungodliness, and worldly lusts, and to live soberly, righteously, and godly in this present world, Tit. 2:11, 12, 13, 14, 15.

[Fifthly], I might be large in the declaring and proving by the scriptures that Christ saves his people (even poor lost sinners) from Hell also, both from the fears of Hell in their hearts, delivering them, who for a long season through fear of wrath, and everlasting death, were held in bondage, Heb. 2:15, and from the power of the pit. Also how he saves them from Satan's deluding temptations and the enticing allurements of the world.

And indeed, I might justly treat upon all that good blessing and covenant grace, which poor lost sinners, from the first conversion to the faith, receive the end of their faith, the salvation of their souls; for these two terms of seeking and saving includes all from the beginning of grace to the end of glory, but this may suffice for the present.

1. *Reason.* Jesus Christ must see and save lost sinners because the Father sanctified him, sealed him, and sent him from heaven to finish this work of redemption. And this is the Father's will, which has sent me, that of all which he has given me I should lose nothing and that everyone who believes on the Son may have everlasting life, John 6:38, 39, 40. This was the

great errand of Christ from Heaven to the inhabitable parts of the earth: to save sinners, 1 Tim 1:15.

Christ came into the world to save sinners. And this was the work his Father gave him to finish. Therefore, he must perfect it. "I came from Heaven" (says Christ) "not to do my own will, but the will of him that sent me," John 6:38.

2. *Reason.* The man Christ Jesus must seek and save lost sinners, because (the Father having exalted him to be a prince, and a Saviour, and promised in his everlasting covenant of grace that all Israel shall be saved, Rom. 11:26, 27) "There is no other name under heaven given among men, whereby we must be saved," Acts 4:12. Neither is there salvation in any other. Truly in vain is salvation hoped for from the hills and from the multitude of the mountains. Truly in Jehovah our God is the salvation of Israel, Jer 3:23. Therefore, the Lord said by his prophets, Isa. 45:22, "Look unto me and be you saved all the ends of the earth; for I am God and there is none else."

3. *Reason.* The Lord Jesus Christ must seek and save lost sinners, because God will not have any one of those, whom he has given to his Son, to perish, Matth. 18:14. Therefore, the Son of Man is come to save them that are lost, v. 11. Christ must give an account to God the Father of all, which he has given him: he must keep them and preserve to himself when he gives up the Kingdom to God the Father, John 17:12 and 18:9. Therefore, Christ promises to give them eternal life, and they shall never perish, neither shall any man pluck them out of his hand, John 10:28. For he said, "Surely they are my people"; so he was their Saviour, Isa. 63:8, 9. And in their affliction, the angel of his presence saved them.

1st *use.* Seeing that this is a truth, that the man Christ Jesus must seek and save lost sinners, let us make use of this doctrine to discover the ground of much trouble and disconsolation in some professors touching their salvation. They see that they are lost, undone, and in a perishing condition, but they look not to Christ to be saved. They think to save themselves by seeking, praying, mourning, reforming, etc. And consider not that Christ must seek and save them. They will take the work out of his hand and think to do it themselves by their humiliations, duties, etc. And such professors either have no comfort, or their joys last no longer then their humiliations and duties, and when they cannot pray, mourn, overcome sin, and perform holy duties with that enlargement and broken heartedness, as sometimes they have done, then all their joy is ceased, all their hopes are perished, all their comforts are gone; and they are marvellously disconsolate and cry out they are hypocrites, they have no grace, etc. Now they look not to Christ, who must save them, but to themselves, and to their performances, duties, and humiliations, and truly in vain is salvation hoped for from these hills and mountains. Although most professors confess with their mouths that Christ must save them, yet many do in their hearts deny him, and would make their prayers, their humiliation, and their duties their saviours: and no marvel if they be often sorrowful and disconsolate, for this they have at God's hand to lie down in sorrow after they having kindled a fire and compassed themselves about with the sparks of their performances, Isa. 50:11, they walk in the light of that fire and sparks, which they themselves kindled; but when that light goes out, and those sparks die or vanish away, then all their joy, peace, comforts, and hopes are lost.

2nd *use*. This doctrine may also be useful for examination: Christ came to seek and save lost sinners. This is the work he has to do for poor souls: to seek and to save them that are lost. Let it therefore put you upon trial, whether you be such as Christ must seek and save. Are you sinners? Yes, we are all sinners will some say. And if any may say he has no sin, he deceives himself, and the truth is not in him, 1 John 1:8, 10. Yes, that is truth: all men are sinners, but has this general truth been brought home to your heart in particular, with such a divine light and power of the Spirit in the world, that it did so convince your conscience, that if you had not known any other man in the world to be a sinner, yet you could not but have believed that you were a sinner. "Ah," says a poor seeking soul, "I know by woeful experience of my own heart and ways that I am a sinner indeed, a sinner with a witness. I was a blasphemer, a drunkard, an unclean person, etc. My heart is still hard and proud, carnal and desperately wicked, I find and feel it so to be daily." Well, but have you had a thorough conviction that you are a sinner? Have you been convinced of your gospel sins? That is, piercing Christ, slighting God's offer of him to you upon gospel-terms, and despising him, though tendered in a covenant of grace? Alas, the thoughts how I have abused, slighted, and neglected free mercy and rich grace pierces my heart. I have stood out against God, preferred the world, and the things of this life, yes, my own base sinful lusts before Jesus Christ. I cannot speak of the vanity and deceitfulness of my heart in this kind without tears. Oh, it breaks my heart so oft as I seriously consider what injury I have done to Christ in his people by scorns and reproaches, and persecutions, what hard thoughts I have had of him (unbelieving thoughts, blasphemous thoughts, carnal thoughts), and what hard speeches I have spoken against Christ, his ways, messengers, ordinances, churches, and people. But could you not reform yourself, humble yourself, deny yourself, forsake your sins, perform duties and so save yourself from this your miserable estate? On no, I did think that I might amend my ways, leave my sins, and reform myself, and I went about it, hoping to be saved by my own righteousness, but all in vain. For either I had no power to forsake my sins, nor grace to pray, mourn, and humble myself, or if I did overcome some temptations and resist some corruptions (through the power of God) or was assisted (by his grace) to perform holy duties, I rested in them, and raised all my hopes, confidence, and comforts from them, grew proud, self-confident, and so miscarried, lost all my hopes and comforts. But even though you could not get heaven this way, yet could you not easily believe and so be saved? "Truly," says the poor sinner, "I think it is as hard a thing to believe in Jesus Christ with all the heart as to keep all the commandments; when I was convinced that my own righteousness could not save me, and saw I could never get to heaven in a way of works, I was complaining to some of my miserable condition, and they bade me believe, which at first I thought was easier, and I resolved to believe. But presently, after an unmortified corruption breaking forth in my heart put me into sad fears, I went to pray, but my heart being hardened by the deceitfulness of sin, I could not pray. Thereupon I doubted of my condition more still, then I would have affected my heart with sorrow, but I could not mourn. I began to feel my heart cold, hard, and dead, and thereupon I called all into question, and being under many fearful temptations, concluded that I was a hypocrite and saw myself utterly lost, having no hopes. I could not but bewail my sad condition to godly friends, who still exhorted me to believe in Christ. But, alas, I could not believe, and I was also afraid to believe, lest it should be upon false grounds, and truly I think had not the day of God's exceeding great power come upon me, and set home a promise of free grace by his Spirit, with divine light and mighty power upon my heart, I should never have believed. But when that promise came, it was so suitable to my present condition, my heart objections were so answered by it, and it pleased God so clearly to reveal his rich and free love in Christ Jesus to my soul in it, that I could not but with tears and much heartbreakings admire the infinite goodness of God to me, and I was so self-ashamed and abased, as that I saw myself the chief of sinners, which promise of the Spirit I received by faith, applied to myself, and in the believing that Christ was mine and I his, I was filled with joy unspeakable and glorious; and ever since God has drawn out my heart more and more after himself, and after holiness, so that he has caused me more to desire, yes hunger and thirst after righteousness and sanctification, then after heaven."

3rd *use*. This doctrine will make much for the consolation of true believers, that Christ must seek and save lost sinners, and that first for themselves, secondly in regard of theirs. Believers themselves are much troubled with their corruptions, and although they pray against them, mourn under them, and resist them, yet sometimes they are carried captive, Rom. 7:23. Now this doctrine may be applied for the consolation of such, Christ must save you from your sins, Matth. 1:21, and sin shall not have dominion over you, Rom. 6:14. His grace is sufficient for you, 2 Cor. 12:8, 9. Christ shall turn away ungodliness from Jacob, and this is his covenant with them, to take away their sins, Rom. 11:26, 27.

Also, believers may, from this doctrine, have some ground of hope and so of comfort, with respect to their yokefellows, parents, brethren, children, or other friends or kinsfolks after the flesh, who yet remain in their natural estate. It may be you have spent many a prayer, some tears also, upon them, you still do make mention of them day and night in prayer, and so often as you have access to the throne of grace, you remember them to your Father. You spread their blind, ignorant, dead, naked, and miserable condition before God, and still they abide in their sinful estate, and you have sad thoughts, doubts, and fears that they will perish. But yet there is hope in Israel touching this thing; for Christ must lose none that the Father has given him, he must seek them and save them. And what know you but that carnal yoke-fellow, or parent, or brother, or child, or sister, or neighbour may be of that number; and if so, they shall not perish. Consider what the Apostle propounds, 1 Cor. 7:16, and let me thus apply it: what know you, whether Christ will save your husband or wife, etc. Therefore pray in hope and wait on God in hope. Who can tell? God may have chosen him, or her, and then Christ must seek and save them.

4th *use*. This doctrine may afford us a word of exhortation to poor seeking, waiting, and mourning souls, who are made sensible of their lost condition and see themselves almost ready to perish for want of Christ. I would exhort such to believe that they shall be saved, for Christ came to seek and to save that which was lost. Christ must seek and save lost sinners, this is a ground to believe it.

Objection. You will say this is a ground to believe Christ will save some lost sinners. But all who were lost in Adam shall not be saved by Christ, and how can I know, that I am one of the few, who shall be saved?

Solution. I answer, when God by his Holy Spirit shall bring home this general truth, particularly to your soul with divine light, life, and power of manifestation, He will so clearly witness that Christ came to seek and to save you, who was a lost sinner, that you shall have a spiritual understanding given to know it, and to believe it, yes, and you shall be filled with joy and peace in believing.

Outline That we should be Holy

Eph 1:4

Doctrine—God will have his people to be a holy people

1. Scriptural Support
   a) Because God has chosen them in Christ to this end Eph 1:4
   b) God calls his to holiness I Thess 4:7
   c) God has given to everyone of his Holy Spirit to sanctify them Rom 15:16
   d) God affords them his Holy Word, which is a means of sanctification John 17:17
2. Reasons that they should be holy
   a) That he may be justified in justifying the ungodly
   b) For the honour and glory of His Son to Whom He has given them
   c) That they may enjoy spiritual communion with Him in this life and the next
3. Application (Use)
   a) How does God make us holy?
      1) A real change of the whole person
      2) It is a work of the Spirit through the Word
   b) By this we can determine who are not the people of God
      1) Those who are legal professors
      2) Those who are formal professors
      3) Those who are carnal professors
   c) By this believers are brought to a deep humiliation and godly sorrow for their unholiness
   d) By this every true believer should be encouraged, particularly when under persecution
      1) Knowing that God has chosen you to be holy
      2) Knowing that God has made you an everlasting covenant of grace and holiness
      3) Knowing that Christ has prayed to the Father for your sanctification

    4) Knowing that Christ sanctified Himself for your sake to be sanctified

    5) Knowing that God has given you the Spirit of His Son who sanctifies you

    6) Knowing that God is faithful who called you

  e) Exhortation to holiness at all times, in all relations and in every condition

EPHESIANS 1:4
That we should be holy.

In this chapter, you have: first, the inscription of the epistles, verse 1, and therein is declared both the pen-man Paul; and his office, an Apostle of Jesus Christ by the will of God; also the persons to whom the Epistle was written, the saints, and to the faithful in Christ Jesus, which are at Ephesus.

Secondly, a salutation, verse 2, and therein is expressed the matter of the salutation, grace and peace; the persons saluted you, that is, the saints; the author from whom grace and peace comes to the saints: from God our Father, and the Lord Jesus Christ.

Thirdly, congratulation, verse 3, for spiritual blessings in general, etc. Who has blessed us with all spiritual blessings, etc., or with every spiritual blessing. Of which the Apostle mentions some particularly in the following verses, that is, election, predestination, adoption. In this fourth verse, Saint Paul hints to us:

First, that there is an election.

Secondly, that the elect are chosen in Christ.

Thirdly, that election was before the Word was founded.

And fourthly, that the elect of God should be holy, and without blame in his presence, in love.

Thus, you see the occasion and dependence of the words of the text, which offers to your religious consideration this plain doctrine.

Doctrine. God will have his people to be a holy people. This point of doctrine needs no explanation; And it is a truth so generally assented to by all professors, that I shall give you but one scripture to confirm it: 1 Thes. 4:3. "This is the will of God," your sanctification, And indeed it appears manifestly in the scripture of truth that this is God's holy will.

First, because God has chosen them in Christ to this end, Ephes. 1:4, that they should be holy.

Secondly, God calls his to holiness, 1 Thes. 4:7. God has not called us to uncleanness, but unto holiness.

Thirdly, God has given to every one of his the Holy Spirit to sanctify them, Rom. 15:16, being sanctified by the Holy Spirit.

Fourthly, God affords them his Holy Word, which is a means of sanctification, John 17:17. "Sanctify them through your truth, your Word is truth." Yes, when they sin against God, he will chastise them for their profit; that they may be partakers of his holiness, Heb. 12:10. So that God would have his people holy.

Reason 1. God will have his people to be holy, that he may be justified in justifying the ungodly, Rom. 3:26. That he might be just, that justifies the ungodly, Rom. 4:5. God justifies the ungodly, that is, He is finding men and women in their blood or in their sins, Ezek. 16:6, 8. He (in the time of love) forgives them all their sins, covers their nakedness with the skirt of Christ's righteousness, and bids them live. This is done when God enters into covenant with them, and so they become his. Now that God may be justified in so doing, though he found them ungodly, unbelievers, impenitent, profane, etc. He does not only forgive them all their sins, and so leave them ungodly to go on in their wicked ways; but he gives them his Holy Spirit of sanctification, who changes their hearts, renews the spirit of their minds, sanctifies their wills and affection, and produces all those fruits of the Spirit in them mentioned in Gal. 5:22, 23, whereby they are made holy in all manner of conversation. 1 Pet. 1:15, 16. And this reason the apostle gives, Ephes. 1:4, 6, that we should be holy to the praise of the glory of his grace, and verse 12, that we should be to the praise of his glory. And herein is God justified in justifying the ungodly, in that he does make and keep them holy, Jude 1.

Reason 2. God will have his people to be holy for the honour and glory of his Son Jesus Christ to whom he has given them. "All mine are yours" (says Christ in his prayer to his Father, John 17:1, 10) "and yours are mine, and I am glorified in them," also verse 19. "And for their sakes, I sanctify myself, that they also might be sanctified." Christ shall be glorified in his saints, especially in his kingly office, Rev. 15:3, 4. Just and true are your ways; you king of saints; who shall not fear you, O Lord, and glorify your Name, for you only are holy. And even though now Christ and his poor saints are scorned, and despised of men; yet that prophesy of Enoch, the seventh from Adam, will have its accomplishment, Jude 14. "Behold, the Lord comes with ten thousands of his saints. The Lord Jesus shall be revealed from heaven with his mighty angels when he shall come to be glorified in his saints," 2 Thes. 1:7, 10. And in that day, it will appear to all the world that it is the great glory of Jesus Christ that his Father has given him so many ten thousands of saints to be his subjects, and himself to be their king, Isa. 33:37, 22.

Reason 3. God will have his people holy, that they may enjoy spiritual communion with him in this life and eternal communion with him in heaven. The saints do enjoy spiritual communion with God in this life, 1 John 1:3. Truly our fellowship is with the Father, and with his Son Jesus Christ, and with the Spirit, Phil. 2:1. And they shall have eternal communion with God in heaven, in that kingdom prepared for them, which then they shall receive, Matth. 25:34. Now this communion with God, none can have without holiness, Heb. 12:14. Therefore, God will have his people to be holy.

1st Use. Will God have his people to be holy? Let it be useful to us, first for enquiry, what holiness is? And how God makes his holy? 1 Thes. 4:3, 7.

Holiness or sanctification is a real change of the whole man from the pollution of sin to the purity of the image of Christ, Rom. 6:22. But now being made free from sin, and become servants of God, you have your fruits unto holiness. Here was a real change in them from the pollution of sin, 2 Cor. 3:18. But we all with open face beholding, as in a glass, the glory of the Lord are changed into the image. Here was the other part of that real change in them; that is, into the purity of the image of Christ. For as men in their natural estate bear the image of the earthly first man—Adam—so men in their spiritual estate bear the image of the heavenly second man—Christ—1 Cor. 15:47, 48, 49. This holiness or sanctification (if you have respect to the author and efficient cause of it) is called the sanctification of the Spirit, 2 Thes. 2:13 and 1 Pet. 2. (If unto the divine act of God, it is called renovation or renewing of the mind, Ephes. 4:23 and Rom. 12:2. If unto the acts and fruits of holiness in believers, it is called faith, love, long suffering, gentleness, goodness, meekness, temperance, etc., Gal. 5:22. If unto the root, fountain, and foundation of holiness, the scripture says Christ is our sanctification, 1 Cor. 1:30). Thus, you hear what holiness is.

Now God makes His holy by his Spirit and Word; whereby he does convince them that they are without Christ, Ephes. 2:12. Makes discovery to them of the worth of Christ, their need of him, and God's offer of him in a covenant of grace upon gospel terms; changing their hearts into the image of Christ, 2 Cor. 3:18. Gives them faith in Christ, repentance from dead works, love to all the saints, etc. "And so the very God of peace sanctify this people," 1 Thes. 5:23. Thus much may suffice touching the inquiry.

2nd *Use.* Will God have his people to be holy? Let us make use of this to discover who are the people of God and who are not. Those people that are ungodly, unsanctified are not the people of God: such may boast of their justification, but they deceive themselves, for God has not justified unsanctified people, 1 Cor. 6:9, 10, 11. They may talk of the free grace of God manifested to them, and bringing them salvation, but they are deluded; for the grace of God that brings salvation teaches us to deny ungodliness and to live godly lives, Titus 2:11, 12. Now there are three sorts of professors who would be esteemed the people of God, and yet are not sanctified by the Holy Spirit: they are not holy, and therefore are not the Lord's people in covenant.

The first sort are all those legal professors who, having been by the Spirit and Word of God much convinced of sin, John 16:8, sorely wounded in their consciences, Proverbs 18:14, and somewhat reformed in their conversations by hearing godly preachers, as Herod was, Mark 6:20, after all this go about to establish their own righteousness, and rest upon their duties, humiliation, and legal reformation. And never have their hearts changed, and renewed, nor Christ given of the Father unto them. These are not sanctified, are not the Lord's. Hear what the Apostle speaks to such among the Galatians. "Are you so foolish? Having begun in the Spirit, are you now made perfect by the flesh? Have you suffered so many things in vain? If it be yet in vain." Well, such of you as God has chosen in Christ that you should be holy, etc. He will also by His Spirit and Word convince you of righteousness, that is, that all your own righteousnesses are as filthy rags, Isa. 6:6. That being ignorant of God's righteousness, you have gone about to establish your own righteousness, Rom. 30:3, and that you must be found in Christ, not having your own righteousness, which is of the law; but that which is through the faith of Christ, the righteousness which is of God by faith, Phil. 3:9.

The second sort are all those formal professors who seem to be only religious, James 1:26. "Having a form of godliness, but denying the power of it," 2 Tim. 3:5. These will tell you they rest not on duties, trust not to their own righteousness, confide not in their humiliation, as legal professors do; But they (after much trouble of conscience for their sins) got comfort, joy, and peace in applying some promises of the gospel to themselves. Consider I pray you, the parable of the stony ground hearers: they on the rock are they, which when they hear, receive the

Word with joy, and these have no root, which for a while believe, and in time of temptation fall away, Luke 8:13. Here was some (plowing though it went not deep enough) and some harrowing also to cover the good seed; after this there was some joy, but no root. Here was the Word convincing and wounding and comforting but no Christ (who is called the root, Col. 2:6, 7) to quicken, renew, and sanctify: And therefore, though they believed awhile, yet they fall away in the time of temptation. And this is the condition of formal professors: they get comfort in promises, but they receive not Christ and his sanctifying comforting Spirit in the promises. Let such hear what the Lord by his prophets speaks to a formal professing people, Isa. 50:11. "Behold all you that kindle a fire that compass yourselves about with sparks. Walk in the light of your fire, and in the sparks that you have kindled. This shall you have at my hand; you shall lie down in sorrow."

The third sort are all those carnal professors who say they are the people of God and hold the common faith, Titus 1:4, which is the faith of God's elect, Titus 1:1. And believe the common salvation: Jude 3. That is to say, common to everyone that believes, both Jew and Gentile: Rom. 1:16. But notwithstanding all this profession of general redemption, they themselves are the servants of corruption: 2 Pet. 2:19. For they take liberty to live in sin, and walk after the flesh, fulfilling the lusts of it, turning the grace of God into lasciviousness, and denying the only Lord God and our Lord Jesus Christ: Jude 4. They are so far departed from the faith, which they sometime professed, and seemed to have, 1 Tim. 4:1, that they question whether the scriptures of truth are the Word of God? Whether Christ is the Son of God? Whether the first day of the week is the Sabbath of God? And they are so far from living godly and walking in the way of holiness that they totally omit all holy duties. They refrain from prayer, they speak not of the word of God when they rise up, nor when they lie down, nor as they sit in the house together with their family. They do not partake of any ordinances, nor perform any worship to God. And as for sin, they make a mock at it; some of them say God takes no knowledge of their sins, he sees no iniquity in them; others affirm that they have no sin, they are born of God, and they cannot sin. And some others are bold, to say, they are justified persons, and therefore all their words and actions are alike acceptable to God, and well-pleasing in his sight, etc. But these carnal professors are not holy, are not the people of God. This may make some discovery of those whose hearts are not right with God; to whom I would give the Apostle's exhortation, Acts 8:22.

3rd *Use*. Will God have His people to be holy? Then may this doctrine occasion a deep humiliation and godly sorrow in believers for their unholiness, carnalness, and sinfulness in heart or life. O beloved, let you and I commune with our own hearts. How much unbelief, hypocrisy, self-filthiness, formality, and wickedness, shall we, upon diligent examination, find still remaining in us? What vanity of mind and carnality is in our hearts? How many hard thoughts of God have we still? Notwithstanding all the experiences God has given us of his unchangeableness, his faithfulness, and his everlasting loving-kindness in Jesus Christ, how apt are we, by an evil heart of unbelief, to depart from God? Alas, what sinful contemplations have we in our spirits? What evil concupiscence? How do our hearts run out after the creature-comforts of this world, and how are our affections still set upon the things below Christ and God? How many idols are set up in our hearts? How great is our self-love, self-seeking, self-confidence, self-dependence, and self-sufficiency! O what high thoughts have we sometimes of ourselves, our gifts, our graces, our experiences, our performances? Surely we have just cause (if God will in mercy work in us godly sorrow) to be ashamed to mourn after a godly manner, and to loathe ourselves for the abominations of our own hearts. But my brethren, let us examine our lives, and search and try our ways, as well as commune with our hearts, for the eye of the world is open upon us; God, and angels, men and devils all observe us (who are believers). They hear what we say, and take knowledge what we do. O beloved, how much vain, carnal, and sinful communication comes out of our mouths that ministers no grace to the hearers? How many idle words do we speak? What unprofitable talk have we among ourselves and with others: not gracious, not seasoned with the salt of truth and holiness, but very unsavory speeches. And when we meet together, and speak one to another of religion, we are apt to speak slightly, rashly, formally, inconsiderately, and not soberly, humbly, and graciously, as becomes the saints. Yes, our conferences sometimes turns to vain jangling and unedifying disputes, wherein we strive for victory, or to maintain our own opinion, more than truth; But besides all this, how much ungodliness is there in our actions? Even though God prevents us by his grace from doing actions simply and grossly evil and ungodly, such as drunkenness, uncleanness, etc. Yet in doing lawful things, we often miscarry; the messengers of Christ do sometimes preach themselves, fathers of families do correct their children sometimes after their pleasures, provoking their children, being bitter to their wives sometimes. Oh how uneven do we walk in our callings and relations, wherein we should especially show forth the power of godliness! Oh, had we tender hearts and were we truly sensible of our sinful miscarriages, we could not speak of those particulars without tears of godly sorrow. Can we consider how many years we have possessed the gospel, how long we have enjoyed the word preached in season and out of season unto us, and yet how little our conversation is as becomes the gospel, how little we have profited, how little we have grown in grace, and in the knowledge of Jesus Christ, and not be affected to mourn under the feeling of our unprofitableness and great barrenness? But I hope God will give us repentance unto salvation, not to be repented of for all our unrighteousness.

4th *Use*. Will God have his people to be holy? Let it be useful for the consolation of every true believer; especially such as at present groan under the tyrannical power or captivation bondage of any corruption; And sigh to God for supply from Christ of any grace wanting, or weak in their apprehension, sense, and feeling. Hearken poor mourning soul, and consider what may be said for your comfort, and search the scriptures, whether it is so or not.

Know first that God's eternal purpose toward you (who are a true believer) in choosing you in Christ was that you should be holy, Ephes. 1:4 and Rom. 8:30. "I have purposed it" (says God); "I will also do it," Isa. 46:11.

Secondly, that God has made with you an everlasting covenant of grace and holiness, wherein he has given you many great and precious promises, to pardon sin, to subdue iniquity, and to put his law in your mind, and write it in your heart, Jer. 3:31, 34, and 32:40 with Heb. 8:10, 11, 12. Micah 7:18, 19, 20 with 2 Pet. 2:3, 4, to the 11th verse.

Thirdly, that Christ has prayed to his Father for you, that he would sanctify you, John 17:1 and 17:20.

Fourthly, that Christ sanctified himself for your sake, that you also might be sanctified, John 17:19, 20.

Fifthly, that God has given you the Spirit of his Son, Gal. 4:6, who is a comforting, sanctifying Spirit, yes, the Comforter, John 14:16, 17, 18. And he that sanctifies all the people of God, 1 Thes. 5:23.

Sixthly, that faithful is God who called you, who also will do it, 1 Thes. 5:24. He called you unto holiness, 1 Thes. 4:7, and he will both make you holy. [He has said you shall be holy, Levit.

11:44, 45, and 19:2. That is such a command as has the force of a promise in it; And though that place, Levit. 20:7, is "Sanctify yourselves therefore and be you holy"; yet the 70 interpreters[10] render it *Et sanctificabimi* and *eritis sancti*. And so does the Chaldees Paraphrase render it also. And Jerome translates that place, in the first of Pet. 1:16, "Be you holy," *Sancti eritis*, "You shall be holy"; And indeed, God can put a being to his Word. And therefore be of good comfort, your sins are forgiven you, Matth. 9:2. And sin shall not have dominion over you, Rom. 16:14. The grace of Christ is sufficient for you, 2 Cor. 12:9. He is full of grace, John 1:16. According as his divine power has given us all things that pertain unto life and godliness, 2 Pet. 1:3.

5th *Use.* Will God have his people to be holy? Let me conclude with a use of exhortation to holiness; "As he that called you is holy, so be you holy in all manner of conversation," 1 Pet. 1:15. God will have his people holy at all times, in all relations, and in every condition.

Therefore, I beseech you brethren, and exhort you in the Lord, and for his sake, to be holy in all manner of conversation, holy in your callings, for godliness is great gain. Holy in your families, in your shops, in your journeys, in all your ways, and in all your relations. Godliness has the promise both of this life, and that which is to come. Piety has a majesty in it; it will give you a throne in the consciences of others that they dare not sin in your presence. Holiness is an ornament to your callings, to your persons, to your families, and to the place where you live. The more holy, the more like your Heavenly Father, and the more you glorify your Heavenly Father, and the more you adorn the doctrine of Christ; yes, the more communion you have with the Father and with Christ. Having therefore these promises, dearly beloved, let us cleanse ourselves from all filthiness of the flesh and spirit, perfecting holiness in the fear of God, 2 Cor. 7:1, 4. Great is my boldness or speech toward you in this exhortation, because I desire fruit that may abound to your account; and give me leave to press this exhortation upon such believers present who have carnal parents, yoke-fellows, or other carnal friends. You would have your natural friends converted, and to that end you pray for them, mourn over them, many a sigh, and many a tear, it may be, they have cost you; but they live in the flesh still, are carnal still.

Oh, let not a holy conversation be wanting, that may further their conversion, 1 Cor. 7:16, 17. And if any obey not the

---

10. The Septuagint translators.

Word; they also may be won without the Word by your godly conversation, 1 Pet. 3:1. And if they be not drawn thereby to the love of the truth, yet their mouths will be stopped, that they cannot speak against it. Would it not be comfortable thing to have a carnal father speak thus of his godly son or daughter; that is, "I was unwilling my children should go so often to hear sermons, and be so often at conferences, and private fasts; and the like; But I have observed that, since they professed religion, and gave themselves to pray, and read the scriptures, they have been much more dutiful to us their parents than before, and they are more diligent in their callings. If this be the worst, they shall have liberty to profess the gospel still. The like I might speak of other relations." But should carnal parents or friends have cause by your loose or uneven walking to speak evil of the ways of God, it would be very uncomfortable to you and dishonourable to the gospel. I shall conclude in the words of the Apostle, Phil. 4:8. "Finally, Brethren, whatsoever things are true; whatsoever things are honest, just, pure, lovely, or of good report, if there be any virtue, and if there be any praise, think on these things, and the God of peace shall be with you," verse 9.

One objection had need to be answered before I end, and that is this; may some say, "You have exhorted us to holiness," and the Apostle tells us, 2 Tim. 3:12, all that will live godly in Christ Jesus shall suffer persecution."

Objection. How may we be encouraged and strengthened against the fears of persecution?

Solution. I answer, first, pray to God that he will furnish you with suffering graces against persecuting times, Col. 1:9, 10, 11. Secondly, improve your interest through Christ in the promises, and believe that the more sufferings for Christ, the more comfort by Christ, 2 Cor. 1:5. The more sufferings, the more holiness, Heb. 12:10. The more sufferings, the more happiness, 1 Pet. 4:14. Only take heed of sufferings as an evildoer, verses 15, 16. And if any suffer as a Christian, Christ will suffer with him, Isa. 63:9. Christ will share with you in your suffering persecution, Acts 9:4, 5. And you shall share with Christ in glory, Rom. 8:17. But you must be holy in sufferings, also praying for them that persecute you, as Christ taught and practised: and so did his martyr Steven, Acts 7:60. "Lord, lay not this to their charge." And so let us pray for them that now disturbed us.

FINIS.

3

Parable of the Kingdom of Heaven Expounded

Introduction

The Parable of the Kingdom of Heaven Expounded was written during the Restoration period (1660–1689) in the year 1674. It is the second of Knollys six eschatological writings but differs from most of the others in that its focus is much more exhortational than theological. Both this work and the *World that now is and the World that is to come* have a strong emphasis on the church in the present era with exhortations to all who profess faith in Christ. Knollys is deeply concerned in the *Parable* for those who attend church but are not committed to Christ in a life of godliness. Consequently, exhortation to professors is a recurring theme in this work.

This is one of his longer published works and was likely preached to his congregation in some form. One of the quite noticeable marks of the *Parable* is the number of scripture passages quoted throughout. It is clear that Knollys knew the Scriptures well, and truly believed the authority and power of the Word by his full text quotes throughout.

In the *Parable* Knollys argues that the kingdom of heaven refers to three different eras in scripture: 1) the kingdom of glory which comes into existence after the resurrection of the dead and the final judgment; 2) the spiritual kingdom of grace in the hearts of believers in which we are presently living; and 3) the mystical kingdom of the church of Christ under the gospel. This parable is referring to the third meaning.

For Knollys this kingdom follows the present era which, for him, was yet in the future. This is Christ's virtual and spiritual coming in his saints and will last for a thousand years. It is not his personal bodily coming which will not occur until the end of the 1000 years.[1] It is, however, a powerful coming of Christ whereby the churches of the saints will be reformed and restored unto a virgin state of primitive purity and spiritual glory, as in the days of the apostles. At this time and during this era the life of the church/His people will be reformed as will also the discipline and government of the churches. The churches will be ruled by the holy, righteous and good laws of Christ. In addition, the ministry of the gospel, the gifts of the Holy Spirit, and ordinances of the church will be restored worldwide in all churches. The *Parable* is addressing the inauguration of this era with the coming of the Bridegroom (Christ) for his bride (the church). The bride, the present era church, is symbolized by the ten virgins. When the Bridegroom comes some virgins will enter into the kingdom of heaven, that is, the 1000 year reign of Christ on earth, and some will be shut out. Consequently, the emphasis of the *Parable* is on those who profess faith that they may be found as the wise virgins and not the foolish ones.

Knollys sees the difference between the wise and foolish virgins, not in their form of godliness but the power of godliness in them. The wise virgins are those who have both, that is they not only carry out their religious duties such as attend church and partake of the ordinances, but they also live the gospel every day. They are not professors of faith but livers of the faith from their hearts. They are the regenerate and true believers. They are the ones in the parable that had oil in their lamps, that is, the unction of the Holy Spirit. It is the oil of grace and sanctification, the gifts and the fruits of the Holy Spirit, even the power of godliness in heart and life.

He warns all in the church, wise and foolish, to not be found sleeping (slack in their spiritual lives) when the bridegroom comes. But his clear focus is on those who profess faith but do not demonstrate the power of godliness in their lives. He calls them to wake up and seek to get the oil of grace, and so conform to the revealed will of God in His Word. The door of grace will shut when no man can come into Christ's kingdom. As we have seen in *Christ Exalted*, Knollys has a passion for Christ and his church that she be prepared for His return. He longs for the day that the church will be as it should be. When the kingdom of heaven comes, it will be. So all, sinners, professors and believers should be ready.[2]

---

1. Anachronistically, this view would be called postmillennialism. Knollys is one of the early proponents of this view. It was popularized by Jonathan Edwards in the eighteenth century.

2. Knollys categorizes his audience into three groups throughout the work and makes application to each. They are believers (true regenerate followers of Christ), professors (those who appear religious but are really not regenerate) and profane persons (those who are sinners in the world). The emphasis is, however, on the professors.

Knollys was clearly concerned for the church at this time. According to his other eschatological writings he believed that the coming of the Kingdom would take place soon.[3] When he wrote this work he was probably addressing not simply members of his own congregation or even of other reformed congregations but also those of the Church of England.[4]

The Parable of the Kingdom of Heaven Expounded

Or an exposition of the first thirteen verses
of the twenty-fifth chapter of Matthew

Matth. 13:34. *"All these things spoke Jesus to the multitudes in parables, and without a parable spoke he not among them."*

Luke 8:10. *"Unto you it is given to know the mysteries of the Kingdom of God, but to others in parables, etc."*

Psal. 78:2. *"I will open my mouth in a parable, I will utter dark sayings of old."*

Psal. 49:4. *"I will incline my ear to a parable."*

———————————

By Hanserd Knollys

———————————

London. Printed for Benjamin Harris, and to be sold at the Stationers Armes in Sweeting, Rents, in Cornhill, near the Royal Exchange. 1674.

---

3. See the final chapter on Knollys's eschatology.

4. A couple of years before the publication of the *Parable*, King Charles proclaimed an Act of Indulgence that permitted Dissenting churches, like Knollys', and Catholic churches to meet without penalty. For over ten years it had been illegal for these groups to meet and sometimes the persecution was quite severe if caught. There were five acts put forward by Parliament against dissenters, entitled the Clarendon Code. They were the Corporation Act, the Act of Uniformity, the Conventicle Act, and the Five Mile Act. Later in the 1670s two more Acts were imposed, the Second Conventicle Act and the Test Act. Persecution depended on where you might live and would arise during particular periods of time. John Bunyan, a Baptist, during this time was imprisoned several times for preaching and meeting. It doesn't appear that the Act of Indulgence or its repeal in 1673 had anything directly to do with the writing of the *Parable*.

To The Reader

Are you a professor? I entreat you, do not rest in the form of godliness without the power of it that undid the foolish Virgins to eternity. It's a vain thing for any person to seem to be religious, and be not so in truth. The fig tree that had leaves was cursed by Christ because it bore no fruit, and it suddenly withered.

Are you a believer? Ponder, then, what is propounded in this little treatise, and search the Scriptures, whether what is affirmed within be so or not. I know but in part, yet am I willing to impart my knowledge for your edification. And if any truth here asserted shall profit your understanding, my earnest request to you is that you will give all the glory to God.

Are you a profane person and one that does scoff at the doctrine of the coming of Christ? Then know that, yet a little while, and he that shall come will come and will not tarry. But if, in the meantime, you die in your sins, you will be damned to eternity. Be serious, therefore, in reading this little book. It may be God will make it a blessing to your soul, and then I have my end.

Your soul's friend,

Hanserd Knollys

The Parable of the Kingdom of Heaven Expounded

Matth. 15:1 to the end of the thirteenth verse:

> 1. Then shall the kingdom of Heaven be likened unto ten Virgins, who took their lamps, and went forth to meet the Bridegroom. 2. And five of them were wise, and five were foolish. 3. They that were foolish took their lamps, and took no oil with them. 4. But the wise took oil in their vessels with their lamps. 5. While the Bridegroom tarried, they all slumbered and slept. 6. And at midnight there was a cry made, "Behold, the Bridegroom comes; go you out to meet him." 7. Then all those Virgins arose and trimmed their lamps. 8. And the foolish said unto the wise, "Give us of your oil; for our lamps are gone out." 9. But the wise answered, saying, "Not so; lest there be not enough for us and you: but go you rather to them that sell, and buy for yourselves." 10. And while they went to buy, the Bridegroom came, and they that were ready went in with him to the marriage: and the door was shut. 11. Afterward came also the other Virgins,

saying, "Lord, Lord, open to us." 12. But he answered and said, "Verily I say unto you, I know you not." 13. Watch therefore, for you know neither the day nor the hour in which the Son of Man comes.

The Lord Jesus Christ, being asked by his disciples what shall be the sign of his coming, Ch. 24:3, answered and said, verse 12, "Iniquity shall abound and the love of many shall wax cold," and verse 21, "Then shall be great tribulation, such as was not from the beginning of the world to this time, no nor ever shall be." So the Apostle testified also, 2 Tim. 3:1. But says our Saviour, verse 29, "immediately after the tribulations of those days," verse 30, "Then shall appear" (not the person but) "the sign of the Son of Man in heaven—And they shall see the Son of Man coming in the clouds of heaven with power and great glory—Then shall the Kingdom of Heaven be likened to ten Virgins," Chap. 25:1.

These thirteen verses contain a parable and the application of it to Christ's disciples. In the parable are three general parts, namely, 1., *Parabola*, verses 1-5; 2., verses 6-9; and 3., verses 10-13. And the exhortation or application of the parable is in verse 13.

In the parable, observe 1. The time then, that is, when the Kingdom of God and coming of Christ in power and great glory is at hand, or near, even at the door: 2. The subject or matter that our Saviour spoke of: the Kingdom of Heaven, 3. The resemblance of that "likened unto ten Virgins" who are described in this verse by their preparation: "They took their lamps" and by their action, "They went out to meet the Bridegroom." Then "shall the Kingdom of Heaven," etc.

By the Kingdom of Heaven in some places of the Holy Scripture, we are to understand the Kingdom of Glory, Matth. 5:3. "Blessed are the poor in spirit, for theirs is the Kingdom of Heaven." In other places of Scriptures by "the Kingdom of Heaven," we are to understand the spiritual kingdom of grace in the hearts of sanctified believers, Matth. 13:31. "The Kingdom of Heaven is like unto a grain of mustard-seed." By the Kingdom of Heaven in some other places of Scripture, we are to understand the Mystical Kingdom of the Church of Christ under the gospel, Matth. 16:18, 19. "Upon this rock" (that rock is Christ, 1 Cor. 10:4.), "I will build my church—and I will give you the keys of the Kingdom of Heaven."

By the Kingdom of Heaven in this verse, we may not understand the Celestial Kingdom of Glory, for there are no foolish

Virgins in that heaven, nor the Spiritual Kingdom of Grace, which is the Kingdom of God within us, Luke 17:21. But the Mystical Kingdom of the Church of God under the gospel, in which there are both wise and foolish Virgins.

1. *Meditation.* Every true visible constituted church of Christ under the gospel did in the Apostles' days, and shall in the latter days, bear some resemblance to the Kingdom of Heaven. For confirmation of this doctrine, read Isa. 60:1, 2, 3, 7, 13, 14, 15, 19, 22. "The glory of the Lord shall arise upon you and his glory shall be seen upon you," verse 2. "I will glorify the house of my glory," verse 7. "And I will make the place of my feet glorious," verse 13. "I will make you an eternal Excellency," verse 15. "The Lord shall be unto you an everlasting light, and your God your glory," verse 19. "I, the Lord, will hasten it in his time," verse 22, that is, in Christ's Day.

In the explication of this point, two things are to be enquired into: 1. What is a true visible constituted Church of Christ under the gospel, 2., in which the Church of God on earth bears proportion with and resemblance unto the Kingdom of Heaven?

Touching the first particular, a true visible constituted church of Christ under the gospel is a congregation of saints, 1 Cor. 1:2, called out of the world, Rom. 1:7, separated from idolaters and idol temples, 2 Cor. 6:16, 17, from the unbelieving Jews and their synagogues and all legal observations of holy days, Sabbath days, and Mosaical rites, ceremonies, and shadows, Acts 19:9 and Col. 2:16, 17, and assembled together in one place, 2 Cor. 14:23. On the Lord's Day, "the first day of the week," Acts 20:7, to worship God visibly by the spirit and in the truth, John 4:23, 24. In the holy ordinances of God, 2 Cor. 11:2, according to the faith and order of the gospel, Col. 2:5.

Touching the second particular to be enquired into, it consists of two parts. 1. The church is called a kingdom. 2. The church is called the Kingdom of Heaven.

The church is compared to a kingdom because

1. Christ, the head of the church, is the King of Saints, Rev. 19:3, and the King of Zion, Psalm 2:6 and 149:1, 2. "Let the Children of Zion (the congregation of saints, verse 1) be joyful in their king."

2. The Church of God is Christ's throne, Jer. 17:13. "A glorious high throne from the beginning (of his mystical kingdom) is the place of our sanctuary," Rev. 4:4. "A throne was set in heaven, the church, and ONE sat on the throne, namely, Christ; And round about the throne were twenty four seats or thrones; And upon the seats I saw twenty four elders (the spiritual priests of

God) sitting clothed in white raiment, and they had on their heads crowns of gold."

3. Christ, the king of his church, is their law-giver, Isa. 33:22. The Lord is our statute-maker, and the Bible is his statute-book in which are published all the Laws of God's house, Ezek. 43:10, 11, according to which laws the church of saints are to be governed by their elders whom Christ has set over them to rule and govern them, Heb. 13:7, 17, according to the laws of his house.

The Church is compared to the Kingdom of Heaven,

[1] With respect unto the gracious and glorious presence of God the Father, Son, and Holy Spirit in the Church: God dwells in Zion, Psal. 9:11, Joel 3:21, for it is his rest, Psal. 132:14. Matth. 18:20. "For where two or three are gathered together in my Name, there am I in the midst of them," Rev. 2:1. "Christ walks in the midst of the golden candlesticks." God's presence makes heaven to be heaven, and that makes a heaven on earth, a heaven in the heart, and a heaven in the congregation of saints.

[2] With respect unto the spiritual glory of the Church of God in the latter days, Isa. 60:7, 13, the beauties of holiness, Psal. 110:3, makes Zion the perfection of beauty, Psal. 50:3. The temple was filled with the Glory of God, Ezek. 43:5 and 44:4. "And the glory of the Lord filled the house of the Lord." The house of the Lord is the church of the living God, 1 Tim. 3:15. And the temple was filled with smoke from the glory of God, Rev. 15:8.

3. With respect unto the great company and number of saints in the assemblies and churches of Christ (called the churches of saints, 1 Cor. 14:33), among whom and in whose assemblies are the holy angels, because of whose presence the women were to be veiled, 1 Cor. 11:10. This will be more evident in the last days, when the Holy City, the New Jerusalem, shall come down from God out of heaven, prepared as a bride adorned for her husband, Rev. 21:1, 2, 3. And when we are come to Mount Zion, unto the City of the Living God, the heavenly Jerusalem, to the general assembly and church of the first born, and to Jesus the Mediator of the new Covenant, Heb. 12:22, 23, 24, then will the Church of God on earth bear some greater proportion with and resemblance unto the Kingdom of Heaven.

Then shall the Kingdom of Heaven be likened unto ten Virgins, etc. Ten is a mystical number, as in Dan. 7:7, 20, 24, "ten horns," Jude 14, "ten thousand of saints," Rev. 2:10, "ten days," and so ten Virgins; that is a definite number for an indefinite. By Virgins we are to understand gospel professors and church members

(2 Cor. 11:2 . . . "I have espoused you to one husband that I my perfect you as a chaste Virgin to Christ") who have escaped the pollutions of the world through the knowledge of Christ, 2 Tim. 3:9. Some are foolish Virgins, formal professors denying the power of godliness, only seeming to be religious, James 1:26, who after they have escaped the pollutions of the world through the knowledge of the Lord and Saviour Jesus Christ, are again entangled in them and overcome, whose later end is worse than their beginning, 2 Pet. 2:20.

Others who are wise Virgins, having not only the form but the power of godliness also, and being partakers of the divine nature, have escaped the corruption that is in the world through lust, 2 Pet. 1:4. These being not defiled with spiritual whoredoms do follow Christ wherever he goes, Rom. 14:4. "These are they which are not defiled with women" (neither the great whore of Rome, Mystery Babylon, the Mother of Harlots, Rev. 17:1, 5, nor the daughters of that whore, false Churches, whose mother Mystical Babylon is, though some of those daughters be as Nineveh was called, Nahum 3:4, well-favoured harlots, because of the multitude of their spiritual whoredoms).

2. *Meditation.* The churches of saints in the last days shall be reformed and restored unto a virgin state of primitive purity and spiritual glory, as in the Apostles' days.

For the confirmation of this doctrine, read and consider these Scriptures, namely, Isa. 2:2, 3, 4, 5. "And it shall come to pass in the last days that the mountain of the Lord's house shall be established in the top of the mountains," etc. Isa. 60:2, 3, 4, 5, 6, "He that is left in Zion and he that remains in Jerusalem shall be called holy," etc. Isa. 60:17, 13, 21. "I will glorify the house of my glory, and I will make the place of my feet glorious," etc. Isa. 65:17, 18, 19, 25. "For behold I create new heavens and a new earth," etc. Rev. 20:1, 2, 3, 4, 5—"Behold I make all things new," 2 Pet. 3:13, 14, Rev. 14:1, 2, 3, 4, 5. "These are they that follow the Lamb— for they are Virgins."

In the explication of this point, we are to consider two particulars:

1. What reformation will be in the churches of saints in the last days?

2. What things shall be restored then which are or have been wanting in the churches of saints since the Apostles' days?

Touching the first particular,

1., professors of the gospel and members of churches will be much reformed from many corruptions in their judgements and conversations. The Apostles tell us and foretold the churches that, in the later days, some professors would be corrupted in their judgements. Compare 1 Tim. 4:1, 2, 3 with 2 Pet. 2:1, 2, 3. "And many shall follow their pernicious ways, by reason of whom the way of truth shall be evil spoken of." And in the last days, other professors would be corrupted in their conversation, 2 Tim. 3:1, 2, 3, 4, 5. "Covetous, proud, promise, and covenant breakers, lovers of pleasures more than lovers of God, having a form of godliness but denying the power of it"; and are not too many members of churches ("who seem to be religious," James 1:26) very much corrupted in their judgments, and some also in their conversations? But the days are coming when there shall be a great reformation in both these respects.

For God will return to the people a pure language, Zeph. 3:9, 13. "The Remnant of Israel shall not do iniquity nor speak lies, neither shall a deceitful tongue be found in their mouth." And those Virgin professors that follow the Lamb, Rev. 14:4, 5, "shall be redeemed from the earth," verse 3, "and from men," verse 4. "And in their mouth was found no guilt, for they are without fault before the throne of God," verse 5.

2. The discipline and government of the churches will be very much reformed in the last days, for then Christ the LORD "will reign in Mount Zion, and in Jerusalem and before his Ancients gloriously," Mich. 4:6, 7, "from henceforth even forever." The churches of saints shall be ruled and governed by the holy, righteous, and good Laws of the Lord Jesus Christ, Isa. 33:22, who is the Son over the house of God, Heb. 3:1, 6, Ezek. 43:10, 11. "Show them all the Laws of the house and let them measure the pattern," etc. Isa. 9:6, 7. "The government shall lie upon his shoulders." Christ is the legislator, the lawgiver, the Bible is his and his churches' statute book, and all the churches, ministers, and saints of God are to be governed by his royal law of liberty, in obeying and keeping of which there is a blessing promised, James 1:25.

Touching the second particular,

1. The ministry of the gospel will be restored in the later days. Jer. 13:14, 15. "I will bring you to Zion and I will give you pastors according to my heart, they shall feed you with knowledge and with understanding."

2. The gifts of the Holy Spirit shall be restored in the last days, Joel 2:21, 23, 28, 29, 30, 31. "The Lord will do great things—be glad then you children of Zion—I will pour out my Spirit upon all flesh," etc. Acts 2:17, 18. "And it shall come to pass in the last days (says God); I will pour out of my Spirit upon all flesh," etc. This is that which God has promised and will again perform.

3. The ordinances of God will be restored to his churches in the later days. The Antichrist has made void the commandments of God by the traditions of men (as the Scribes and Pharisees did, Mark 7:6, 7, 9). And he has changed the ordinances of Christ, and brought in the ordinances of men, Col. 2:20, 22, 23. "Why are you subject to ordinances (or traditions) after the commandments and doctrines of men?" which is will–worship, verse 23, and vain worship, Matth. 13:8, 9. "But in vain do they worship me," etc. The ordinances of God (which have been corrupted by men's inventions and superstitions) shall be restored to their primitive purity and first institutions. Read Jer. 32:38 and 30:40, and compare it with Zeph. 3:9. "Then will I turn to the people a pure language (or a clean lip) that they may call upon the Name of the Lord and serve him with one shoulder (or consent). In that day, the LORD shall be ONE and his Name ONE"; that is, in the later days, Christ and his saints shall be ONE kingdom: and his way and worship but ONE in all the earth.

Which took their lamps. The virgin professors of the gospel and worshippers of God in the churches of Christ have lamps, that is, the presence of God in his worship and ordinances, Matth. 18:20. "For where one or three are gathered together in my name, says Christ, there am I in the midst of them."

God manifested his presence with Abraham when he was offering a sacrifice to the Lord, Gen. 15:17, 18. "Behold a smoking furnace and a burning lamp passed between these pieces; And God made a covenant with Abraham." Read Exod. 19:18, 27 and 20:11 and Isa. 4:5, Rev. 15:9. God appointed seven lamps to be lighted and supplied with sweet oil of olives, both in his wilderness tabernacle, Exod. 25:37, and in his Canaan temple, 2 Chron. 4:20, 21, that they might burn continually before the Lord, which typed forth the seven Spirits of God, Rev. 3:1, 4, 5. "And there were seven lamps of fire burning before the throne which are the seven spirits of God," that is, the variety and abundance of the gifts and fruits of the Holy Eternal Spirit. There are diversity of gifts, but the same Spirit, 1 Cor. 12:4, and so there are diversity and many fruits of the Spirit, Gal. 5:22, 23.

"These ten Virgins having received their lamps," that is, a commandment from the Lord (for the commandment is a lamp, Prov. 6:3) to worship him by the Spirit in truth, and spiritual gifts and grace to perform the gospel-instituted ordinances of Christ according to the holy will of God unveiled in his written word, "for his Word is a lamp unto the feet of his saints, and a light unto their paths," Psal. 119:105.

3. *Meditation.* The virgin professors of the gospel and worshippers of God in the churches of saints shall have gospel light and spiritual gifts in the later days to worship God in the order and ordinances of the gospel according to the written Word of God.

First, virgin professors shall have gospel light in the later days to worship God aright. The written Word of God (through the teachings of the Holy Spirit), that is, the commands of Christ and the examples of his Apostles, churches, and saints approved by Christ (recorded in the Holy Scripture of truth) will be a lamp and a light unto them, Psal. 119:105, Prov. 6:23, and 1 Cor. 11:1, 2; 14:37. Phil. 3:16, 17 and Isa. 60:1, 2, 3. "Arise, shine, your light is come—And the Gentiles (or heathen nations) shall come to your light," etc.

Secondly, virgin professors in the churches of Christ in the later days shall have spiritual gifts qualifying and enabling them to worship God by the Spirit and in the truth in the order and ordinances of the gospel, Acts 2:17. "And it shall come to pass" (says God) "in the last Days, I will pour out my Spirit upon all flesh," etc., I Cor. 12:4. "There are diversities of gifts, but the same Spirit." As in the days of the Apostles, so shall it be in the last days, Joel 2:21, 28, 29, much more poured forth.

And went forth to meet the Bridegroom. The Bridegroom is the Lord Jesus Christ, John 3:29. "He that has the Bride is the Bridegroom," that is, Jesus Christ, to whom his churches and saints are espoused, 2 Cor. 11:2, whom Christ has betrothed to himself in loving kindness and faithfulness forever, Hosea 2:19, 20. They are his sister and his spouse, Cant. 4:10, the Lamb's wife, Rev. 19:7, 8, and he is the Bridegroom, Isa. 62:5. "With the joy of the Bridegroom over the Bride shall the LORD rejoice over you."

To meet the Bridegroom does imply two things.

First, that the Virgins did know and believe that Christ was coming, Psal. 96:9, 11, 13. "O worship the Lord in the bounty of holiness. Let the heavens rejoice, and let the earth be glad and rejoice before the Lord, for he comes, for he comes," etc. Had not the foolish Virgins known and believed that Christ would come, yea, and that he was coming, they would not have gone out to meet him, but would rather have scoffed at his coming, when the wise Virgins had spoken of it, as those scoffers will do, 2 Pet. 3:3, 4. "There shall come in the last days scoffers saying, 'Where is the promise of his coming?'"

Secondly, that all the Virgins did know and believe that the coming of the spiritual Bridegroom Christ Jesus was near, and that he would come quickly or shortly: the Bridegroom's coming was even at the door, therefore they went out to meet him, Heb. 10:37. "Yet a little while and HE that shall come will come, and will not tarry. Now the just shall live by faith." The Virgins believed this and went out to meet the Bridegroom, and they had Scripture grounds to believe it, because Christ had revealed it in his written word, Rev. 22:12. "Behold I come quickly," verse 20, "HE which satisfies these things says surely I come quickly," Amen.

They went out to meet the Bridegroom, that is, the virgin professors in the churches of saints in the later days knowing and believing the coming of Christ the Bridegroom will go out from their nearest and dearest relations, their great professions. They will forsake father and mother, wife and children that will not go out with them to meet the Bridegroom, and will follow him wherever he goes, as his disciples did, Matth. 19:27. So will the Virgins do, Rev. 14:1, 4. And it is the duty of all Christ's disciples to do, Luke 14:26, 27, Matth. 20:37, 38, 39. And they that forsake all their relations, estates, lands, houses, goods, and all for Christ shall not lose by so doing, Luke 18:28, 29, 30 and Mark 10:28, 29, 30, Rev. 22:12. "Behold I come quickly and my reward is with me."

4. *Meditation*. That such gospel light will be revealed to Virgin professors in the later days, and such anointing of the Spirit will be poured out upon them, as will cause them and make them willing to sell all, lose all, and forsake all, and go out to meet the Bridegroom.

1. Gospel light touching the kingdom and coming of the Spiritual Bridegroom our Lord Jesus Christ will be revealed in the later days, Matth. 24:14. "And this gospel of the Kingdom shall be preached in all the world—And then shall the END come," Zech. 14:6, 7. "It shall come to pass, that at evening time it shall be light.—And the Lord shall be King over all the earth. In that DAY shall there be ONE Lord and his Name ONE." And Rev. 22:5. "The Lord God gives them light—And they shall see

his face, and his Name shall be in their foreheads, And they shall reign forever and ever— Which must shortly be done," "Behold, I come quickly," etc.

2. The anointing of the Spirit, the gifts and powerful operations of the Spirit will be upon virgin professors in the later days, Joel 2:28,29, Isa. 43:3, 5, 6, and Chap. 32:15, 16, 17, 1 John 2:13, 14, 20, 27. The fathers, the young men, and the little children shall have the unction of the Holy ONE, etc. Then it will be with virgin professors as it was in the Apostles' days, 1 Cor. 12:4, 5, 6, 7, 8, 9, 10, 11, etc. "There are diversities of gifts but the same Spirit; and there are diversities of operations but the same God; All these work one and the self same Spirit."

3. This gospel light, anointing, and operation of the Holy Spirit upon virgin professors in the last days will engage them and make them willing to go out to meet the Bridegroom, Psal. 110:2, 8. The "Lord will send the rod of your strength out of Zion: Rule you in the midst of your enemies. Your people shall be willing in the DAY of your power, in the beauties of holiness," etc. God will put his Spirit within them and cause them to walk in his ways, Ezek. 36:27. He will pour his Spirit upon them, Ezek. 39:29, and they shall obey his voice, Matth. 25:6. "Behold the Bridegroom comes, go you out to meet him." And they went out to meet the Bridegroom.

Verse 2. "And five of them were wise and five were foolish."

In this parable, virgin professors in the churches of saints are variously distinguished by Christ; namely, "Five of them were wise and five were foolish." 2. The foolish took no oil with them, but what was in their lamps, verse 3. The wise took oil in their vessels with their lamps, verse 4. 3. The lamps of the wise Virgins (being trimmed and supplied with oil in their vessels) continued burning. The lamps of the foolish Virgins (being trimmed but not supplied with oil) went out, verses 7, 8. 4. The wise Virgins, being ready, went in with the Bridegroom to the marriage; but the foolish Virgins, not being prepared, were shut out, verses 10, 11, 12.

This verse contains the full distinction of virgin professors. Five were wise, and five were foolish. Five is a definite number put for an indefinite, and thereby a small number is here put for a great number, and a few for very many. The five foolish Virgins, for all sorts of gospel professors, who having a form of godliness, lack the power of it, 2 Tim. 3:5. And the five wise Virgins, for all sorts of worshippers of God that make not only a profession of

Christ, but have also profession of Christ dwelling in their hearts, Ephes. 3:17, both which particulars will plainly appear in the exposition and handling of the 3rd and 4th verses.

Meditation. There are some wise, and many foolish Virgins.

The Holy Spirit has given many distinguishing characters in the Scripture of truth between these wise and foolish Virgins, of which some in this parable, which I have already mentioned in general, and shall afterwards show particularly. And the Scripture distinctions between sanctified believers and hypocrites; between them that only seem to be religious and them that are sincerely so in deed and truth; between those that are in Christ, having an everlasting and inseparable union with him, and those that are without Christ, who make a profession of Christ, but have not profession of Christ in their hearts; I say all those Scripture distinctions are applicable, and may be accommodated unto wise and foolish professors, but especially that Scripture distinction, 2 Tim. 3:1-5, which the Holy Spirit makes between them that have the form, and them that have the power of godliness, which Christ in this parable does metaphorically express by the foolish Virgins, verse 3, who took their lamps, but took no oil with them, and the wise Virgins, that took oil in their vessels with their lamps, verse 4.

> *Verse 3, 4. "They that were foolish took their lamps, and took no oil with them. But the wise took oil in their vessels with their lamps."*

By lamps, we are to understand temple light, namely, divine knowledge and spiritual gifts, as has been proved in the exposition of the first verse, by which our Saviour did mystically and metaphorically show that the foolish Virgins had a form of godliness.

By oil in their lamps is meant that shining outward profession of Christ, which went out at last, verse 8. "Give us your oil for our lamps are gone out." The light of the knowledge of Christ and of the prophecies and of the mysteries of his kingdom and coming, which shined in the professions they made and in the witness and testimony that they had born for Christ against the Antichrist, withered away and died. And all their common gifts and graces faded and failed; and they all fell away like the stony ground hearers, Luke 13:8. "Who believe for a time, but in time of temptation fall away."

By oil in the wise virgin's vessels we are to understand Jesus Christ, and the Spirit of Christ, the sanctifying knowledge of Christ, and the saving grace of the Lord Jesus Christ in their hearts and in their souls. For their souls are vessels of mercy prepared for glory, Rom. 9:23, 24. And their mystical and spiritual oil is the unction of the Holy ONE, which they have received, 1 John 2:20, 27. By which our Saviour did figuratively and mystically show "that the wise Virgins had the power of godliness." And in this part of the parable of the Kingdom of Heaven, Christ declares and testifies that they are foolish Virgins, who rest satisfied and content themselves with the form of godliness without the power of godliness; who have lamps but no oil.

. . . That they are wise Virgins who have both lamps and oil in their vessels (that is, Christ and his Spirit and his grace in their hearts) having both the form and power of godliness.

Meditation. It's not the lamp-light of protection and the form of godliness; but the oil of grace, and sanctification, even the power of godliness in heart and life, that will put the denomination of and distinction between wise and foolish virgin professors in the last days.

Though this be very clear and plain by what has been already said in this exposition; yet because I do think it may be profitable, first, for the conviction of some formal professors, who are foolish Virgins, especially sinners in Zion, unconverted Church members. And, second, for the edification and establishment of sanctified believers in the visible constituted churches of Christ, especially weak Christians: I am therefore willing (through divine assistance) to treat more largely of the form and power of godliness (and in it to demonstrate the wisdom and folly of virgin professors) than I shall do of some other things held forth in this parable, which I judge less necessary to enlarge upon.

That which I shall offer to consideration touching the form and power of godliness does consist in these three following propositions:

1. *There is the form of godliness and the power of godliness.* All the Virgins had burning and shining lamps, and some of them had oil in their vessels with their lamps, verse 3.

2. *The form of godliness may be where the power of godliness is not.* The foolish Virgins took their lamps, but took no oil with them, verse 3, that is in their vessels. That is, they had the form of godliness in their profession, but

they wanted the power of godliness in their hearts and conversation.

3. *That some virgin professors in the church of saints, having the form of godliness, will deny the power of it in the last days*, of whom the Apostle spoke expressly and foretold, 2 Tim. 3:5.

Touching the first proposition, the Greek signifies any form, or kind of worship, or godliness, and having no article joined with it, it does not signify this, that, or the form of godliness properly, or strictly; but indefinitely, any form, and every form of godliness, and consequently the form of godliness.

There are diverse forms of religion in which men worship and serve God according to the different oppressions and persuasions of persons professing godliness; of which some, yea several, are of man's devising: Matth. 15:8, 9 compared with Col. 2:20, 22, 23. But there is a form of godliness, which is of God's own institution under the gospel, in which men ought to worship God in spirit and truth, John 4:23, 24, according to his own appointments, Psal. 3:3, 16.

The form of godliness (of God's own appointment) consists in the external religious performance of all those evangelical duties which he has commanded us in his holy Word, Ezek. 43:10, 11, according as he has commanded, in which persons seem to be religious and godly. Formal professors do perform those religious duties:

1. From a principle of self, which is the common and highest principle that formal professors and hypocrites act by in the worship of God. They pray for themselves, fast and mourn for themselves, and live to themselves, Zech. 7:4, 5. 6. Self-love, self-seeking, self-confidence, self-dependence, self-sufficiency, self-righteousness, and self-salvation is the frame and end of a formal professor. Self is the spring and main principle of all he does in his religion, Hosea 10:1, 2. Israel is an empty vine; he brings forth fruit unto himself.

2. From a principle of tradition which they have received from their fathers by custom and education; so did the Apostle Paul worship God before his conversion, being zealous of the traditions of his fathers, Gal. 1:14, 15. "I profited in the Jews' religion above many—Being more exceedingly zealous of the traditions of my fathers." Thus many formal professors now worship God after the traditions and customs of their fathers and teachers, as the Scribes and Pharisees did, whom Christ reprehended, Mark 7:8, 9, 13. "You hold the tradition of men," and in vain

did they worship God, making the Word and commandments of God of no effect by their traditions, Jer. 7:18 and 44:16, 17. "The children gather wood and the fathers kindle the fire, and the women knead their dough to make cakes to the Queen of Heaven and to pour out drink offerings unto other gods, that they may provoke me to anger.—As for the word that you have spoken unto us in the Name of the Lord, we will not hearken unto you—But we will certainly do whatsoever thing goes forth out of our own mouth to burn incense unto the Queen of Heaven, and to pour out drink offerings unto her, as we have done, we and our fathers, our kings and our princes in the cities of Judah, and in the streets of Jerusalem; for then had we plenty of victuals, and were well, and saw no evil."

3. From a principle of fear: legal fear (that is, the fear of hell, wrath or curse, etc.). This fear causes many professors to pray, hear sermons, perform holy duties, and to partake of God's ordinances. Also, a servile fear of the anger and displeasure of men causes many children and servants to worship God formally, and they seem to be religious because they are afraid to anger and displease their godly parents, masters, or some other godly relations. And that their fear of God is taught by the commandments of men, Isa. 29:13. And thereby they are made conformable unto the external parts of God's worship, and attain unto a form of godliness, yet are without the power of it.

4. From a principle of superstition, many are like the idolaters of Athens, who worshipped the unknown God, Acts 17:23, 23. They were very superstitious in their will-worship of God. The zeal and superstition of the Scribes and Pharisees made them so formal in their legal ceremonial worship of God, Luke 18:12. I fast "twice a week," etc., and Rom. 10:2. Many of the Jews being zealous in their devotion but wanting knowledge, worshipped God according to the superstitious inventions of men, which things, says the Apostle, have indeed a show of wisdom in will-worship, Col. 2:20, 23. And do make formal professors subject to the ordinances of God after the commandments and doctrines of men.

This may suffice to evince and demonstrate that there is a form of godliness. And indeed none can externally worship God without some form of godliness, in which persons do seem to be religious and may seem to be like God in holiness and righteousness both in worship and conversation in some measure.

As there is the form of godliness, so there is the power of godliness. The power of godliness consists, 1. In the truth of grace, 2. In the lively acts and exercise of grace, and 3. In the growth and perfection of grace.

The power of godliness consists, first, in the truth of grace. In whatsoever form of religion, any professors worship God; yea though that external form be ordained of God, instituted by Jesus Christ and practised by the Apostles, churches, and saints; yet for all this without the truth of grace, they are void of the power of godliness. And therefore the primitive saints did not only receive the ordinances but the truth of grace also by the ministry of the Apostles in the dispensation of the gospel, Col. 1:4, 5, 6, 7, 8. And knew the grace of God in truth.

True grace is the incorruptible seed of the new birth, 1 Pet. 1:23, and of the Kingdom of God in the hearts of believers, Matth. 13:31, 32, which Kingdom of God within us, Luke 17:21, is not in Word only, but in power and in the Holy Spirit, 1 Cor. 4:20, and 1 Thes. 1:4, 5.

Now the power of godliness does demonstrate itself by true saving sanctifying grace, 1. In denying all ungodliness. In living soberly, righteously, and godly in this present evil world, Tit. 2:11, 12. This is the constant frame of a believer's heart. He would not sin, he hates all sin. He would be holy; he loves holiness, and desires to be more holy, Rom. 7:15, 16, 19, 20, 21, 22.

Secondly, the power of godliness does consist in the lively acts and exercise of grace; as the form of godliness appears in the frequent exercise of the holy duties, so does the power of godliness appear in the lively acts and exercise of the holy graces, that is, in the life and lively work of faith, 2 Thes. 1:11, 12. Also in the labour of fervent love, 1 Pet. 1:22. Bearing all things, enduring all things with all brotherly kindness, Rom. 13:4, 7 and Heb. 6:10. Likewise in the consistent exercise of patience, humility, meekness, and self denial, taking up the cross daily, bearing it patiently, following the steps of Christ, who humbled himself unto death, even the death of the cross. Yea, and he endured the cross. Now believers who have the power of godliness are armed with the same mind, 1 Pet. 4:1, and desire to be like minded to Christ, Phil. 2:5, 8. They suffer patiently; knowing that tribulation (which is the trial of their faith) works patience and are desirous that patience may have her perfect work, James 1:2, 3, 4.

Thirdly, the power of godliness does consist in the growth and perfection of grace, grace is of a growing nature, 2 Pet. 3:18. For,

1. It grows in its root, which is Jesus Christ, Col. 2:6, 7. As the good seed that is sown in good ground and brings forth fruit, Luke 8:8, 15. The reason why some formal professors fall

away is because they are not rooted nor grafted into Christ, Luke 8:13. And the reason why those believers that are engrafted into Christ grow as cedars in Lebanon, as a green olive tree in the House of the Lord, and bring forth fruit as the vine, is because they are trees of righteousness, the planting of the Lord, Isa. 61:3, which take root downward into Christ and so bring forth fruit upward by that sap and nourishment which they receive from that spiritual root, that is, those divine influences of the Spirit of grace that they are made partakers of by being engrafted and rooted into Christ. This growth in grace is very secret, hidden, not seen nor always discerned, like the growth of corn underground or of trees in winter or of the child in the womb, yet it does afterwards appear and is visible.

2. Grace grows in its lovely acts and exercise. As a child after its natural birth grows in all parts and members of the body, so a child of God being regenerated and born again of the incorruptible seed of the Word does grow in grace and in the knowledge of Jesus Christ by adding one grace to another, unto faith, virtue; to virtue, knowledge, temperance, patience, godliness, etc. 2. Pet. 1:5-11. This growth in grace demonstrates the power of godliness: by this spiritual growth in grace, the weak in faith, Rom. 14:1, become strong in faith, 1 John 2:14, and little faith becomes great faith; like the grain of mustard seed that becomes a great tree, and very fruitful, whereunto Christ likened the kingdom of his grace within us, Matth. 13:31, 32 with Luke 17:21.

3. Grace grows in its fruits unto perfection, and hereby is the power of godliness demonstrated, that is, in bringing forth much fruit, John 15:5, 8, namely, the fruits of the Holy Spirit, Gal. 5:22, 23, which are the fruits of holiness and righteousness unto eternal life, Rom. 6:22. Thus fruitful were the saints in the church of the Thessalonians, 2 Thes. 1:3. And the Apostle Paul exhorted the primitive saints to perfect holiness in the fear of God, 2 Cor. 7:1. And the Apostle Peter exhorted the called ones of God to be holy in all manner of conversation, 1 Pet. 1:15, 16, because he knew that the power of godliness consisted in the life of holiness and righteousness, and is demonstrated in a holy conversation. Thus it appears that there is the form of godliness and the power of godliness, which is the first proposition.

The second proposition is this: *That the form of godliness may be where the power of godliness is not.*

Simon Magus seemed to be religious. He believed and was baptized, and took up the form of godliness, Acts 8:12. But for all this formality, he had not the power of godliness, for he was in the gall of bitterness and bond of Iniquity, and his heart was not right with God, Acts 8:21.

Ananias and Sapphira his wife were both professors and church-members; they had taken upon them the Name of Christ and the form of godliness, seemed to be very charitable, and pretended much brotherly love to the poor saints, for they sold a possession and gave a part of the price of it unto the poor, Acts 5:1, 2, and yet they were void of the power of godliness.

Professors that are proud, covetous, carnal covenant-breakers, false accusers, inconsistent, fierce, heady, high-minded, lovers of pleasures more than lovers of God, etc. Many of them have a form of godliness, but they have not the power of godliness, 2 Tim. 3:2, 3, 4, 5.

When professors and church members are generally formal in the performance of the duties of religion, very perfunctory and superficial in the worship of God, or lukewarm (neither hot nor cold), very indifferent whether they observe the Lord's Day or another day, or no day at all to the Lord, so whether they hear the Word preached, pray in their families or in their closets, or pray not at all, whether they come to the Lord's Table or stay away, it argues they are so far from having the power of godliness, that they can scarcely be said to have the form of godliness.

Again, when professors and members of churches are very frequent and constant in assembling themselves together to worship God, very zealous and precise in the external part of the worship of God, and seem to be very conscientious and scrupulous in such things as appertain to the form of godliness, asserting and contending that all things ought to be exactly done in the Church of God according to the rule of the written word of God, and yet walk very disorderly at home, are heady and unruly in their own houses, let no rules nor bounds to their obstinate and perverse wills, to their inordinate and vile affections, to their worldly and covetous hearts, who seem to be religious yet bridle not their tongues but deceive their own hearts, "their religion is in vain," James 1:26. These professors have a form of godliness, but they lack the power of it.

Thus, it appears that the form of godliness may be where the power of godliness is not. Professors may have leaves without fruit, as the fig tree had; lamps and lighted, but no oil in their vessels like the foolish Virgins; seem very religious in the congregation of saints and be very irreligious in their conversation among sinners.

The reasons why professors rest in and hold up a form of godliness without the power of it are these:

1. Because they would have a name to live though they are dead, Rev. 3:1. They are very desirous to have a name in the house of God, to be accounted religious, and to be numbered among the saints; therefore, they take up a form of godliness and rest in it.

Those foolish professors, Matth. 25:1, 2, had gotten a name among the wise, and were called "Virgins." And they seemed to be religious; they had lamps of gospel profession, and the form of godliness with which they were satisfied, and in it they rested securely till the Bridegroom came, and then it appeared they lacked oil, that is, the truth of grace and power of godliness; for lack of which they were excluded and rejected by Jesus Christ, Matth. 25:8, 11, 12.

2. Because a form of godliness will comport with a spirit of worldliness, earthly-mindedness, covetousness, pride, uncleanness, drunkenness; so that these lusts be but secretly committed. A professor and church member may be a self-lover and a lover of pleasures, a covenant or promise-breaker, and yet have and hold up a form of godliness without the power of it, 2 Tim. 3:1-5.

3. Because professors and church members may avoid troubles and persecutions, while they enjoy Sabbaths, sermons, and ordinances in an external form of public worship; whereas the power of godliness will expose them to suffer persecution, 2 Tim. 3:12. So that the form of godliness may be where the power is not. This is the second proposition.

There is a third proposition, namely: *That some professors and church members having and holding up the form of godliness, deny the power of it.*

Professors they must be and church members they may be, that have and hold up the form of godliness, and seem to be very devout and religious in the worship of God, and yet some of them deny the power of godliness. We have showed in the handling of the first proposition in which the form of godliness and in which the power of godliness does consist, and have treated briefly both of the form and power of godliness. Now it remains that, in handling this third proposition, we show, 1. What it is to deny the power of godliness, and 2. The reasons why they deny the power of godliness.

To deny the power of godliness is, 1., to have an aversion against it in their affections, not to love and affect the power of godliness, which aversions against the power of godliness does arise and spring from that cursed and sinful enmity in their carnal minds against God, Rom. 8:7. The carnal mind is enmity against God, and therefore carnal professors do not love nor like godliness in the truth and power of it, though they may be found in the form and profession of it. "O," says a formal professor in his heart, "I do not love this preciseness, this is to be righteous overmuch. I like not those that are so strict, so zealous, and so scrupulously conscientious. What necessity is there to deny myself my liberty, my lawful recreation, content and delight in things indifferent? Must my liberty in that be judged by another brother's or sister's conscience?" He loves not, he likes nothing, it crosses his interest in the world or it is contrary unto some of this beloved and indulged lusts to be so zealous, so religious, so conscientious as the power of godliness requires, and would engage him to be: therefore he is averse from it, and so may be said to deny it.

To deny the power of godliness is, 2., to refuse all the offers of Christ and grace, which God makes them in the ministry and administration of the gospel by his Holy Spirit, Isa. 53:1, 2, 3, Acts 3:13, 14. "But you denied the Holy ONE." That is, they refused Christ, and would not have him to be their Saviour, King, Priest and Prophet, saying, "We will not have this man to reign over us." Formal professors know not the worth of Christ; they are not sensible of their want of grace, therefore they slight, neglect and refuse the offers of grace. They are willing to seem religious, but as for the truth of grace and the power of godliness, they regard it not. They like Christ as a Saviour, but refuse him as a Sovereign; though they would be saved, they care not to be sanctified, they refuse to enter in at the straight gate of grace, and to walk in the narrow way of holiness, and yet they would go to heaven, and to that end they cry, "Lord, Lord," Matth. 7:21, 22. They pray and prophesy in Christ's name, Luke 13:23, 27. They worship God, seem to be very religious, and partake of all God's holy ordinances, having a form of godliness, but yet they deny the power of godliness by refusing the offers of Christ and grace in the gospel and ordinances of God.

To deny the power of godliness is, 3., to live in the practice of known sins, secretly indulging and allowing them, Tit. 1:16. "They profess that they know God, but in works they deny him."

When professors' lives are loose, carnal, and worldly, and their works are the works of darkness, and they themselves are workers of iniquity, they deny God and the power of godliness.

The power of godliness consists in practical holiness. Some professors seem to be holy in God's house, who live very ungodly in their own houses. They seem to be religious in the church and in the worship of God, but they are irreligious at home, in their shops and callings, trading and living in sin and ungodliness. These having a form of godliness deny the power of it.

Now the reasons why formal professors deny the power of godliness are,

1., because their hearts are not right with God. Simon Magus believed and was baptized, and worshipped God, but his heart was not right with God, Acts 8:21, 23. There is a carnal enmity in their hearts against God, and the power of godliness, Rom. 8:7, though they like the outward form, yet they love not the inward power of godliness.

2. Because the inward power of godliness is cross to their outward and worldly interests, therefore they deny the power of it. The formalist says within himself, "Though I be religious, a church-member, etc., yet I am resolved to make my religion and church fellowship comport with my interest in the world, and to be subservient unto my honour, credit, profit, yea and my pleasure, delight, and contentment, etc."

When formal professors discern that the power of godliness will not only check and curb their vile affections, perverse wills, and sinful desires, but also will mortify, kill, and destroy their lusts and corruptions, root and branch, then they refuse and deny the power of godliness.

Rather than the formalist will hazard the loss of life, liberty, or estate, and expose himself to poverty, prison, banishment or death for his religion, he will deny Christ, deny God, and the power of godliness.

3. Because the power of godliness engages professors to follow holiness, and to deny all ungodliness, Tit. 2:11, 12, such professors as have the form of godliness only are very apt to rest in the external part and performance of holy duties and sacred ordinances without the enjoyment of God and Jesus Christ. But the truth and life of grace and the power of godliness will not suffer the soul to rest in the duties and ordinances without the enjoyment of fellowship and communion with God, therefore the formalist will not close with the power of godliness, but

refuses and denies it, because he is unwilling to leave his sins. I shall now make some application of what I have said touching the form and power of godliness.

1. Use of instruction to virgin professors.

There are three things necessary unto the form of godliness, namely,

1., the knowledge of the revealed will of God in his written Word touching Christ's institution of gospel ordinances, and his constitution of the worship of God in it and because of it. How can any person worship God in spirit and truth (as true worshippers ought to do, John 4:23, 24.) unless they understand and know the truth revealed in the Holy Scriptures?

Ignorant persons are not capable to perform the external part of the worship of God; for they do not know it. The Athenians worshipped the unknown God, which the Apostle told them was their great superstition, Acts 17:22, 23. And our Saviour told the woman of Samaria that the Samaritans worship they know not what, John 4:21, 22. So then knowledge is necessary unto the form of godliness.

Many persons think it is enough that their ministers know how they ought to worship God, and so are willingly ignorant, whose fear towards God is taught by the precepts of men, and they willingly walk after the commandment, Hos. 5:11, which formality of conformity Christ reprehended, Matth. 15:9. "In vain they do worship me, teaching for doctrine the commandments of men."

2. In the form of godliness, there must be a conformity unto the revealed will of God in his Word, especially in the external part of the instituted worship of God in the gospel.

Uniformity in worship in any nation or congregation without conformity unto the rule or canon of the Holy Scripture is but superstition and a worship of God after the inventions and traditions of men, which the Apostle reproved in the Colossians, and called "will-worship," Col. 2:20, 21, 22, 23. The temple, the altar, and they that worship (that is, the church, the worship of God, and the worshippers of God) are to be measured by the reed or rod of the sanctuary, that is by the written word of God, Rev. 11:1. Moses was commanded to do all things according to the pattern that God showed him in the Mount, Heb. 8:5, and the Prophet Ezekiel was commanded to show the house of God's worship to the House of Israel and admonished them to measure the pattern, Ezek. 43:10.

3. In the form of godliness, there ought to be a uniformity among all the churches of God in every nation, in every city, and in every village. All that worship God in one place are to worship him in one way, with one accord, and with one shoulder. It was so in the Apostle's days, Acts 1:4, 24, Phil. 2:2. "Being of one accord, of one mind," Acts 4:32. And so it shall be in the last days, Jer. 32:36, 38, 39. "And I will give them one heart, and one way that they may fear me, (i.e.) worship me, forever."

This uniformity was tacitly hinted by the Apostle, in reproving that confusion that was in the church of Corinth, 1 Cor. 14:26, 33, for God is not the author of confusion but of peace, as in all the churches of saints.

Uniformity in worship not after the invention of men, but according to the written Word of God, makes for peace, unity, and edification in the churches of saints, and is a special means to avoid confusion and disorder in the Worship of God, 1 Cor. 14:40.

2. Use of Conviction. 1. Of those foolish virgin professors who rest in the form of godliness without the power of it. They may hereby be convinced,

1. That their hearts are not right with God, though they do materially that which is right in the sight of God; but are like Amaziah who did that which was right in the sight of the Lord, but not with a perfect heart, 2 Chron. 15:1, 2. And whosoever rests in a form of godliness, without the power of it, deceives his own heart, and his religion is in vain, James 1:26.

Such may be convinced, 2., that in all their solemn appearing before God, and their approachings nigh unto him, their hearts are far from him, Isa. 29:13 and Matth. 15:8. And testifies that all their worship is in vain, Matth. 15:8, 9. And they themselves hypocrites, verse 7. As the heart is, so is the worshipper in the sight of God. If the heart be proud, covetous, vain, foolish, lukewarm, formal and hypocritical, all that professor's duties, performances and worship is abhorred of God, his soul hates them, Isa. 1:12, 13, 14, 15 and Chap. 66, verse 3. "Bring no more vain oblations, incense is an abomination to me, the New Moon and Sabbaths, the calling of Assemblies, I cannot away with. It is iniquity, even the solemn meetings, —Your New Moons, and your appointed feasts my soul hates, they are a trouble unto me, I am weary to bear them.—And when you spread forth your hands, I will hide my eyes from you; yea, when you make many prayers, I will not hear; your hands are full of blood. He that kills an ox is as if he slew a man, he that sacrifices a lamb as if he cut off a dog's neck, he that offers an oblation as if he offered swine's blood, he that burns incense as if he blessed an idol; yea they have chosen their own ways, and their soul delights in their abominations."

They may be convinced, 3. that they shall never see God in heaven, Heb. 12:14, "for without holiness" (the power of godliness) "no man shall see the Lord." They are declared by God in his Word to be hypocrites, Matth. 15:7, 8, 9, and if they repent not, they shall have their portion with hypocrites, Matth. 24:51, in the lowest and deepest of eternal flames and of everlasting darkness, there shall be weeping and gnashing of teeth.

3. Use of consolation unto the wise Virgins. Are you an Israelite indeed? Do you worship God in spirit and truth? Have you both the form and power of godliness? Then be of good comfort. For,

1., Christ is yours, and all is yours, 1 Cor. 3:21, 22, 23. God is your father, grace is your portion, and heaven is your inheritance, holiness is your way, and happiness will be your end, Matth. 5:8.

2. You do and shall enjoy spiritual communion with God in holy duties and in his sacred ordinances. The power of godliness does make the believer fruitful under that form of godliness which Christ has instituted for the worship of God; and affords him fellowship with the Father, Son, and Spirit, 1 John 1:1, 2, 3.

3. Know for your comfort, that the power of sin, Satan, hell cannot, shall not, prevail against the power of godliness in you, so far as to provoke the Lord to forsake you forever, or to cause you to forsake God for ever, for he has said, Heb. 1:3, 5, "I will never leave you, never ever forsake you." Read for your comfort, Jer. 32:38, 40. "And they shall not depart from me." But the power of godliness in you will, by the power of Christ, prevail against, conquer, and overcome the power of darkness, and all the wiles of the wicked one, 1 John 2:13. Also, the power of this world, Eph. 6:12, 13 and the threats, allurements, etc. of it, 1 John. 5:4, 5. And likewise the power of sin, both the reigning power of it (called the "dominion of sin," Rom. 6:14, "sin shall not have dominion over you, because you are not under the Law, but under grace"), and the tyrannizing power of it (called the "captivity of sin," Rom. 7:2, 3, and 8:2). "But the Law of the spirit of life in Christ Jesus has made me free from the Law of sin and death. Rejoice therefore in the Lord and bless him," 1 Pet. 1:3, 4, 5, 6, 8.

4. Use of exhortation, 1., to the profane, 2., to professors, and 3., to true believers.

1. [First] A word to all profane persons who have neither the power nor the form of godliness. I exhort such to consider the woeful state and miserable condition, being all of them without Christ, having no hope, and without God in the world, Ephes. 2:12. David tells profane sinners, "The wicked shall be turned into hell; and all the people that forget God," Psal. 9:17. You can live without Christ, trade without Christ, marry and give in marriage without Christ; but tell me, you profane sinners, what will you do if you die without Christ? Can you think seriously of going to Hell, and being tormented there to eternity? Will the enjoyment of the pleasure of sin for a season compensate the loss of your souls and the pains of Hell forever?

Secondly, a word to the foolish virgin professors who, having a form of godliness, deny the power of it. I exhort such to consider seriously whether seeming to be religious, and saying "Lord, Lord," will save your immortal souls, Matth. 7:21, 22, 23. "Not everyone that says unto me, 'Lord, Lord' shall enter into the Kingdom of Heaven, but he that does the will of my Father which is in heaven—Many will say to me in that day, 'Lord, Lord, have we not prophesied in your Name, and in your Name have cast out Devils, and in your Name done many wonderful works?'—And then will I profess unto them, 'I never knew you, depart from me you that work iniquity.'" Remember professors that the foolish Virgins had their lamps lighted, and they shined in the form of godliness, but they found the door of the Kingdom of Heaven shut against them. And when they said "Lord, Lord, open to us," Christ said unto them, "I know you not," Matth. 25:10, 11, 12, because they had not the power of godliness, Luke 13:24, 28. "Strive to enter in at the straight gate, for many I say unto you, will seek to enter in and shall not be able.—There shall be weeping and gnashing of teeth, when you shall see Abraham, Isaac, and Jacob, and all the prophets in the Kingdom of God, and you yourselves shut out."

Do not rest in a form without the power of godliness, lest you sitting down in any church of saints and under the sacred ordinances of God without Christ come short of heaven, for without holiness no man shall see the Lord, Heb. 12:14. The Kingdom of God is not in word but in power, 1 Cor. 4:20.

Thirdly, a word to the wise Virgins that have not only the form but the power of godliness, whom I exhort, 1. To exercise the power of godliness in the performances of holy duties and in partaking of God's holy ordinances, and not to rest in the form and external part of the worship of God. 2. To demonstrate unto all that you have the power of godliness by being holy in all manner of conversation, both in the house of God and in your own houses, showing forth the virtue of him that has called you; by which the faith, humility, self-denial, patience, the love and life of Jesus Christ may be manifested in your life.

Query 1. How may professors attain unto the power of godliness and so become wise Virgins?

Sol[ution]. 1. Professors must come to Christ in the ordinances of God, 1 Cor. 1:18, 24. Christ complained of the Jewish professors that they would not come to him, John 5:40, many come to sermons, to duties, to ordinances but few come to Christ. Most rest in the form without the power of godliness, satisfying themselves in coming to sermons and attending upon ordinances without going to Christ in them, Isa. 55:3.

2. The gospel must come to professors not in word only, but also in power and in the Holy Spirit, 1 Thes. 1:5, before they can come to Christ to attain the power of godliness.

3. The ministers of Christ must declare the testimony of God not with excellency of speech, not with enticing words of man's wisdom, but their speech and their preaching must be in the demonstration of the Spirit and in power, 1 Cor. 2:1, 2, 4, 5, before the gospel can come to their hearers' hearts in power and in the Holy Spirit, and before their hearers can come to Christ, and before they can attain to the power of godliness. The plain and powerful preaching of the gospel is the ordinary means by which God draws sinners with cords of love to Christ, and makes the ministry of the word powerful and effectual to call, convert, sanctify, and save sinners, Rom. 1:16, 17, Rom. 10:14, 17.

Query 2. How many professors know that they have attained unto the power of godliness, and that they are wise Virgins?

Sol[ution]. Professors may know that they have attained unto the power of godliness, and are wise Virgins, 1., By the victory they have obtained over the world, Satan, and their own sins. There's none but true believers have overcome the world, 1 John 5:4, 5. None but those that are strong in faith have overcome the Devil, that wicked one, John 2:14. It's the truth of faith and the power of godliness by which sanctified persons do overcome their sinful lusts and corruptions; the grace of God teaches all men to deny ungodliness and worldly lusts, Tit. 2:12.

[2.] By the lively acts and constant exercise of grace in whomsoever the power of godliness is, it will appear in the growth and exercise of grace, 1 Pet. 3:18. Such Christians are fruitful under God's holy ordinances, John 15:5. The gospel came to them not in word only but in power and in the Holy Spirit, 1 Thes. 1:5, and their faith did grow exceedingly, and the love of them all exceeded, 2 Thes. 2:3.

[3.] By their holy conversation in the world, 2 Cor. 1:12. "This is our rejoicing, the testimony of our conscience that in simplicity and godly sincerity by the grace of God we have our conversation in the world." The power of godliness will appear in a holy life and heavenly conversation, as it did in the primitive saints, Phil. 3:20, to which they were exhorted, 1 Pet. 1:15, namely, to be holy in all manner of conversation.

Query 3. Are they that have the power of godliness obliged to the form of godliness?

Sol[ution]. Yes, the Apostle commended the Church and saints in Corinth for keeping the ordinances of God, 1 Cor. 11:1, 2, and the Apostle Peter commanded them to be baptized with water, who had received the Holy Spirit, Acts 10:47, 48. All the Apostles, the churches of saints, and all true believers looked at themselves to be obliged to the external form of godliness and worship of God in external gospel ordinances, as it appears in the Acts of the Apostles and in their epistles.

Verse 5. "While the Bridegroom tarried, they all slumbered and slept."

The Bridegroom is the Lord Jesus Christ, verse 1, who is here said to tarry or delay his coming, Chap. 24:48, which he will not do in respect of the time appointed of the Father. Then he that shall come, will come, and will not tarry, Heb. 10:37. But Christ is said to tarry or delay his coming;

1. Because he came not when they prayed for his coming, and earnestly desired his presence and appearance: thus Jesus tarried two days after Lazarus' sisters had sent him word that he was sick, John 11:1, 3, 6 and yet came in due time and manifested himself with power and great glory in raising Lazarus from the dead, verses 23, 40, 43, 44.

2. Because he came not when they looked for him, and at the time when they expected his coming. The Apostles tells us, Heb. 9:28, "Unto them that look, for him he shall appear the second time without sin unto salvation." But of that day and hour

knows no man, no not the Angels of heaven, but my Father, said Christ, Matth. 24:36.

They all slumbered and slept. All the Virgins, both the foolish and the wise Virgins. First, they all slumbered or nodded, that is to say, they did not wake and watch as formerly they had done, while they waited for and expected the glorious appearance of their LORD, and bore their testimony of his coming, but began to be careless and secure, neglecting their duty. They became drowsy and indisposed to wait any longer for the coming of the Bridegroom, grew weary, silent and sleepy as the spouse did, Cant. 4:16; 5:1, 2, between her entreating and inviting her beloved to come into his garden, and his coming, "I sleep but my heart wakes," verse 2.

Secondly, they all slept or were fast asleep, that is to say, the wise Virgins as well as the foolish were fallen into a state of security, as persons are when they are fast asleep in the night season, fearing neither fire, thieves, nor any other danger. So all these ten Virgins (it being now near midnight) were fast asleep (as it were in a dead sleep) through their carnal security and careless neglect of their watch and other holy duties. And some of them backslid into a deep apostasy, and so continued until the cry at midnight awakened them out of that deep sleep of carnal security, backsliding, and apostasy, into which they were fallen, as appears in the 6th and 7th verses of this chapter.

Meditation. Many virgin professors, being mistaken about this time of Christ's coming, who tarried longer than they expected, will fall into the slumber of sinful silence and careless security. And some professors will fall into a dead and deadly sleep of backsliding and apostasy. This meditation consists of four propositions.

First, many virgin professors have been and are mistaken about this time of Christ's coming. And that does appear by what many learned and godly men have written and witnessed touching the coming of Christ, many have looked for the coming of Christ, as the judge of the quick and the dead, 2 Tim. 4:1. "I charge you therefore before God and the Lord Jesus Christ, who shall judge the quick and the dead at his appearing and his kingdom." And that at the end of the world, 2 Pet. 3:3, 10, 12, when he shall give up his kingdom to the Father, 1 Cor. 15:24-28. But few have expected the coming of Christ as the Bridegroom, and the New Jerusalem to come down from heaven as a bride adorned for her husband, Rev. 21:1, 2. Who looks for the Marriage of the Lamb? And who will grant that his bride shall make herself ready, Rev. 14:7, 8, to be married to Christ and to live and reign with

Christ a thousand years here on earth between the final destruction of the Beast and the false Prophet and the eternal judgement of the last day? Rev. 20:4. But more will be spoken of the coming of Christ in the exposition of the next verse.

Secondly, the Bridegroom tarried longer than the Virgins expected, "while the Bridegroom tarried," says the text. They expected his coming while they were awake, watching and witnessing, praying and looking for him, but he tarried till they all slumbered and slept. And then he came at midnight, verse 6, at an hour (in a dispensation) when they looked not for him, Matth. 24:44, 50. "Therefore be you also ready, for in such an hour as you think not, the Son of man comes. —The Lord of that servant shall come in a day when he looks not for him, and in an hour that he is not aware of," Matth. 25:13. "Watch therefore for you know neither the day not the hour in which the Son of Man comes," and 1 Thes. 5:2, "For you yourselves know perfectly that the day of the Lord so comes as a thief in the night."

Thirdly, the generality of virgin professors will fall into the slumber of a sinful silence, neglect to watch and wait for the Spiritual Bridegroom, and grow careless and secure while he tarries.

So long as virgin professors will be speaking of Christ's coming and kingdom, and talking of his power (as was prophesied the latter day saints shall do, Psal. 145:11), while they are praying continually for the coming and Kingdom of Christ (as he taught his disciples to pray, Matth. 6:10, "Your kingdom come"). And while they are watching and waiting for the Lord from heaven in his glorious appearance with kingly power and majesty, as the saints were exhorted by the Apostle to do, 1 Thes. 1:9, 10, "To serve the living God and to wait for his Son from heaven"; I say, so long as virgin professors are so doing, they will not, cannot, shall not slumber nor sleep. But when they begin to be silent in bearing their testimony for the Kingdom of Christ against the Kingdom of the Antichrist, and will not, do not, speak of his glorious coming and kingdom as the Bridegroom, but give over praying for it and waiting for him; then they begin to be careless of his coming, and to grow secure, and being at ease in Zion, begin to slumber, and at last some of them fall fast asleep.

Fourthly, some professors will fall into a deep and deadly sleep of backsliding and apostasy. As some of the latter day saints will be shining believers, Isa. 60:1, 2, so some of the virgin professors in the last days will prove backsliding formalists and damnable apostates, and this grand and greater apostasy has these four steps or gradations:

1. A liberal inordinate resting and reposing their hearts in and upon worldly contentments.

2. A cooling in their affections and careless neglect of holy duties, ordinances, and the pure worship of God.

3. A fearlessness of declining and backsliding.

4. A benumbed deadness, hardness, insensibleness, security and contentedness, being at ease and rest, and so fall asleep in that condition, and this will happen a little before the coming of Christ, 2 Thes. 1:2, 3. "Now we beseech you, brethren, by the coming of our Lord Jesus Christ, and by our gathering together in him—That you be not soon shaken in mind, or be troubled, neither by spirit nor by word, nor by letters as from us, that the day of Christ is at hand—Let no man deceive you by any means, for that day shall not come except there come a falling away first, and that man of sin be revealed, the son of perdition." This apostasy was foretold also by the Apostle Peter in his second epistle, the third chapter, and the 3rd and 4th verses. "Knowing this first, that there shall come in the last days scoffers, walking after their own lusts and saying, 'Where is the promise of his coming for, since the fathers fell asleep, all things continue as they were from the beginning of the creation?'" The Apostle Paul also foretold Timothy, that in the last days, (which will be perilous times) men eminent for professions (having the form of godliness) will deny the power of it through their own lusts, 2 Tim. 3:1, 2, 3, 4, 5. There are two expressions used by both those Apostles touching this grand and last apostasy, which does confirm my opinion that they both prophesied and wrote of the same apostasy. Paul says, 2 Tim. 3:1, "This know also that, in the last days." And Peter says, 1 Peter. 3:3, "Knowing that first —that in the later days," etc.

The root of this grand and last apostasy is self-love, and the love of pleasures, which the Apostle in his epistle to Timothy notes to be the chief character of the formal professors and apostates in the last days, 2 Tim. 3:2, 4. The men of Name shall be "Lovers of their own selves and lovers of pleasures, more than lovers of God." These sinful pleasures and worldly contents cause professors to slumber, and some to fall fast asleep in apostasy. Self-love is that root of bitterness out of which those unblessed, yea those cursed branches of sinful lusts (there mentioned) do sprout and grow, especially covetousness, pride, and covenant breaking. And the love of pleasures is the corrupt fountain from whence the bitter waters of those sinful lusts spring and flow.

Let him that has understanding judge what I say. If MEN, not profane only but professors also, not only the men of the world, but also members of churches, do love themselves more than truth and righteousness and love the world more than faith and a good conscience, yea, love their vain sinful delights and pleasures more than God and Jesus Christ, may not those and such as those be ranked and numbered among the apostasies and backsliders of the last days? By how much the more we see and know men that have been very eminent in profession above many others, and have been highly esteemed in the churches of saints, men of name, chief men among the brethren, yea among the elders for knowledge, gifts, zeal, etc., who have born a glorious testimony for Christ against the Antichrist. But yet they have afterwards (through love of themselves and love of pleasures and other sinful lusts) backslid, revolted, and apostatized from what they formerly practised and professed before many witnesses. May we not conclude them to be among the number of the apostates of the last days?

Verse 6. "And at midnight there was a cry made, 'Behold the Bridegroom comes, go you out to meet him.'"

[First,] Night does mystically and metaphorically signify

[1.] A time of rest, ease, and quietness, also drowsiness, sluggishness, and a lazing disposition; likewise a condition of a sinful careless security, Rom. 10:11, 12. "And that knowing the time that now it is high time to awake out of sleep, for now is our salvation nearer than when we believed—The night is far spent, the day is at hand, let us therefore cast off the works of darkness, and let us put on the armour of light.—1 Thes. 5:2, 6, 7. For your selves know perfectly that the day of the Lord comes as a thief in the night.—Therefore, let us not sleep as do others, but let us watch and be sober—For they that sleep, sleep in the night, and they that are drunken are drunken in the night—Matth. 24:48, 49, 50. But and if that evil servant shall say in his heart, 'My Lord delays his coming,' and shall begin to smite his fellow servants, and to eat and drink with the drunken, the Lord of that servant shall come in a day when he looks not for him and in an hour that he is not aware of."

2. A condition and time of great darkness, discomfort, sore afflictions and heavy judgements, Exod. 12:29. "And it came to pass that, at midnight, the LORD smote all the firstborn in the land of Egypt": Mich. 3:6, 7. "Therefore night shall be unto you, that you shall not have a vision, and it shall be dark unto you that you shall not divine, and the sun shall go down over the prophets and the day shall be dark over them—then shall the

seers be ashamed, and the diviners confounded, yea they shall cover their lips, for there is no answer of God," Joel 3:1. "Gird yourselves and lament you priests, howl you ministers of the altar: come lie all night in sackcloth you ministers of my God; for the meat-offering and the drink-offering is withheld from the house of your God."

3. A time of greatest retirement and repose for most serious devotion and spiritual meditation, and holy contemplation, Psal. 4:4, "Commune with your own heart upon your bed, and be still," etc. Psal. 16:7, "My reins shall instruct me in the night season." Cant. 3:1, "By night on my bed I sought him whom my soul loves, I sought him but found him not."

This midnight dispensation in the text does mystically and metaphorically signify all these three particular conditions at the time of the Bridegroom's coming, with respect to the several sorts of persons who will be then and in that day concerned in that place, namely,

[F]irst, the foolish Virgins will then be found in a sluggish disposition and condition of a sinful careless security, so sleepy that their lamps go out, verse 8. And the wise Virgins will be too secure and careless at that time, verse 5.

Secondly, worldly professors who are taught to worship God according to the commandments and precepts of men and the inventions and superstitions of men will then be found under great darkness, discomfort, and amazement, Luke 21:25, 26, 27, "And there shall be signs in the sun, and in the moon, and in the stars, and upon the earth distress of nations with perplexity, the sea and the waves roaring—Men's hearts failing them for fear, and for looking after those things which are coming on the earth, for the powers of heaven shall be shaken—And then shall they see the Son of Man coming in a cloud with power and great glory"; Because of the sore afflictions and righteous judgements of God, Matth. 24:21, 29, 30. "For then shall be great tribulation such as was not from the beginning of the world to this time, no nor ever shall be— Immediately after the tribulations of those days shall the sun be darkened, and the moon shall not give her light, and the stars shall fall from heaven, and the powers of the heavens shall be forsaken—And then shall appear the sign of the Son of Man in heaven, and they shall see the Son of Man coming in the clouds of heaven with power and great glory."

Thirdly, there will be some, a few, a small remnant of Virgin saints who will accompany the Bridegroom when he comes, even in the midnight dispensation, and they are those hundred forty-four thousand who have their Father's name written on their foreheads, Rev. 14:1,2, 3, 4, 5, being in their retirement, repose, and secret devotion formerly sealed for the servants of God, Rev. 7:3, 4. And now come with the Bridegroom and shall stand with the Lamb upon Mount *Zion* being without fault before the throne of God.

"There was a cry made," etc. The questions are: 1. What cry was this? 2. Who made this cry? 3. Who heard this cry?

Touching the first question, "What cry was this?" I answer that the Greek word does both here and in many other places of Scripture signify a very loud, fierce, and vehement cry, as Acts 7:57. "They cried out with a loud voice," Acts 19:28. As a herald at arms cries out with a loud voice when he proclaims an edict, or when the common crier makes proclamation, Rev. 7:2, "He cried with a loud voice," etc., and Rev. 10:3, Rev. 19:17.

Touching the second question, "Who made this cry?" I answer, either the LORD himself, or the ministers of Christ, or the people of God. For this cry is either by preaching the coming of Christ publicly, Isa. 58:1, "Cry aloud, spare not, lift up your voice like a trumpet," etc., Matth. 24:14. And the gospel of the kingdom shall be proclaimed or preached publicly in all the inhabited world, or else a cry raised by the voice of a great number of the saints and servants of God in the temple of God that was opened in heaven, Isa. 66:6. "A voice of the LORD, a voice from the temple," after the Resurrection of the two prophetical witnesses of Christ which the beast had killed, compare Rev. 11:7, 11, 12, 17, 19. "And they heard a great voice from heaven, saying unto them, 'Come up hither,'" verse 12 with Rev. 19:1, 4, 5, 6, 7, 8, 9. "And a voice came out of the throne, and I heard as it were the voice of a great multitude saying 'Alleluia, for the Lord God Omnipotent reigns. Let me be glad and rejoice, and give honour to him, for the marriage of the Lamb is come. Blessed are they that are called to the marriage supper of the Lamb.' These are the true sayings of God, or by the Lord Himself," Joel 3:16. Jehovah also shall roar out of Zion, and utter his voice from Jerusalem, and the heaven and the earth shall shake, read Hag. 2:6, 7, and Heb. 12:16, 27 and verse 25. "See that you refuse not him that speaks from heaven."

Touching the third question, "Who heard the cry?" I answer: all the Virgins both wise and foolish heard this cry. "The Bridegroom comes, go you out to meet him," as appears in the next verse. For they all (being awakened by that loud cry) rose and trimmed their lamps, verse 7, and probably there were many others, even great multitudes, that heard this cry or proclamation of the Bridegroom's coming, who were glad and rejoiced that the marriage of the Lamb was come, and that does appear by what is prophesied and recorded, Rev. 19:1 to the 9th verse.

The sum and substance of this cry is contained in these words, "Behold the Bridegroom comes, go you out to meet him." In which are three things to be observed, namely,

1. The attention, "Behold."
2. The assertion, "The Bridegroom comes."
3. The obligation or duty enjoyed and commanded, "Go you out to meet him."

[1.] When God would have some wonderful and glorious thing made known unto the world and unto his people, he stirs up their attention by this word, "Behold," Isa. 65:1, Zeph. 3:19, 1 Cor. 15:21, 1 John 3:1, Rev. 15:5 and 21:5, especially when God speaks of his Son Jesus Christ, Isa. 28:16, John 1:29, Rev. 1:7, 16, 15:22, 7. "Behold he comes," etc. "Behold I come quickly." So in the text, "Behold the Bridegroom comes" this is a matter which is worthy of and calls for the churches', ministers', and saints' attention.

[2.] "The Bridegroom comes."

It's not said HE will come, though that is true, Heb. 10:37. Yet a little while and "HE that shall come, will come, and will not tarry." But HE comes, HE is upon his march, Rev. 19:11, 12, 13, 14, 15, HE has been coming a great while, HE went forth long ago, Rev. 6:2, and now HE is very near even at the door ready to enter into the Bride chamber; Only HE stands and stays at the door until the Bride has made herself ready, Rev. 19:7, 8, verse 10 of this chapter, "And they that were ready went in with him to the marriage and the door was shut."

Seeing that many both learned and godly men have been mistaken in their opinions about the coming of Christ as was hinted in the exposition of the former verse; it concerns the churches of saints, the ministers of Christ, and all sanctified believers to search the Holy Scriptures and pray that God will, by his Holy Spirit, open the Scriptures to us and open our understanding thus in this his coming.

And now let not the churches ministers, not any of the saints, be offended with me for showing my opinion, touching this coming of Christ and the Scripture grounds and reasons for the same, which I humbly offer with all submission unto their judgement.

I do believe and am persuaded that the coming of Christ (spoken of in this parable, verse 6:10) is not the coming of Christ in his own person upon the earth (though I do believe Christ will come the second time in his own person upon the earth, Heb. 9:28, Zech. 3:4, 5), but this is his virtual, spiritual, powerful, and glorious coming in his saints and sanction "as the Bridegroom of his Church, and new Jerusalem, who shall also come down from God out of heaven, prepared as a Bride adorned for her husband." Our David's mystical kingdom on earth among his saints, when HE shall be king of all the earth and all the kingdoms of this world shall be Christ's. And when the Lord's redeemed ones, whom HE has made kings and priests to God, shall have the kingdom and dominion under the whole heaven given to them, and they shall reign on earth. And the reasons grounded on Scripture are as follows: 1. Negatively. 2. Affirmatively.

Negatively, that the coming of Christ spoken of in the 6th and 10th verses of this parable is not the coming of Christ in his own person upon the earth.

First, because, at the personal coming of Christ on earth (called "his appearing" the second time, Heb. 9:28), all his saints shall come with him, Zach. 14:5. "And Jehovah my God shall come and all the saints with you," 1 Thes. 3:13. At the coming of our Lord Jesus Christ with all his saints. The living bodies of the saints shall be changed and glorified. And the bodies of the saints deceased shall then be raised and also glorified, Phil. 3:20, 21, "For our conversation is in heaven, from whence also we look for the Saviour our Lord Jesus Christ—who shall change our vile body that it may be fashioned like unto his glorious body, according to the working by which he is able even to subdue all things unto himself." 1 Thes. 4:14, 15, 16, 17, "For if we believe, that Jesus died and rose again, even so them also which sleep in Jesus will God bring with him. For this we say unto you by the word of the LORD, that we which are alive and remain unto the coming of the Lord shall not prevent them which are asleep— For the Lord himself shall descend from heaven with a shout with the voice of the Archangel and with the Trump of God, and the dead in Christ shall rise first—Then we which are alive and remain shall be caught up together with them in the clouds to meet the Lord in the air, and so shall we ever be with the Lord." But there will not be such a general and physical resurrection at the coming of Christ as the Bridegroom, for then the living saints only shall enter into the bride chamber, and those wise Virgins who never came personally into the kingdom of the Father in heaven shall be admitted into the kingdom of the Son on earth, Rev. 3:21. "To him that overcomes will I grant to sit with me in my throne; even as I also overcame and am set down with my Father in his throne," which Christ himself expounds, Rev. 2:26 saying, "To him will I give power over the nations. Even as (or the same power that) I received of the Father."

Secondly, because at the personal coming of Christ on earth, will be the universal physical resurrection of all that are dead (and the physical change of all their bodies that are then alive), 1 Cor. 15:51, 52. "Behold I show you a mystery—we shall not all sleep, but we shall all be changed in a moment in the twinkling of an eye at the last trump (for the trumpet shall sound, and the dead shall be raised incorruptible and we shall be changed)." Which resurrection Christ in John 6:39, 40, 44 three times together testifies shall be at the last day, and Matth. 25:31, 32. "When the Son of Man shall come in his glory and all the holy angels with him, then shall he sit upon the throne of his glory," compared with Rev. 20:11, 12, 13, "And I saw a great white throne and him that sat on it, from whose face the earth and the heaven fled away, and there was found no more place for them. And I saw the dead small and great stand before God, and the books were opened, and another book was opened which is the Book of Life, and the dead were judged out of those things which were written in the Book, according to their works— and the sea gave up the dead which were in it, and death and hell delivered up the dead which were in them, and they were judged every man according to his works"; together with the eternal judgement, Matth. 25:33, 34, 46; 2 Thes. 1:7, 8, 9, 10; 2 Tim. 4:1; Jude 14, 15; Rev. 20:12.

Thirdly, because when Christ comes virtually and spiritually as the Bridegroom, then will begin the times of the restitution of all things. Then God will restore our judges as at the first, and our counsellors as at the beginning, Isa. 1:25, 26, 27. Then Christ will restore Israel, and restore the kingdom to Israel, Mich. 4:7, 8. Even the first dominion shall come to the Daughter of Zion, the kingdom shall come to the Daughter of Jerusalem. Then Christ will make all things new, Rev. 21:5. But when Christ shall come personally upon the earth (as the judge of the quick and the dead) then will be the dissolution of the material heavens and earth, and the final consumption and conflagration of all things, 2 Pet. 3:4, 7, 12, "When the heavens being on fire shall be dissolved." Now consider that this great desolation of all things, yea of the material heavens and earth (which the Scripture testifies will be at Christ's second coming) cannot be at the beginning of his kingdom here on earth for above a thousand years, after that time Gog and Magog will be gathered together and compass the camp of saints about and the beloved city, Rev. 20:4, 5, 7, 8, 9.

Objection. Does not this opinion exempt and exclude Christ from rule and sovereignty in his monarchical kingdom on earth, contrary to Rev. 20:4, "They lived and reigned with Christ a thousand years"?

Answer. No.

Consider first, Christ may be said to be with a person or people, and they with him virtually by his Spirit and power or his powerful spiritual presence, Isa. 57:15; 1 Cor. 6:16; Rev. 2:1; Rom. 6:4; Col. 2:12, 13. As it is said, Jer. 8:9, "Is not the LORD in Zion? Is not her King in her?" Though not personally, but spiritually.

Secondly, as Christ is said to be in his mystical kingdom the church of God here on earth; where his laws, his statutes, and his ordinances are dispensed in his Name, and by the power of his Holy Spirit; so will he be in his monarchical kingdom, the throne of his Father David here on earth, Luke 1:32, 33. "And the Lord God shall give unto him the throne of his Father David. And he shall reign over the House of Jacob forever, and of his kingdom there shall be no end"; not personally at the beginning of it, but virtually by his laws, etc.

Did not the Caesars and Roman Senate govern the world by their laws and edicts, and by those kings and governors of provinces whom they commissioned and made rulers for them? Is not the King of Spain said to rule and reign in those parts of America, and in other parts of the world (which he or his ancestors conquered) by his laws, civil and ecclesiastical, although he himself was never present there in his own person? And does not the Pope reign over the kings and kingdoms of the earth, who have agreed and given their kingdom to the Beast, Rev. 17:17, 18, though he was never personally in those kingdoms, but gives commissions to his kings, his nuntios, his cardinals, and his prelates to rule in his Name and by his laws and edicts, canons and constitutions to govern the people in those his kingdoms?

So shall Christ reign over all the nations and kingdoms of the world, whom he shall conquer, and they shall become his, Rev. 11:5. And HE shall be King of all the earth, Zach. 14:9. And God shall give him the throne of his father David, Luke 1:32, 33. And the judgement shall be given to the saints of the most high, and they shall possess the kingdom and govern the nations by Christ's laws, Dan. 7:14, 21, 27, and in his Name, and by his commission with his Holy Spirit and power, and in great glory, Isa. 60:1, 2, 3, 7, 11, 12, 13, 14, 15. "Arise, shine, for your light is come and the glory of the Lord is risen upon you—The sons also of them that afflicted you shall come bending unto you, and all they that despised you shall bow themselves down at the soles of your feet, and they shall call you the city of the LORD, the Zion of the holy one of Israel—While you have been forsaken and hated, so that no man went through you; I will make you an eternal excellency and joy of many generations"; from the beginning of the thousand years' reign, Rev. 20:4, until the end of it, which is Christ's Davidical and monarchical kingdom. And after that, Christ has put down all rule, all authority, and all power that are his enemies by the hands of his saints, who shall bind kings in chains and nobles in fetters of iron, and execute the judgement written, "This honour have all the saints," Psal. 149:7, 8, 9. Then will the Lord Jesus Christ himself come in his own person, and all his holy angels and saints shall attend him, Matth. 25:31, 32. "When the Son of Man shall come in his glory and all the holy angels with him, then shall he sit upon the throne of his glory—and before him shall be gathered all nations, and he shall separate them one from another, as a shepherd divides his sheep from the goats." Then shall he sit upon the throne of his glory, and the saints shall sit upon thrones with Christ, Matth. 19:28. "And Jesus said unto them, 'Verily I say unto you, that you which have followed me in the regeneration, when the Son of Man shall sit on the throne of his glory; you also shall sit upon twelve thrones, judging the twelve tribes of Israel,'" Rev. 3:21. "'To him that overcomes will I grant to sit with me in my throne, even also as I overcame and am set down with my Father in his throne.'"

This personal coming of Christ had its typical vision and mystical appearance at his transfiguration, Matth. 17:1, 2, 9. "And after six days, Jesus took Peter, James, and John his brother, and brought them up into a high mountain, and was transfigured before them, and his face did shine as the sun, and his raiment was white as the light. And as they came down from the mountain, Jesus charged them saying, 'Tell the vision to no man until the Son of Man rise again from the dead.'" Those Apostles Peter, James, and John his brother were they of whom Christ spoke, Matth. 16:27, 28. "For the Son of Man shall come in the glory of his Father, with his angels, and then he shall reward every man according to his works—'Verily, I say unto you, there are some standing here which shall not taste of death till they see the Son of Man coming in his kingdom.'" And Peter being one of those three bore his testimony and record of it, 2 Pet. 1:16, 17, 18. "For we have not followed cunningly devised fables, when we made known unto you the power and coming of our

Lord Jesus Christ, but were eyewitnesses of his majesty. For he received from God the Father honour and glory, when there came such a voice to him from the excellent glory. 'This is my Beloved Son in whom I am well pleased'—And this voice which came from heaven we heard when we were with him in the holy Mount." And it shall be visible indeed, Matth. 24:27. For as the lightning comes out of the east, and shines even unto the west, so shall also the coming of the Son of Man be, Acts 1:11. He shall so come in like manner as you have seen him go into heaven. And very glorious; for Christ shall come in the glory of his Father, Mark 8:38. In his own glory, and his Father's, Luke 9:26. In the glory of the holy angels also, Matth. 25:31, and likewise in the glory of all his saints, 2 Thes. 1:7, 8, 9, 10.

Then shall Christ, the King of saints, the King of Zion, and the King of Nations be admired of all them that believe, 2 Thes. 1:10, "and praised, saying, 'Who would not fear You, O King of Nations?'" Jer. 10:7, 10, "The blessed and only potentate, the KING of Kings and LORD of Lords," 1 Tim. 6:15, Then also shall the saints be glorified. Phil 3:20, 21, "For our conversation is in heaven, from whence we look for the Saviour, the Lord Jesus Christ—who shall change our vile body, that it may be fashioned like unto his glorious body," etc. 1 John 3:2, "Behold now we are the sons of God, and it does not appear what we shall be, but we know that, when he shall appear, we shall be like him, for we shall see him as he is": and rewarded, Rev. 22:12, "'Behold I come quickly, and my reward is with me.'" Matth. 25:34, "'Come you blessed of my Father, receive the kingdom prepared for you from the foundation of the world.'"

Then wicked men and wicked angels shall by Christ and his saints be judged according to their deeds, 1 Cor. 6:2. "Do you not know that the saints shall judge the world?" verse 3. "Know you not that we shall judge angels?" and 2 Tim. 4:1, "I charge you therefore before God and the Lord Jesus Christ who shall judge the quick and the dead at his appearing, and his kingdom." And then shall Christ deliver up the kingdom to God the Father, 1 Cor. 15:24, 28. That as Christ is now All and in All, Col. 3:11, so God the Father then shall be All in All, 1 Cor. 15:28. Thus much negatively.

Affirmatively. That the coming of Christ in the 6th and 10th verses of this chapter is his virtual, spiritual, powerful, and glorious appearance in his saints and sanction ("As the Bridegroom of his church, the New Jerusalem, the holy City, the general assembly and church of the first born, written in heaven, who also shall come down from God out of heaven prepared as a bride adorned for her husband") and in his Davidical kingdom on earth.

For proof of this my opinion, search those places of Holy Scripture, Isa. 60:2, 3, 7, 13; Psal. 110:3; 2 Thes. 1:10; Rev. 14:1, 2, 3, 4, 5; Heb. 12:23; Rev. 21:1, 2, 3, 4, 5. "Arise, shine, for your light is come, and the glory of the Lord is risen upon you." — "For behold darkness shall cover the earth and gross darkness the people: but the LORD shall arise upon you and his glory shall be seen upon you"—"And the Gentiles shall come to your light, and kings to the brightness of your rising"—"All the flocks of Kedar shall be gathered together unto you, the Rams of Nebajoth shall minister unto you, they shall come up with acceptance on my altar, And I will beautify the house of my glory; the glory of Lebanon shall come unto you, the fir tree, the pine tree and the box together to beautify the place of my sanctuary, and I will make the place of my feet glorious." "The LORD said unto my Lord, 'Sit on my right hand, until I make your enemies your footstool.'" "Your people shall be willing in the day of your power, in the beauties of holiness from the womb of the morning, you have the dew of your youth"—"When he shall come to be glorified in his Father, and to be admired in all them that believe (because our testimony among you was believed) in that day"— "And I looked and saw a Lamb on the Mount Zion, and with him an hundred forty-four thousand having his Father's Name written in their foreheads"—"And I heard a voice from heaven as the voice of many waters, and as the voice of a great thunder; and I heard the voice of harpers, harping with their harps. And they sung as it were a new song before the throne, and before the four Beasts, and the elders, and no man could learn that song, but the hundred and forty and four thousand which were redeemed from the earth. These are they which are not defiled with women, for they are Virgins. These are they which follow the Lamb wherever he goes. These were redeemed from among men, being the first fruits unto God, and to the Lamb. And in their mouth was found no guile, for they are without faults before the throne of God." "To the general assembly and church of the first born which are written in heaven, and to God the Judge of all, and to the Spirits of just men made perfect. And I saw a new heaven, and a new earth, for the first heaven and the first earth passed away, and there was no more sea. And I, John, saw the Holy City New Jerusalem coming down from God out of heaven prepared as a bride adorned for her husband. And I heard a great voice out of heaven, saying, 'Behold the Tabernacle of God is with men, and he will dwell with them, and they shall be his people, and God himself shall be with them and be their God. And God shall wipe away all tears from their eyes, and there shall be no more death, neither sorrow nor crying, neither shall there be any more pain, for the former things are passed away.'" "And he that sat upon the throne said, 'Behold, I make all things new. And he said unto me, 'Write, for these words are true and faithful.'" Read Isa. chapter 62, particularly verse 5. Christ not in his own person, but by his substitutes, does marry his Church, so shall your sons marry you.

[3. Picking up the third point of the sum and substance of this cry from verse 6,] "Go you out to meet Him." The Virgins went out before and that of their own accord, and very early too; But now they are called out, and that by a loud voice, and are commanded, "'Go you out to meet him.'" They who at first were so forward, are now at last so backward, that they must be provoked, stirred up, yea roused out of their slumbering, sleep, careless security, and commanded if not compelled to go out again to meet the Bridegroom.

The spouse of Christ said within herself, Cant. 3:2. "I will rise now; I will seek him whom my soul loves." And she said to her beloved, "Come my Beloved, let us go up early to the vineyards, there will I give you my love," Cant. 7:11, 12. But for all this her fervency, she cooled in her spiritual affections towards Christ, was sleepy and indisposed for spiritual communion with her beloved, she framed excuses, being lazy and loath to open the door, though she heard him call her, and knew his voice, Cant. 5:2, 3. "I sleep but my heart wakes, it is the voice of my beloved that knocks, saying, 'Open to me my sister, my love, my dove, my undefiled, for my head is filled with the dew, and my locks with the drops of the night. And I have put off my coat how shall I put it on, I have washed my feet how shall I defile them?'"

It has been hinted in the exposition of the first verse in what respects the Virgins went out at first to meet the Bridegroom.

Let us consider what is further intended and here commanded them in these words, "Go you out to meet him."

By going out again to meet the Bridegroom, we may here understand three things,

1. A rising and shaking of all security, carelessness, and indisposition to watch and wait for the appearance of Christ, Rom. 13:11, 12, 13, 14. "And that knowing the time that now is, it is high time to awake out of sleep, for now is our salvation nearer than when we believed"—"The night is far spent, the day is at hand. Let us therefore cast off the works of darkness, and let us put on the whole armour of God. Let us walk honestly

as in the day, not in rioting and drunkenness, in chambering and wantonness, not in strife and envying. But put you on the Lord Jesus Christ, and make no provision for the flesh to fulfil the lust of it."

2. A recovering themselves out of their backsliding and apostatising condition, by prayer, repentance, and reformation, Jer. 3:12, 13, 14, 22. "Go and proclaim these words towards the north and say, 'Return you backsliding Israel, says the Lord, I will not cause my anger to fall upon you, for I am merciful says the LORD, and I will not keep anger forever'" —"'Only acknowledge your iniquity, that you have transgressed against the LORD your God, and have scattered your ways to the strangers under every green tree, and you have not obeyed my voice,' says the LORD." "'Turn, O backsliding children,' says the LORD, 'for I am married unto you, and I will take you one of a city, and one of a family, and I will bring you to Zion." —"'Return you backsliding children, and I will heal your backslidings.' Behold we come unto you, for you are the LORD our God," Hos. 14:1, 2, 3, 4, 5, 6, 7. Read the whole chapter.

3. A preparing to meet the Lord, Amos 4:12; 2 Chron. 30:19. "Prepare to meet your God, O Israel." —"That prepares his heart to seek God the LORD God of his Fathers, though he be not cleansed according to the purification of his sanctuary," Luke 1:17. "To make ready a people prepared for the Lord." So did those Virgins, the foolish seemingly, the wise sincerely, verse 7. "Then all those Virgins arose and trimmed their lamps."

1. *Meditation.* There will be a midnight dispensation of mystical and spiritual darkness upon professors, Isa. 60:2. "Darkness shall cover the earth and gross darkness the people," etc. Distress and perplexity, and great tribulation upon the inhabitants of the earth, Luke 21:25, 26, 27. "There shall be upon the earth distress of nations with perplexity; Men's hearts failing them for fear," etc. Matth. 24:21, 29. And too great security, formality, and drowsiness upon some of the wise Virgins, sanctified believers, before the coming of the Lord Jesus in his kingdom here on earth, Matth. 26:40, "What, could you not watch with me one hour?" 41. "Watch and pray," etc. Rev. 3:3, "If therefore you shall not watch, I will come on you as a thief, and you shall not know what hour I will come upon you." Cant. 5:2, 3, "I have put off my coat, how shall I put it on?" etc. Matth. 24:37, 38, 39 and Luke 17:26, 30. "As it was in the days of Noah and Lot, so shall it be in the days of the Son of Man. So shall also the coming of the Son of Man be. Even thus it shall be in the day when the Son of Man is revealed," Luke 17:30.

Parable of the Kingdom of Heaven Expounded 121

2. *Meditation.* That there will be such a voice of the LORD, such a voice from the city, and from the temple, such a loud cry in the time of the midnight dispensation, that will awake and rouse up all the slumbering and sleeping Virgins, Isa. 66:6, "A voice of strife from the city, a voice from the temple, a voice of the LORD that renders recompense to his enemies." Rev. 11:12, And they (the slain or dispirited witnesses, verse 7) "heard a great voice from heaven, saying, 'Come up hither.'" Joel 3:6, "Jehovah also shall rear out of Zion, and utter his voice from Jerusalem."

3. *Meditation.* That the next glorious appearance of the Lord Jesus Christ will be his virtual and spiritual coming in his saints and sanction (as the Bridegroom of his church) to marry her by her sons, Isa. 62:4, 5 and by them to reign over the nations with power and great glory a thousand years here on earth, Dan. 7:27.

There are but three special kinds and times of Christ's coming:

1. His coming in the form of a servant in the days of his flesh, Phil. 2:7.

[2.] His coming as a judge at the last day, when he shall judge the quick and the dead, 2 Tim. 4:1, called his appearing the second time, Heb. 9:28. Both these are his personal appearances or his coming in his own person.

[3.] But between these two appearances or comings of Christ in his own person, there is witnessed by the Holy Prophets and Apostles, and recorded in the Holy Scripture of truth, another kind of Christ's coming at another time. And that is his coming as the Bridegroom, and as the only potentate, Kind of Kings and Lord of Lords, 1 Tim. 6:14, 15, Rev. 19:16, which is his virtual, spiritual, powerful, and glorious coming in his saints and sanction, and by them to marry his Jerusalem, Isa. 62:4, 5. So shall your sons marry you, and with them to reign over the nations and kingdoms of the world, a thousand years on earth, Rev. 11:15, 16, 17. "And the seventh angel sounded, and there were great voices in heaven, saying, 'The kingdoms of the world are become the kingdoms of our Lord and of his Christ, and he shall reign forever and ever.' And the four and twenty elders which sat before God on their seats, fell upon their faces and worshipped God, saying, 'We give you thanks O Lord God Almighty, which are, and was, and are to come, because you have taken to you your great power and have reigned.'" Rev. 19:1, 4, 6, 7, 8, 9, 16, "And I heard as it were the voice of a great multitude, and as the voice of many waters, and as the voice of many thunderings, saying, 'Alleluia, for the Lord God omnipotent reigns. Let us be glad and rejoice, give honour to him, for the marriage of the Lamb is come, and his wife has made herself ready,'" Rev. 20:4, 5, 7, 9. "And I saw thrones, and they that sat upon them, and judgement was given unto them. And I saw the souls of them that were beheaded for the witness of Jesus, and for the Word of God, and which had not worshipped the Beast, neither his image, neither had received his mark upon their foreheads, or in their hands, and they lived and reigned with Christ a thousand years. But the rest of the dead lived not again until the thousand years were finished. This is the first resurrection—And when the thousand years are expired, Satan shall be loosed out of his prison—And they went upon the breadth of the earth, and compassed the camp of the saints about, and the beloved city, and fire came down from God out of heaven and devoured them."

4. *Meditation.* It is the duty of all virgin professors, especially sanctified believers who are wise Virgins, to go out and meet the Bridegroom when he comes by his spiritual power and glory in his saints and sanction to set up his kingdom and to reign on earth.

First, the Lord Jesus Christ who is King of saints, Rev. 15:3. King of Zion, Psal. 149:1, 2, and the King of Nations, Jer. 10:7, shall be the only potentate, 1 Tim. 6:14, 15, and king of all the earth, Zach. 14:9. And all the kingdoms of the world shall be his, Rev. 11:15, and his saints, Dan. 7:14, 22, 27. And they shall reign with Christ on earth a thousand years, Rev. 5:10, and Rev. 20:4.

Secondly, the God of heaven will set up this kingdom and his saints in the days of those kings of the fourth monarchy that oppose him and his saints, Dan. 2:14. And give it unto Christ as he is the Son of David, Luke 1:32, 33. "He shall be great and shall be called the Son of the Highest, and the Lord God shall give unto him the throne of his Father David, and he shall reign over the house of Jacob forever, and of his kingdom there shall be no end. —And unto the saints of the Most High," Dan. 7:27. "And the kingdom and dominion, and the greatness of the kingdom under the whole heaven shall be given to the people of the saints of the Most High, whose kingdom is an everlasting kingdom, and all dominions shall serve and obey him, who shall take it and possess it a thousand years."

Thirdly, when Christ comes to set up his kingdom and to reign on earth virtually and spiritually in his saints and sanction, with power and great glory; it's the duty of all virgin-professors, especially sanctified believers who are wise Virgins to go out to meet the Bridegroom, verse 6.

To meet the Bridegroom implies,

1. To be walking in the same way of Truth, in which Christ comes, etc. To own that truth, and to witness unto that truth of the kingdom, power, and glory of our Lord Jesus Christ, against the kingdom, power, and glory of the Antichrist, which is the finishing testimony of all the faithful witnesses of Christ, Rev. 11:7. "And when they shall have finished their testimony, the Beast that ascends out of the bottomless pit shall make war against them and overcome them and kill them." Which testimony is that gospel of the Kingdom of Christ that must be preached in all the world for a witness unto all nations, Matth. 24:14.

2. To meet the Bridegroom implies a progress and going on in that way of truth without weariness, fainting, sitting down and slumbering, Isa. 40:28, 29, 30, 31. "Have you not known, have you not heard, that the Everlasting God is LORD, the Creator of the ends of the earth, faints not, neither is weary. There is no searching of his understanding"—"He gives power to the faint, and to them that have no might he increases strength. Even the youth shall faint and be weary, and the young men shall utterly fail: but they that wait upon the Lord shall renew their strength, and they shall walk and not faint."

3. To meet the Bridegroom implies a diligent and continual watching and waiting for the virtual, spiritual, powerful, and glorious appearance of Christ the Bridegroom, Isa. 26:8, 9. "Yea, in the way of your judgements have we waited, O LORD, have we waited for you. The desire of our soul is to your name, and to the remembrance of you, in the night, yea with my Spirit within me will I seek you early; For when your judgements are in the earth, the inhabitants of the world will learn righteousness." Habak. 2:3, 4, "For the vision is for an appointed time, but at the end it shall speak, and not lie; though it tarry, wait for it, because it will surely come, it will not tarry. Behold, his soul, which is lifted up, is not upright in him; but the just shall live by his faith." Matth. 25:13, "Watch therefore, for you know neither the day, nor the hour in which the Son of Man comes."

> *Verse 7. "Then all those Virgins arose and trimmed their lamps," or cleansed their lamps.*

The Virgins, being awakened by the cry at midnight, did all arise, that is to say, All those virgin professors began to shake off the carnal security, and rise from their beds of spiritual ease of sloth, and laziness, and lukewarmness, Isa. 32:9. "Rise up you women that are at ease," Cant. 3:2. And went out again to meet the Bridegroom, as they were commanded, verse 6, being glad to hear that Christ was now coming in that midnight dispensation. They do as David did, Psal. 119:62, "At midnight will I arise and give thanks unto you." As Jonathan arose and went to meet David, 1 Sam. 23:16, so those virgin professors arose and went out again to meet the Bridegroom, Christ Jesus the Son of David. Now the Virgins are awakened, and they call upon one another like the watchmen of Mount Ephraim, saying, Jer. 31:6, "'Arise ye, and let us go up to Zion, unto Jehovah our God.'" The coming of Christ the Bridegroom will be a morning of such glorious light that shines from one end of the heavens unto the other, that will shine upon all the virgin professors, and cause the wise Virgins to arise and shine as was prophesied, Isa. 60:1, 2. "'Arise, shine, for your light is come, and the glory of the LORD is risen upon you.'" —"For behold the darkness shall cover the earth, and gross darkness the people, but the LORD shall arise upon you, and His glory shall be seen upon you." And in order to their shining profession, the Virgins, being risen, are said to trim their lamps.

"And trimmed their lamps." It seems, while the Virgins slumbered and slept, their lamps decayed; that is to say, the oil in their lamps wasted, and was spent, and the wick and smoking flax was burnt, and the light that had shined for some time began to grow dim, and was going out, and some of their lamps went out, being foul and unsavory, verse 8.

By "trimming their lamps" is meant all the means and endeavours those virgin professors used to cleanse and purge their lamps, to supply them with oil, and wick or flax, and so to repair their light and prepare themselves to meet the Bridegroom, that is to say, Now that the Virgins are awakened and are risen up, they, especially the wise Virgins, begin again to speak of the glory of Christ's Kingdom, and to talk of his power, Psal. 145:10, 11, 12, and to prepare themselves for the coming and Kingdom of Christ. The wise Virgins, having oil in their vessels, get their lamps supplied. And like the Bride, the Lamb's wife, Rev. 19:7, 8, they make themselves ready, verse 10. "And they that were ready went in with him" (with Christ the Bridegroom) "into the marriage." But the foolish Virgins, having no oil in their vessels, that is, they being without Christ and having not the spiritual unction of the grace of God in their hearts, their lamps went out, and they were shut out of the Marriage Chamber, verse 10, 11, 12. While they went to buy oil, even while they were seeking after

Christ, Prov. 1:22, 23, 28. "How long you simple ones will you love simplicity, and scorners delight in their scorn and fools hate knowledge?" —"Turn you at my reproof": "'Behold, I will pour out my Spirit upon you, I will make known my words unto you. Then shall they call upon me, but I will not answer, they shall seek me early, but they shall not find me.'" And Luke 13:24, 25, 26, 27, "Strive to enter in at the straight gate, for many I say unto you shall seek to enter in, and shall not be able. When once the master of the house is risen up and has shut the door, and you begin to stand without and to knock at the door, saying, 'Lord, Lord open unto us,' and he shall answer and say unto you, 'I know you not, whence you are'; Then shall you begin to say, 'We have eaten and drunk in your presence, and you have taught in our streets'—But he shall say, 'I tell you, I know you not whence you are. Depart from me all you workers of iniquity.'"

1. *Meditation.* The public testimony of the nearness of Christ's coming as the Bridegroom with spiritual power and great glory in his saints and sanction will awaken and raise some virgin professors out of their security, backsliding, and apostasy.

That there will be a cry at midnight, namely, a loud voice from the Lord, a voice from the city, a voice from the temple, that is, a public ministerial testimony even in the midst of the midnight dispensation, and saying, "Behold the Bridegroom comes," has been showed in the exposition of the sixth verse, and the words of this seventh verses testifies that loud voice or cry did awake and cause the Virgins to rise, "Then all those Virgins arose," that is, out of the slumber and sleep of their sinful silence, worldly ease, carnal security, careless formality, backsliding, and apostasy, and some of them with their loins girt, and their lamps burning, did arise and shine, and went out again to meet the Bridegroom.

2. *Meditation.* That some of the virgin professors shall be recovered out of their security, backsliding, and apostasy, and shall rise and shine at the coming of Jesus Christ as the Bridegroom of his church.

God has promised to heal the backslidings of his people upon their repentance and returning to the Lord, Jer. 3:22. "Return you backsliding children, and I will heal your backslidings; Behold we come unto you, for you are the LORD our God," Hosea 14:1, 4. And he will cause the light of the knowledge of the glory of God to shine in their hearts, 2 Cor. 4:6. And make them shine in a holy gospel conversation, Isa. 60:1, 2, 3, to the praise and glory of God, "Arise, shine, for your light is come, and the glory of the LORD is risen upon you."—"For behold the darkness shall cover the earth, and gross darkness the people; but the LORD shall arise upon you, and his glory shall be seen upon you. And Gentiles shall come to your light, and kings to the brightness of your rising."

3. *Meditation.* It's the duty of virgin-professors and church-members to prepare themselves for the coming of Christ as the Bridegroom, Matth. 24:44. "Therefore, be you also ready, for in such an hour as you think not, the Son of Man comes," Luke 12:35, 36, 40. "Let your loins be girded about, and your lights burning— And you yourselves like unto men that wait for the Lord, when he will return from the wedding, that when he comes and knocks, they may open unto him immediately. Be you therefore ready also, for the Son of Man comes at an hour when you think not."

To be so prepared and ready, the wise Virgins must put on their beautiful garments, Isa. 52:1, and rejoice as Zion did, Isa. 61:10, "I will greatly rejoice in the LORD, my soul shall be joyful in my God for he has clothed me with the garments of salvation, he has covered me with the robe of righteousness, as a Bridegroom decks himself with ornaments, and as a Bride adorns herself with her jewels." And those that have spotted their garments of profession by any sinful conversation or compliance ought to wash their robes, and make them white in the blood of the Lamb, Rev. 7:14, that so, they all being clothed with fine linen, white and clean (which is the righteousness of the saints, Rev. 19:8), as a bride adorned for her husband, Rev. 21:2, may walk with Christ in white. And (being thus adorned and made ready to meet the Bridegroom) may be counted worthy to enter with him into the marriage chamber. Of this preparation you will read more in verse 10.

> *Verse 8. "And the foolish said unto the wise, Give us*
> *of your oil, for our lamps are gone out."*

In these words, consider

1. The request that the foolish Virgins made unto the wise, "Give us of your oil."
2. The reason of their request, "For our lamps are gone out."

The foolish virgin-professors were now at last made sensible that they wanted oil, and that it was their great folly that they did take no oil with them (as the wise Virgins did in their vessels) when they took their lamps, and went out to meet the Bridegroom.

1. *Meditation.* It argues and demonstrates very great folly in those virgin-professors and church-members, who seem to be religious, having a form of godliness, and are looking for and bearing testimony unto the spiritual kingdom and glorious appearance and coming of Christ, the church's Bridegroom, to be without Christ and to lack the Spirit of Christ, and the saving and sanctifying grace of Jesus Christ in their hearts.

Doubtless now at last, the foolish Virgins were very sensible of their folly in resting satisfied and contented with a profession of Christ, without a profession of Christ, with having their lamps and the form of godliness without the oil of grace and the power of godliness; And with being in a gospel church state, and thus partaking of the holy ordinances of God and enjoying fellowship with the wise virgin-saints, and yet not being partakers of the divine nature, nor having communion and fellowship with God the Father, Son, and Holy Spirit in the ways and ordinances of God.

Now those foolish virgin-professors wish they had some of the wise Virgins' oil; "O," say they, "that we had Christ, the Spirit of Christ, and the grace of Christ in our hearts!" Now they ask and beg, they seek unto and entreat the wise virgin-saints, saying, "Give us of your oil, communicate of your saving and sanctifying graces to our souls."

2. *Meditation.* The time will come when foolish professors and formal church members will see and sadly experience their being without Christ, and their want of the spirit and grace of God.

Many professors now can live without Christ, and without God, and without grace in the world, yea, in the churches of saints, and in the ordinances of the gospel, sometimes making a shining profession of Christ, and witnessing of, and bearing their testimony to the kingdom and coming of the Lord Jesus Christ; and at other times slumbering and sleeping in a carnal security, lukewarmness, formality, and backsliding apostasy: who, when they are awakened by some midnight dispensation of God, will see and be convinced, and made sensible of their want and need of Christ, and the spirit of Christ, and the grace of Christ.

The time will come when they shall see and know by a thorough conviction and woeful experience that none but Christ, nothing but grace, will supply their [desires], nor satisfy their souls. "Give us of your oil": "Oh! that we had possession of Christ as you have; Oh! that the saving sanctifying grace of God, and spirit of God were in our hearts, as they are in yours; We now see our lack of the power of godliness, truth of grace, and union and communion with Christ, which you have and enjoy."

And though men and women, yea some professors and church members can live without Christ, buy and sell without Christ, build and plant without Christ (for they will be very busy about such things, when the Son of Man comes, Luke 17:26, 27, 28, 29, 30) and some professors can have and hold communion with the saints in the churches and holy ordinances of God, without Christ and grace: Yet, when Christ comes, yea when death comes, and they are awakened by that midnight dispensation, then they see themselves lost and undone to eternity, then they know not what to do, nor how to die without Christ and without grace. Then they call, and cry, send for, and seek unto the ministers and saints of God, and say, "Pray for us, speak to us, pity us, tell us what we shall do. O men and brethren, what shall we do?" (as they did, Acts 2:37). And as the jailer did, Acts 16:30. "Sirs, what shall I do to be saved?" and as the foolish Virgins did here to the wise Virgins, "Give me of your oil."

For our lamps are gone out; or are going out, as in the margent. This is the reason of their request; as if they had said, "O you wise Virgin saints, sanctified believers, who have union with Christ, who have obtained the precious faith of God's elect, and have received the grace of God in truth, and all the fruits of the Spirit; Give us of your oil, communicate some of your saving sanctifying grace unto us. For our lamps of professed gospel-light, our shining temple-light, all our spiritual gifts and common grace, all our former gospel enjoyments, even all our hopes and comforts are now decayed, withered, perished, and are ready to die, and be utterly extinguished, and we ourselves are in the dark, and must sit down and perish in eternal darkness, unless you can and will supply us with some of your spiritual oil"; "For our lamps are gone out."

3. *Meditation*. That all the gospel light that shines in the spiritual gifts and religious actions of foolish and formal professors will at last be extinguished, and go out, and they will fall away.

1. There are some formal professors that have received spiritual gifts from God, 1 Cor. 12:4 to the 11th verse. "Now there are diversities of gifts, but the same Spirit, and there are differences of administrations, but the same Lord" — "And there are diversities of operations, but it is the same God that works all in all" —"But the manifestation of the Spirit is given to every man to profit as well. For to one is given by the Spirit

the word of wisdom, to another the word of knowledge, by the same Spirit —To another faith by the same Spirit, to another the gift of healing by the same Spirit, to another the working of miracles, to another prophesy, to another discerning of spirits, to another diverse kinds of tongues, to another the interpretation of tongues." One member of the church may have a word of knowledge, another may have a word of wisdom, another may have a gift of prophesy, another may have faith (not sanctifying faith) and all these and several others gifts given them by the Holy Spirit of God, and yet not have Christ, not the graces of faith and love in Christ Jesus, 1 Cor. 13:1, 2, 3, "Though I speak with the tongues of men and of angels, and have not charity, I am become as sounding brass or a tinkling cymbal. And though I have the gifts of prophesy, and understand all mysteries, and all knowledge, and though I have all faith, so that I could remove mountains, and have not charity, I am nothing. And though I bestow all my goods to feed the poor, and though I give my body to be burned, and have not charity, it profits me nothing." Gal. 5:6, "For in Jesus Christ, neither circumcision avails anything, nor uncircumcision, but faith which works by love." The Apostle in these words, "Neither circumcision avails anything," shows and testifies that no privileges, ordinances, gifts, or administrations that the Jews had under the Law; nor uncircumcision, that is to say, no privileges, ordinances, gifts, or administrations, which the Gentiles have under the gospel, will profit or avail them anything in order unto the obtaining of eternal life, and everlasting salvation, without faith in Christ Jesus, that works by love, or as Paul says, Gal. 6:15. "For in Christ Jesus, neither circumcision avails anything, nor uncircumcision, but a new creature," 2 Cor. 5:17; that is, unless the professing Jew or Gentile be a new creature, 2 Cor. 5:17, that is God's workmanship created in Christ Jesus unto good works, Ephes. 2:10 that we should walk in them.

    2. And some foolish and formal virgin-professors may shine for a season in the acts and exercise of those spiritual gifts that they have received from God for the church's edification, 1 Cor. 14:1 and 3. "Follow after charity, and define spiritual gifts, but rather that you may prophesy." — "But he that prophesies speaks unto men to edification and exhortation and comfort." And they may also shine in some kind and degree of gospel-like conversation, and saint-like life, in respect of some external actions and outward performance of holy duties. And they may likewise shine like lamps and temple-lights in bearing their witness and testimony for Christ, his headship, ministry, churches, worship,

kingdom, and government. And lastly, they may shine like lamps and burning lights in enduring the afflictions of the gospel, in suffering the spoiling of their goods, imprisonment, banishment, yea ,and death itself, 2 Cor. 13:1, 2, 3.

3. And yet after all this, their lamps will go out and those foolish and formal professors will fall away, Luke 8:13. "They on the Rock are they which, when they hear, receive the Word with joy, and these have no root, which for a time believe, and in time of temptation fall away." Those hard-hearted hearers believed for a time. They made a profession of the faith of the gospel, and they made a confession, too, and that before many witnesses; "But in the time of temptation fell away." When that hour of temptation comes upon them which Christ has foretold shall come upon all the world, to try them that dwell upon the earth, Rev. 3:10, then they will fall away; and the reason is, because "they have no root," that is, they have not Christ, they are not rooted in him, Col. 2:6, 7. "As you have therefore received Christ Jesus the Lord, so walk you in him: rooted and built up in him, established in the faith: as you have been taught, abounding in it with thanksgiving." Faith in Christ never falls away, 1 Pet. 1:3, 4, 5, "Blessed be the God and Father of our Lord Jesus Christ, which according to his abundant mercy has given us new birth unto a lively hope by the resurrection of Jesus Christ from the dead, to an inheritance incorruptible and undefiled, and that fades not away, reserved in heaven for you, who are kept by the mighty power of God, through faith unto salvation, ready to be revealed in the last time." It's a faith without Christ that foolish professors depart from, 1 Tim. 4:1. "Now the Spirit speaks expressly that, in the later times, some shall depart from the truth, giving heed to seducing spirits and doctrines of devils."

Verse 9. But the wise answered, saying, "Not so, lest there be not enough for us and you, but go you rather to them that sell, and buy for yourselves."

This verse contains the answer that the wise Virgins gave to the request of the foolish Virgins. In which,

1. They gave them a denial, and the reason of it; "But the wise answered, saying 'Not so, we may not, we cannot grant what you desire of us, lest there be not enough for us and you.'" As if the wise Virgins had said, "'It's true indeed, we have oil in our vessels, and supply for our lamps, but we can spare none, our vessels have no more oil in them than we do and shall need for ourselves, not so. The Lord Jesus Christ has given us his saving

and sanctifying grace, but we may not, we cannot give it to you, no not the least measure of it; not a dram nor a drop can we give, nor can we spare any of it, we stand in need to get more grace for ourselves, lest we should not have enough in those hours and times of trials, that we may meet with yet, ere we meet with the Bridegroom, and lest we have not enough for those services of Christ, and sufferings for Christ that our Lord may call us to either before his coming, or when he comes, or after he is come as the Bridegroom.'"

2. They gave the foolish Virgins directions what to do in their condition, "But go you rather to them that sell and buy for yourselves," in which we are to consider,

1. Who they are that sell this spiritual oil?
2. What it is to buy it?

The spiritual oil is the unction of the holy one, 1 John 2:20, 27. That with which Christ was anointed above his fellows, Psal. 45:7, namely, the saving, sanctifying grace of God, the gifts and fruits of the Holy Spirit, of which read the exposition of verse 4.

They that sell this mystical and spiritual oil are Christ and his ministers and servants. The Lord Jesus Christ is the owner of this oil, and he himself does sometimes sell it, or offer it to sell, as he did to the Church of Laodicea, Rev. 3:18, "I counsel you to buy of me gold tried in the fire, that you may be rich, and white raiment, that you may be clothed, and that the shame of your nakedness do not appear, and anoint your eyes with eye salve, that you may see." But ordinarily and commonly Christ authorizes and commands his faithful servants (the ministers of the gospel) whom he appoints, commissions, and sends to offer this spiritual oil for sale, and to sell it unto whomever will buy it, Isa. 51:1, "Hearken to me, you that follow after righteousness, you that seek the Lord: look unto the rock from which you are hewn, and to the hole of the pit from which you are dug." John 7:37, "In the last day, the great day of the feast, Jesus stood and cried, saying, 'If any man thirst, let him come unto me and drink.'" Rev. 22:17, "And the Spirit and the Bride say, 'Come.' And let him that hears, say 'Come.' And let him that is thirsty come. And whosoever will, let him take the water of life freely." For as it was a great sin in Simon Magus to offer money, and to think that the gifts of the Holy Ghost might be bought for material money, so it is a very great sin in any minister to sell that mystical oil for material silver or gold, or any price or earthly commodity. And it is a very great mistake in foolish professors to think they may buy, that is, bargain with God for Christ and grace upon the terms of the old covenant of works, and their own righteousness, which is as menstruous rags, Isa. 64:6.

To buy this spiritual oil implies three things,

1. A sense of want and need of it, which the foolish Virgins now had,

2. Attending upon the ministry of the Word and administrations of the gospel to obtain it, or to get some of this oil, having their heart and hand open and willing to receive it, Acts 16:14, "And a certain woman named Lydia, a seller of purple of the city of Thyatira, which worshipped God, heard us whose heart the Lord opened, that she attended unto the things which were spoken of Paul."

3. A willingness to have it upon Christ's own terms of free grace, without money and without price, Isa. 55:1, 2, 3, and Rev. 21:6, 22:7. "Ho, everyone that thirsts, come you to the waters. And he that has no money, come you buy and eat, yea come, buy wine and milk, without money and without price. Wherefore do you spend money for that which is not bread, labour for that which satisfies not? Hearken diligently unto me, and eat that which is good, and let your soul delight itself in fatness," —"Incline your ear and hear and come unto me, and your soul shall live, and I will make an everlasting covenant unto you, even the sure mercies of David.'" —"And he said unto me, 'It is done, I am the Alpha and Omega, the beginning and the end: I will give unto him that is thirsty of the fountain of the water of life freely'"—"And the Spirit and the Bride say 'Come,' and let him that hears say 'Come,' and let him that is thirsty come, and whosoever will, let him take the water of life freely."

1. Meditation. That virgin-saints who have the greatest and fullest measure of grace and holiness, cannot give or impart any of it unto others.

"And the foolish said unto the wise: 'Give us of your oil; that is, impart some of your grace unto us': but the wise answered and said, 'Not so, we cannot give you grace, nor can we impart any of our grace to you.'" "'Oh!' says a dying father, mother, or some other relation. 'I am without Christ, I have no grace, I am ready to die and be damned and I shall perish to all eternity. O dear wife, child, husband, or other godly relation, that my soul were in your soul's condition. Oh! speak comfort and peace to me. Oh! that I had Christ's grace, pardon or any hopes of eternal life.' 'It is not in me, I cannot impart any grace to you; Christ must give you of his Spirit, and God must give you of his grace, I cannot.'"

Godly parents and relations may and ought to pray that God will give pardoning grace, sanctifying grace, saving grace to their children, or to any other relations, but they cannot give any, nor can they impart any grace to them.

Abraham could not give grace to Ishmael, nor could Isaac impart grace to Esau, nor Jacob to Reuben, no, nor David to Absalom, nor Job to his wife: Neither could Paul impart grace to his countrymen, for whom his heart's desired prayer was that they might be saved; and although he was willing to be accursed for them, as the Holy Scriptures of truth testify.

2. *Meditation.* Every saint and sanctified believer will (ere he gets to heaven) stand in need of all the grace he has.

Sanctified believers, called saints, may meet with such fiery trials, such hellish temptations, such powerful stirrings of corruptions, and so great variety of afflictions, tribulations, persecutions, and sufferings; and such hours and powers of darkness, and so deep desertions that will call for and require the Virgin's lively acts and exercise of all the grace of God they have; yea and they may be necessitated to go to Christ for more grace as the Apostle did, 2 Cor. 12:7, 8, 9. "And lest I should be exalted above measure through the abundance of the revelations, there was given to me a thorn in the flesh, the messenger of Satan to buffet me, lest I should be exalted above measure. For this thing I besought the Lord thrice, that it might depart from me: And he said unto me. 'My grace is sufficient for you for my strength is made perfect in weakness.' Most gladly therefore will I rather glory in my infirmities, that the power of Christ may rest upon me." Believers will have need of all the grace they have when they come to die, and be dissolved.

3. *Meditation.* It's the duty of every person that sees their need and want of Christ, his Holy Spirit, and sanctifying grace to attend upon the ministry of the gospel and administrators of the holy ordinances of God, and to accept and receive Christ and grace offered freely without money or cost.

Many sinners are so blinded, 2 Cor. 4:3, 4, that they see no form nor comeliness in Christ; and when they do see some beauty and excellency in him, yet they are apt to refuse and reject him, until they be thoroughly convinced of their want and need of him, his Spirit and grace, and that there is not salvation in any other, Acts 4:12. And then they begin to desire and say,

'O! that I had Christ; O! that I had grace; O! that I could believe.' Now it is their duty to attend diligently and conscionably upon the ministry of the gospel and means of grace; for faith comes by hearing the word preached, Rom. 10:17; Acts 14:1; Isa. 55:3. "Incline your ears, come unto me, hear and your souls shall live. And I will make an everlasting covenant with you," etc.

And as it is their duty to hear, so it is their duty to believe, 1 John 3:23, and by faith to accept and receive Jesus Christ offered to them upon gospel terms of free grace, without money and without price, John 1:11, 12. "He came unto his own, and his own received him not, but as many as received him, to them gave he the power to become the sons of God, even to them that believe on his Name," Rev. 22:17. "And the Spirit and the Bride say 'Come,' and let him that hears say, 'Come,' and whosoever will, let him take the water of life freely"; and Isa. 55:1, 2, 3.

Verse 10. "And while they went to buy, the Bridegroom came, and they that were ready went in with him to the marriage, and the door was shut."

The foolish Virgins followed the counsel of the wise and went to buy oil for themselves; and so do many formal and foolish professors (when they are convinced of their sins, and of their need of a Saviour) then they seek after Christ and cry for grace, and call upon God for pardoning mercy and salvation but it's too late it may be, Prov. 1:24, 28. "Because I have called and you refused, I have stretched out my hand and no man regarded"—"Then shall they call upon me, but I will not answer, they shall seek me early but they shall not find me. And while they went to buy, the Bridegroom came."

"And they that were ready went in with him to the marriage, and the door was shut." They that were duly prepared for the Bridegroom's coming had an entrance admitted to them into his kingdom and all others were excluded.

"They that were ready" had put off the filthy rags of their own righteousness, and had put on the robes of Christ's righteousness, Rom. 13:14. God had taken away their filthy garments and had clothed them with change of raiment, Zach. 3:3, 4. Thus *Zion*, the holy City, the New Jerusalem is called upon and commanded by the LORD her maker, her husband and her redeemer to loose herself from the bands of her neck, her captivity, to arise and put on her beautiful garments, Isa. 52:1, 2, 3. And so she shall do with great joy and rejoicing. And therefore she is prophetically said to do so, Isa. 61:10. "I will greatly rejoice in the LORD, my soul shall be joyful in my God, for he has clothed me with the garments of salvation, he has covered me with the robes of righteousness; as a bridegroom adorns himself with ornaments, and as a bride decks herself with her jewels."

And to be prepared for the Bridegroom's coming is to be arrayed in fine linen, white and clean, which is the righteousness of the saints, Rev. 19:7, 8. And so the Holy City, the New Jerusalem, was prepared as a bride adorned for her husband in John's vision, Rev. 21:2. Of this glorious marriage and mystery of Christ and his church, David prophesied, Psal. 45. In which we have this great and glorious solemnity of the Bridegroom's coming, and of the marriage of the Lamb mystically and metaphorically sung and penned down by that sweet singer of Israel in that (*epithalamium*) love song or marriage song. Psal. 45:1, 2, 6, 8, 9, 13, 14. "My heart is inditing a good matter. I speak of the things which I have made touching the King. My tongue is the pen of a ready writer." —"You are fairer then the children of men; grace is poured into your lips; therefore God has blessed you forever. Your throne, O God, is forever and ever, and the sceptre of your kingdom is a right scepter. All your garments smell of myrrh, and aloes, and cassia, out of the ivory places by which they have made you glad. King's daughters were among your honorable women. Upon your right hand did stand the Queen in gold of Ophir. The King's daughter is all glorious within; her clothing is of wrought gold." —"She shall be brought unto the King in raiment of needlework; the Virgins, her companions that follow her, shall be brought unto you with gladness and rejoicing they shall enter the King's palace." And so the Prophet Ezekiel (describing the church's condition, from her cradle to her crown, Ezek. 16:13-14) speaks of her inward and spiritual beauty and glory under diverse metaphors and figurative expressions, verse 8, to the end of the 14th verse. "Now when I passed by you, and looked upon you; Behold your time was the time of love. And I spread my skirt over you, and covered your nakedness; yea, I swore unto you, and entered into a covenant with you. Then washed I you with water, yea I washed away your blood from you, and I anointed you with oil, I clothed you also with embroidered work, and shod you with badger's skin, and I girded you about with fine linen and I covered you with silk and decked you also with ornaments, and I put bracelets upon your hands, and a chain on your neck, and I put a jewel on your forehead and earrings in your ears and a beautiful crown upon your head. Thus you were decked with gold and silver, and your raiment was of fine linen and silk and broidered work, you did eat fine flower and honey and oil, and you were exceeding beautiful, and you did prosper into a kingdom. —And your renown went forth among the heathen, for your beauty was perfect through my comeliness which I had put upon you," says the Lord GOD. This prophesy in the mystery of it will be fulfilled when the Bridegroom comes, for then Christ will put on a beautiful crown upon her head, and she will be exceeding beautiful, and she shall then prosper into a kingdom, Isa. 28:5. "In that day shall the LORD be for a Crown of glory, and for a diadem of beauty, unto the residue of his people." Isa. 62:3. "You will also be a crown of glory in the hand of the LORD, and a royal diadem in the hand of your God." When will this day of Zion's glory be? Then it will be when the Bridegroom comes, and marries his Bride, Isa. 62:5. "For as a young man marries a Virgin, so shall sons marry you, and as the Bridegroom rejoices over the Bride, so shall your God rejoice over you." And thus the wise virgin-saints were prepared and ready, and went in with him to the marriage.

"And the door was shut." There is the door of grace, and that is all opportunities and seasons that the Ministers of Christ have and improve to preach, and the people have and improve to hear the gospel of the grace of God; also to administer and partake of the holy ordinances of God in any place and at any time, called to the open door, Rev. 3:8. "A great door and effectual is opened," etc. 1 Cor. 16:9 and 2 Cor. 2:12. "And a door was opened to me of or by the Lord." That was a door of grace. And when God removes the candlestick, takes away the gospel, suffering the adversaries to silence and persecute his faithful ministers and churches of saints, when their ministers by imprisonment or banishment are removed into corners, and their eyes cannot see their teacher, when the people run to and fro, to seek the Word of the Lord, and cannot find it, then the door of grace is shut.

There is also the door of the Kingdom of Christ, Luke 13:25, 26, 27, 28, 29. "When once the Master of the house is risen up and has shut to the door, and you begin to stand without and to knock at the door, saying, 'LORD, LORD, open unto us,' and he shall answer and say unto you, 'I know you not, whence you are': Then shall you begin to say, 'We have eaten and drunk in your presence, and you have taught in our presence, and you have taught in our streets', but he shall say, 'I tell you I know you not, whence you are; depart from me all you workers of iniquity.' There shall be weeping and gnashing of teeth when you shall see Abraham, and Isaac, and Jacob, and all the prophets of the Kingdom of God, and you yourselves thrust out. And they shall come from the east, and from the west, and from the north, and from the south, and shall sit down in the Kingdom of God." This is the door that was shut here in my text, to wit, the door of Christ's marriage chamber, that is to say, an entrance and admittance into the everlasting Kingdom of our Lord Jesus Christ, 2 Pet. 1:10, 11. "Wherefore the rather Brethren give diligence to make your calling and election sure, for if you do these things, you shall never fail, for so an entrance shall be ministered unto you abundantly, into the everlasting Kingdom of the Lord and Saviour Jesus Christ."

1. *Meditation.* That all persons, especially virgin professors, ought to prepare, and to be ready, when Christ, the churches' Bridegroom, comes.

To this end,

1. Sinners, you must get Jesus Christ, if you will not receive and entertain Christ into your hearts, by faith, a true penitent and lively faith, he will not receive and admit you into the marriage chamber of his kingdom, when he comes as the Bridegroom. If sinners will not let Christ live in them, and reign in them, in the kingdom of his grace now, Rom. 15:20, 21, they shall not live and reign with him in his kingdom, Rev. 20:4. Christ will shut the door of his kingdom against them that shut the door of their hearts against him.

Therefore, sinners, while Jesus Christ stands at the door, open the door of your hearts to Christ, and let him come and set up the kingdom of his grace in your hearts according to his gracious promise, Rev. 3:20, 21, 22. "'Behold, I stand at the door and knock, if any man hears my voice, and opens the door, I will come into him and sup with him, and he with me.'—'"To him that overcomes, will I grant to sit with me in my throne, even as I also overcame, and am sat down with my Father in his throne.' He that has an ear let him hear what the Spirit says unto the churches."

2. Saints, you ought to prepare and be ready to meet Christ, the Church's Bridegroom, when he comes, and therefore consider what you have to do ere you and Jesus Christ meet in his marriage Kingdom. O gracious and precious saints, have you not something to do ere you die? Can you heartily desire and earnestly pray to be dissolved and be with Christ before you have overcome the world, John 5:4, 5. Get the victory over sin, I Cor. 15:56, 57, and be refined, vanquished, and made conquerors over the Devil, John 2:13, 14, and in all these to be more than conquerors through Christ Jesus our Lord? Rom. 8:37. Can you expect to inherit all things, Rev. 21:7 until you have

overcome all things? Our Lord Jesus Christ overcame before he sat down with the Father in his throne. And will Jesus Christ grant you to sit down with him in his throne, until you have also overcome? Rev. 3:21, 22.

Again, consider saints, are you prepared as a bride adorned for her husband? Rev. 21:2, 3. Are you clothed in fine linen, white and clean, Rev. 19:8, and so made ready for the Marriage of the Lamb? Rev. 19:7. Or do not some of you stand in need to wash your robes and make them white in the blood of the Lamb, Rev. 7:14, 15, before you can put on your beautiful garments, Isa. 52:1, 2, and adorn yourselves with ornaments as a bride, Isa. 61:10, or as the Bridemaidens, the Virgins, her Companions? Psal. 45:9, 13, 14.

The LORD has washed his people with water, yea, he thoroughly washed away their blood from them, and anointed them with oil, and then he clothed them with embroidered work, girded them with linen and covered them with silk. He decked them also with ornaments, bracelets, jewels, chains of gold and pearl about their neck, and at last he put a beautiful crown upon the churches' head, and they prospered into a kingdom, Ezek 16:9-14. So the Apostle testified that Jesus Christ gave himself for his church that "he might sanctify it, and cleanse it with the washing of water by the word, that he might present it to himself a glorious church, not having spot or wrinkle, or any such thing, but that it should be holy and without blemish." O beloved and blessed Virgin saints, how much cleansing, purging, sanctifying work is there yet to be done in your souls by the Spirit and word of God in the lively and powerful applications of the precious blood of Jesus Christ? Heb. 9:14 and Heb. 13:12 and I John 7:9.

Once more, consider saints, O you wise Virgins, are your vessels full of oil? Are your hearts full of grace? Have you perfected holiness in the fear of God? 2 Cor. 7. And are you come in the unity of faith, and of the knowledge of the Son of God unto a perfect man? Eph. 4:3. If not, you are not yet so prepared, nor are you yet so ready as you should desire and endeavour to be, and may be through the communication of the exceeding riches of the grace of God, Eph. 2:7, and the unsearchable riches of Jesus Christ, you may attain to be ere the Bridegroom come.

1. *Meditation.* While some foolish and negligent virgin-professors are seeking too late to get, and endeavouring too late to buy the spiritual oil of grace to supply their lamps, Christ will come and shut the door of his grace and kingdom against them, and the door was shut.

Some professors being careless and negligent when they enjoy powerful means of grace (as the foolish Virgins were when they first went out to meet the Bridegroom) content themselves and are satisfied with some spiritual gifts without grace, and the form of godliness without the power of it (as the foolish Virgins did that took their lamps, but took no oil with them). And so go on in the broad way of an outward customary and formal performance of holy duties and partaking of gospel ordinances all the day of grace, until the night of security, ease, and darkness overtake them, and they begin to slumber and fall fast asleep in their formality, or in their apostasy, until in some midnight dispensation, a cry with a loud voice from the Lord, from the city or from the temple, awakens them and affrights them; And then they perceive that their lamps are gone out, and that they themselves are in a state of darkness, wanting Christ and grace in their souls (as the foolish Virgins who wanted oil in their vessels and went to buy it). So some formal professors, when it is too late, seek for grace and enquire after Christ; saying as Balaam did, "Let me die the death of the righteous, and let my last end be like his," Numb. 23:10. But their day of grace being past, Christ shut the door of grace, saying "He that is unjust, let him be unjust still, and he that is filthy, let him be filthy still," Rev. 22:11. And Christ will, when he comes as the Bridegroom, shut the door of his kingdom against those foolish virgin-professors who refused the offers, call and invitations of the gospel in the day of grace, read Prov. 1:20 to the end of the chapter. Verses 24, 25, 28, "Because I have called and you refused, I have stretched out my hand and no man heeded"—"But you have set at nought all my counsel, and would have none of my reproof. Then will they call upon me, but I will not answer; they shall seek me early, but they shall not find me." And as does plainly appear in the 11th and 12th verses of this chapter.

Verses 11, 12. "Afterward came also the other Virgins, saying 'LORD, LORD, open unto me'; But he answered and said, 'Verily I say unto you, I know you not.'"

Afterwards, or last of all, that is after the wise virgin-saints were entered into the Marriage Chamber with Christ the Bridegroom of his Church, and after the door of the Kingdom of Christ was shut, then came the foolish Virgin-professors, a multitude of very many formalists and hypocrites, saying, "Lord, Lord, open to us." They called and cried earnestly, prayed and beseeched the Lord Jesus Christ again and again to open the door of his kingdom unto them, and let them have an entrance admitted into this everlasting kingdom.

But he answering, said, "'Verily I say unto you, I know you not.'" As they were earnest in their request, so was Christ very positive in his answer, "Verily," assuredly, indeed, and the truth, "I know you not," I love you not, I do not approve of you, I own you not to be of the number of those that my Father gave me, and whom I redeemed with my blood, and whom I called and sanctified by my Spirit and grace, and who sought to worship God by the Spirit and in truth, I know you not to be the adopted children of my Father, justified and sanctified by faith that is in me. You are formalists and hypocrites, impenitent backsliders and apostates, who have denied my headship, my kingly office, and would not that I should reign over you. In a word, you are workers of iniquity. "Depart from me," I profess I do not know you, so as to approve of you, to own you, to open the door of my kingdom to you, Luke 13:24, 25, 26, 27. "Strive to enter in at the straight gate, for many I say unto you, will seek to enter in and shall not be able." —"When once the master of the house is risen up and has shut the door, and you begin to stand without, and to knock at the door, saying, 'Lord, Lord, open unto me,' and he shall answer and say unto you, 'I know you not whence you are.' Then shall you begin to say, 'We have eaten and drunken in your presence, and you have taught in our streets'" — "But he shall say, 'I tell you, I know you not whosoever you are. Depart from me you workers of iniquity.'"

Meditation. It will be a sad, admonishing and miserably woeful condition that all foolish virgin-professors will be in when the Lord Jesus Christ shall exclude them and shut them out of his kingdom and disown them forever.

Virgin-professors, having a strong conscience, Hosea 1:8: and great hope and expectations, I Cor. 15:19, of the pardon of all their sins and of eternal life and salvation, and then at last find by woeful experience that the Lord has rejected their confidence, Jer. 2:37, and their expectations be in vain and perish, Prov. 10:28, and their hope like the spider's web, Job. 8:13, 14. "For what is the hope of the hypocrite when God shall take away his soul?" Job. 27:8 and God will not forgive their iniquities, Jer. 14:10 and 16:18, but will give them the wages of their sins, Rom. 6:23, and reward them according to their evil deeds, Rom. 2:6, 9, 11. Yea, and they having had a strong persuasion or presumption, rather that when Christ comes, they shall have an entrance admitted to them into his everlasting kingdom, and at last Christ comes, and shuts the door of the kingdom, and then they come and knock , and say, "Lord, Lord, open to us," and be denied and repulsed, and Christ tell them he knows them not, and say, "Depart from me" you hypocrites, you formal professors, you foolish Virgins, and all you workers of iniquity: what an amazement and astonishment will it be to them? And then "they will begin to say, 'LORD, we have eaten and drunk in your presence, and you have taught in our streets,'" Luke 13:26, 27. That is, we have been under the ministry of the gospel, and all the administrations of it. We have been often at the Lord's Table, and have been partakers of all the holy ordinances of God, Matth. 7:21, 22, 23. "Not everyone that says 'Lord, Lord, shall enter into the Kingdom of Heaven, but he that does the will of my Father which is in heaven.'" —"Many will say unto me in that day, 'Lord, Lord, have we not prophesied in your name, and in your name have done many wonderful works,' and then will I profess unto them, 'I never knew you, depart from me you that work iniquity.'"

> *Verse 13. "Watch, therefore, for you know neither the day nor the hour in which the Son of man comes."*

This verse contains the use that Christ would have his disciples make of this parable and of his doctrine in that contained, and that is to watch, "Watch you therefore," which exhortation he urges from their ignorance of the time when Christ, the Churches' Bridegroom, will come. "For you know neither the day, nor the hour in which the Son of Man comes."

From whence two propositions do arise, namely,

1., That the time of Christ his coming as the Bridegroom is not known to any saint or angel, but to the Father only.

2. That it's the duty of all Christ's disciples to be watching and waiting daily for the glorious appearance of Christ, who will come as the Bridegroom of his church.

Touching the first proposition, read Matth. 24:36, Mark 13:32. "But of that day and that hour knows no man, no not the angels which are in heaven, neither the Son but the Father"— Though God the Father has reserved the knowledge of the day and hour of Christ, the Bridegroom's coming, in his own secret decree, yet he has given forth and revealed some signs of him coming which are recorded in the holy Scriptures of truth, which his disciples being desirous to know, asked him saying. "And what shall be the sign of your coming?" Matth. 24:3, unto which question Christ answered many things but more particularly he told them,

1., That his saints and servants should suffer great persecutions, Matth. 24:9 and Luke 21:12, 16, 17.

2. That iniquity shall abound and the love of many will wax cold, Matth. 24:12.

3. That the gospel of the Kingdom shall be preached in the all the world for a witness unto all nations, Matth. 24:14, 4. That then shall be great tribulations, such as never was, no nor ever shall be, Matth. 24:21. And immediately after the tribulation of those days, the powers of heaven shall be shaken, and then there shall appear the sign of the Son of Man in heaven, Matth. 24:29, 30.

Touching the second proposition, read Matth. 24:42 and 25:13; Luke 21:36. "Watch you therefore, and pray always, that you may be accounted worthy to escape all those things that shall come to pass and to stand before the Son of Man." They that would be accounted worthy to stand before Christ the Bridegroom when he comes must watch and pray continually.

Watching implies:

1. That professors, Christ's disciples, ought to be awake, Rom. 13:11, "And that knowing the time that now it is high time to awake out of sleep, for now is our salvation nearer than when we believed." 1 Thes. 5:2, 6, "For yourselves know perfectly, that the day of the Lord so comes as a thief in the night."

2. That professors are to be in a continual expectation of Christ's glorious appearance "as they that wait for the morning," Psal. 130:5, 6. "I wait for the Lord; my soul does wait, and in his word do I hope. My soul waits for the Lord, more than they that watch for the morning, I say, more than they that watch for the morning." And Luke 12:35, 36, 37, 38. "Let your loins be girded about, and your lamps burning.—And you your selves like unto men that wait for their Lord when he will return from the wedding, that when he comes and knocks, they may open unto him immediately. Blessed are those servants, whom the Lord when he comes shall find watching. Verily, I say unto you that he shall gird himself, and make them to sit down to meat, and will come forth and serve them. And if he shall come in the second watch, or come in the third watch, and find them so, blessed are those servants."

3. That professors be looking out, desirous of and longing for the coming and Kingdom of Christ, 2 Pet. 3:11, 12. "Looking for and hasting unto the coming of the day of God."

Watching is a necessary duty incumbent upon Christians at all times, Luke 21:36, in all things, 2 Tim. 4:5. It's our duty in every duty: we ought to watch and pray, Matth. 26:41, and to watch after prayer, and wait for the return and answer of our prayers. Christians ought to watch their hearts' thoughts and affections; they ought to set a watch before the door of their lips, that their tongues do not offend, and they ought to watch their lives and conversations for godly callings and employments in the world. But especially Christians ought to watch for the glorious appearance of the Bridegroom, our Lord Jesus Christ, Matth. 24:42. And they ought to be in a watching posture, and upon watching work or duty, especially, when they hear of his near approach. Yea, and it is the duty of believers, to be upon their watch all the mystical night, until the Bridegroom comes.

The word "watch" is borrowed from shepherds, or soldiers, or seamen, or porters, or citizens, who used to watch in the night season. The Jews divided the night into 3 watches, of which the first began at twilight, and continued till midnight, called the beginning of the watches, Lam. 2:19. The second watch began at midnight, and continued unto the cock crowing, called the middle watch, Judg. 7:19, and the third watch was from the cock crowing till sun-rising, called the morning watch, Exod. 14:24. And according to this Hebrew dialect and division of the mystical night in this parable, the time this duty was to be attended was the morning watch, for midnight was past, and the day of Christ was dawning, or near approaching, "Behold, the Bridegroom comes; watch you therefore" etc., as they, Psal. 130:5, 6.

Query: Watchmen, what of the night?

Answer. The morning comes, and also the night, Isa. 21:12. "If you will enquire, enquire you," etc. namely, that morning when the righteous shall have the dominion, Psal. 49:14. And also the night, even that night of Mystical Babylon's destruction, foretold Rev. 18:8, 10, 19, 21, 22, 23.

But more particularly that we may the better understand what time of the mystical night it is with us in our Land-Horizon, it may be considered, that after that first sunshine DAY of the gospel, in the days of Christ and his Apostles had continued for some years, a night of great darkness and bloody persecution began, which continued to the reign of Constantine the Great. And that was the first watch of our mystical night. And after the Moonshine Reformation during Constantine's time, the Arian clouds of mystical darkness overspread the face of the ecclesiastical heavens, and at last the Beast opened the bottomless pit, and there arose a smoke out of the pit, as the smoke of a great furnace, and the sky and the air were darkened by reason of the smoke of the pit, Rev. 9:1, 2, 3. And this midnight dispensation will continue until within 3 or 4 hours of the Sun-rising. And this is the second watch of the mystical night of popery, and persecution. So that the morning watch is the third and next, which will continue until the Son of Righteousness arise; which watch will begin at or about the time of the Beast killing Christ's witnesses, and will continue about 3 1/2 prophetical days or years, Rev. 11:7, 11, 15. During that time of the witnesses lying dead, Rev. 11:8, 9, the wise Virgins are commanded to watch, Matth. 25:13.[5]

And they ought to be in a "watching posture," that is to say, waking, waiting, looking, longing for and believing the near approach and sudden coming of the Bridegroom, namely, our Lord Jesus Christ. And also about watching work; that is, doing the work of their Generation in bearing their witness for Christ against the Antichrist, his ministry, churches, worship, ordinances, and discipline and in finishing their testimony of the kingdom and dominion of Christ against the kingdom and dominion of the Antichrist. That when Christ come and finds them so doing, he may say, "Well done, good and faithful servants, enter you into the joys of your master." So the wise Virgins being thus prepared and ready, they may enter into the Marriage Chamber with the Bridegroom when he comes.

Finis.

---

5. See the essay in the final chapter at the end of the book for an understanding of Knollys's eschatology.

4

The World that Now Is and the World that Is to Come

Introduction

The World that now is and the World that is to come is often classified as one of the six eschatological writings that Knollys penned during the Restoration years. However, like the *Parable*, there is much in it that is directly related to the life of church. It was written two years after the Popish Plot[1] and during the height of the Exclusion Crisis.[2] Moreover, Knollys had written a scathing attack upon the Church of Rome in 1679 in two separate treatises on the heels of the Popish Plot.[3] In addition, it is important to note that in one of those writings he predicted, on the basis of his interpretation of the Bible and present day events that the events that precede the "world to come" would begin in 1688. Consequently, he was writing this treatise with a sense of urgency for the church and all who would read it. In it he addresses true believers, professors of faith and the profane of the world to

---

1. The Popish Plot was a conspiracy concocted by Titus Oates between 1678 and 1681. As a result, the kingdoms of England and Scotland were filled with anti-Catholic hysteria. This was an alleged Catholic conspiracy to assassinate Charles II. This hysteria resulted in the execution of at least 22 men and the Exclusion Bill Crisis. Oates was eventually arrested and convicted for perjury but the damage had been done. Knollys and many others believed in the Popish Plot.

2. The Exclusion Crisis took place from 1679 through 1681 during the reign of King Charles II. Three Exclusion bills had been introduced by Parliament which sought to exclude from the throne the King's brother, James, a committed Catholic, who was the heir. Charles did not have an heir, so James was next in line.

3. *Mystical Babylon* and *Exposition of the Eleventh Chapter of Revelation*.

be ready for the return of Christ. This call to be ready is a theme throughout the work but is quite pointed in its final pages.

This book, as the title suggests, is divided into two parts. The first part is *The World that now is* and takes up two thirds of the total work. Knollys's focus in this part is on the life of the believer and the life of the church with a concluding call to be ready for Christ's return. The second part, *The World to Come* is wholly devoted to the order and details surrounding the "world to come," with a pointed call to people to come out of Babylon (the Roman church), and for the leaders of the government to reject Babylon.

According to Knollys there are three worlds: 1) the world that was (before Christ's first coming); 2) the world that now is (between the first and second comings); and 3) the world that is to come (the world that follows Christ's second coming). His concern in the first part of this treatise is with the second world. He maintains that in this second world the "chief work of Jesus Christ in His first coming was to save sinners, to build up his own house, and to institute gospel ordinances necessary for her disciples to worship God in Spirit and Truth." In the next pages he fleshes out this chief work in three parts.

The first part of the chief work of Christ is "to save sinners." Christ brings salvation to sinners through the work of the Spirit and Word in their souls in a general order of experiences. This order is: 1) conviction of sin, righteousness and judgment; 2) the illumination of the saving knowledge of Jesus Christ; and 3) conversion which changes the heart and results in a life of sanctification. In this part there is a strong emphasis on conviction. The reason for this was Knollys's belief that a "lack of a thorough work of conviction [on the soul] is the cause of the lack of a sound and saving work of conversion." Consequently, he counsels pastors "to labour in the Word and Doctrine on a thorough gospel conviction." It is important to note that this conviction is not only a conviction of sin but also of unbelief, that is, that they have not believed on Jesus Christ as the only Saviour provided by God. They have heard but have rejected Him. Knollys does acknowledge that some people are saved without this deep conviction, particularly those who are brought up under godly parents; but even these will see that their righteousness is but filthy rags and will experience conviction of sin.

The second chief work of Christ in this world is to build up his own house which is the church of God. In this part he explains what the church is, but focuses most of his attention on the leaders who work with Christ to build up the church. Christ governs his church through pastors and teachers who are also called bishops, presbyters or elders. One unique aspect of this form of government for Knollys is that, among the pastors in a designated city, one pastor should have the pre-eminence and priority, who is designated as bishop. He emphasizes that this role is not one of lordly pre-eminence but one who is chosen by the other pastors and "acts, guides, rules with the other elders consent and suffrage and assistance according to the laws of Christ."

The third chief work of Christ in this world is to institute gospel ordinances. He follows a regulatory form of church worship and delineates those ordinances that should be practiced in the church. They are: 1) prayers by the elders; 2) reading, expounding and interpreting the Scripture by the teacher; and 3) to "preach the gospel and exhort people to repent and believe the gospel, to be holy and to walk in the commandments and ordinances of the Lord." In addition, the worship should include: 4) baptism of those who believe the gospel; and 5) the partaking of the Lord's Supper for those who believe and are baptized. Besides these standard gospel ordinances Knollys adds: 6) singing in the congregation. The primary songs to be sung in the service are the Psalms; however, a person may compose their own song, and if they have a gift, they ought to sing it unto the congregation for its edification.

Knollys concludes the first part of this treatise with an exhortation to believers and unbelievers in light of the second coming of Christ. He highlights the nearness of this coming by declaring the scriptural signs of his coming which coming he believed would be only several years away.

The second part of this treatise deals with the "World to come" and the events surrounding that world beginning with the Second Coming of Christ. He elaborates on five events which are to be understood as following one another. These events are: 1) the second coming; 2) the making of all things new in the new heavens and earth; 3) the reign of Christ with his saints on earth for 1000 years; 4) the resurrection of the dead; and 5) the final judgment. He maintains his eschatological views which he espoused in the *Parable*. In particular, that Christ Second Coming will be personal, but not visible, with his saints. This will be the time of the first resurrection in which the saints will be raised and will rule with Christ on earth for 1000 years. At the end of the 1000 years he will return visibly and the rest of the dead will be raised and judged.[4]

He concludes this part of the treatise with a call to professors of Christ and to the profane of the world to be ready for this world to come and Christ's return. There is also a word of instruction to the King, the nobles, judges and all magistrates in Britain and Scotland to kiss the Son, as Psalm 2 calls all nations to do.

---

4. This is a version of what we now call postmillennialism. See the final chapter for more on his eschatology.

The World that now is and the World that is to Come
or the First and Second Coming of Jesus Christ
In which several prophecies not yet fulfilled are expounded
By Hanserd Knollys
A servant of Jesus Christ. *Rev.* 1:19

LONDON
Printed by *Tho. Snowden, An.* 1681.

To the Reader
Christian Reader,

So needful is the true knowledge of God and Jesus Christ; so absolutely conducing unto man's eternal wellbeing, John 17:3, as by which alone true happiness is to be attained. To that end, in the former part of this little treatise is set forth, first, what the Lord Jesus Christ has done and suffered for the salvation of sinners.

Secondly, what He does work in them by his Holy Spirit and Word, in order unto their everlasting salvation.

Thirdly, what kind of worship, churches, ministers, and ordinances the Lord Jesus Christ has instituted and appointed under the gospel. And in the latter part of it is briefly and plainly declared that there is a world to come; that the Lord Jesus Christ will come personally, visibly, and suddenly; that he will set up his kingdom, and will reign, raise the dead, and judge both the quick and the dead, 2 Tim. 4:1, at his appearing and his kingdom. It may be some of all sorts of readers will judge and censure me for one thing or another, but with me it is a very small thing that I should be judged by man's judgement. I only entreat the judicious reader to search the Scriptures and thus to prove all things, and hold fast that which is found. I pretend not to infallibility; I know but in part yet I am willing to impart that which I do know unto others that are searching after knowledge and understanding.

And I pray that God will fill you that read what I have written with the knowledge of his will revealed in his written Word, that you may prove what is the perfect will of God. But if any man seems to be contentious, we have no such custom, neither the churches of God. Nor will I contend with anyone otherwise than the apostle Jude exhorts in the third verse of his epistle, that we should earnestly contend for the faith that was once delivered unto the saints; not by vain disputings and janglings, but by sober afflictions and clear proofs of Scripture, Isa. 8:20. Show me, friendly readers, in which I have erred from the truth, and it will be as precious balm, and I shall esteem you my friend indeed that will endeavour to convert me from the error of my way, if it be done in a spirit of love. Nay, if any one shall do it in another frame of spirit, I shall thankfully acknowledge his kindness that will endeavour to convince me, to reprove me (yea, although he should reproach me), and I would bear it patiently, and humbly acknowledge my mistake. And I will not obstinately hold fast any error after conviction, through the grace of God; for I love the truth as it is in Jesus (if my heart does not deceive me) more than myself, or my esteem in the world.

From my study in Bartholomew-Lane, August 3, 1681. Your soul's friend,

Hanserd Knollys

The World That Now Is

The Holy Scripture of truth speaks of this world; namely the world that *was*, 2 Pet. 3:6, the world that *now is*, called this world, Matth. 2:32, and the world *to come*, Heb. 2:5. The world that now is is the subject of the first part of this treatise. And the world to come shall be the subject of the latter part of it.

The principal matter, which we intend to treat touching the world that now is, does concern the first coming of Christ into this world when the word was made flesh and dwelt among us, John 1:14. The chief matter of the latter part of this treatise does concern the second coming of Christ in the world to come. In which there will be a new heavens, a new earth, and a new Jerusalem; and all things will be newly created, Rev. 21:1-5.

CHAP. I.

In which our general position is propounded, proved, and explained

Section 1. The Position Propounded.

That the chief work of Jesus Christ in his first coming into the world was to save sinners, to build up his own house, the church of the living God, and to institute all gospel ordinances necessary for his disciples to worship God in spirit and in truth.

Section 2. The Position Proved.

1. That our Lord Jesus Christ came into the world to save sinners, Luke 5:32. "I came not to call the righteous, but sinners to repentance," Matth. 18:11. "For the Son of Man is come to save that which was lost." And 1 Tim. 1:15. "Christ Jesus came into the world to save sinners."

2. That our Lord Jesus, being come in the flesh, did build up his own house, the church of God, Heb. 3-6. "For this man [Christ Jesus] was counted worthy of more glory than Moses, in as much as he who built the house, has more honour than the house. Moses was faithful in all his house, as a servant, but Christ as a son over his own house," the church of God, 1 Tim. 3:15.

3. That our Lord Jesus Christ has instituted all gospel-ordinances necessary for his disciples, to worship God in Spirit and in truth, 1 Cor. 11:1,2. "Be you followers of me, even as I am of Christ—And keep the ordinances as I delivered them to you," John 4:21, 22, 23, 24—"The true worshippers shall worship the Father in spirit and in truth. God is a spirit, and they that worship him must worship him in spirit and in truth."

Section 3. The Position Explained.

[I.] The first part of our general position to be explained is that our Lord Jesus Christ came into the world to save sinners, 1 Tim. 1:15. Now the method I shall observe in the explanation of this part of our position shall be to show:

1. What kind of saviour Christ is.
2. What salvation sinners may have by Jesus Christ, and
3. How sinners are saved by Jesus Christ.

And of these in order:
First, what kind of saviour is Jesus Christ? I answer,

1. The Lord Jesus Christ is an almighty saviour. As there is none other, Acts 4:12, so there need be no other saviour. None can pull a soul out of Christ's hand, John 10:27-30. Christ is God-Man, Emmanuel, God with us, Matth. 1:23. "Jehovah our Righteousness," Jer. 23:6. The Mighty God, Isa. 9:6. The Almighty, Rev. 1:8, the True God and Eternal Life, 1 John 5:20. There is no saviour, but God, Isa. 43:3, 11. "I even I am Jehovah, and beside me there is no saviour." And Jude verse 25. "To the only wise God our Saviour, be glory, and majesty, dominion and power, both now and ever. Amen." It is absolutely necessary unto salvation to know and believe that the Lord Jesus Christ

is very God as well as very man. So the Virgin Mary believed when she said, "My spirit has rejoiced in God my Saviour," Luke 1:46, 47. And so did all the holy apostles and saints believe and confess, Rom. 9:5; 2 Cor. 5:19; 1 Tim. 2:3; Tit. 1:3; Tit. 2:10; Tit. 3:4; and 1 John 5:20. "Who is the true God and eternal life." They that do not believe, but deny Jesus Christ to be God, deny the Lord that bought them, and bring upon themselves swift damnation, 2 Pet. 2:1, 2, 3. They undervalue his most precious blood, Heb. 1:29, compared with Acts 2:28. "To feed the church of God, which he has purchased with his own blood." And they, in effect, deny the all-sufficiency of Christ's satisfaction for the sins of mankind, whose nature he took, namely, the seed of Abraham, Heb. 2:16. "But he takes hold of the seed of Abraham."

2. The Lord Jesus Christ is a gracious saviour, Eph. 2:5. "By grace you are saved." And verse 8. "For by grace are you saved." This free grace is the kindness and love of God our Saviour towards sinful sinners, Tit. 3:3-7, whom he justifies freely by his grace, Rom. 3:24 and 2 Tim. 1:9. And saves them with an everlasting salvation. And also sanctifies them by faith in him, Acts 26:18, where faith is put sinecdochically for all the graces of sanctification, which our Lord Jesus Christ imparts unto and implants in the souls of justified believers, 1 Cor. 6:9, 10, 11. John 1:16. "And of his fullness have all we received, and grace for grace," Eph. 4:7. "To every one of us is given grace." And James 4:6. "He gives more grace." Such is the unsearchable [and the exceeding riches of his grace, Eph. 2:7] riches of Christ, Eph. 3:8, that he will be gracious to whom he will be gracious, etc. Read Exod. 33:19 and Rom. 9:15.

3. The Lord Jesus Christ is an all-sufficient saviour, Heb. 7:25. "He is able to save to the utmost," etc. Christ has made full satisfaction for the sins of all them whom the Father gave him to redeem, Isa. 53:10. His soul was made an offering for sin, and he gave himself a ransom for all, 1 Tim. 2:5, 6. There's enough in Christ; there's all in Christ, Col. 1:19. "For it pleased the Father, that in him should all fullness dwell: and in him dwelled all the fullness of the God-head bodily," Col. 2:9. He is a full Christ, and has an infinite all sufficiency in himself, to supply all the wants of his saints, 2 Cor. 12:9. "My grace is sufficient for you," etc.

Secondly, what salvation may sinners have by Jesus Christ? I answer,

1. Sinners may be saved from their sin by Jesus Christ, Matth. 1:21. "For he shall save his people from their sins." It is a very great mercy to be saved from our sins. This salvation is not

by any other, Acts 4:12. There are three things in sin from which Christ saves sinners, namely,

First, the dominion of sin. It was David's prayer, Psal. 19:13. Psal. 119:133. "Let not any iniquity have dominion over me"; and Christ's promise, Rom. 6:14, "Sin shall not have dominion over you; because you are not under the law, but under grace." There is a reigning power in sin, Rom. 6:12. "Let not sin therefore reign in your mortal body," etc. Also, Rom. 5:21, which Christ subdues, Mich. 7:19. "He will subdue our iniquities," and destroys, Rom. 6:6.

Secondly, the captivating power of sin. This the apostle sadly experienced, Rom. 7:23, 24. "I see another law in my members, warring against the law of my mind, and bringing me into captivity to the law of sin, which is in my members." But yet he blessed God for Jesus Christ, verse 25, through whom he had deliverance, Rom. 8:2. "The law of the spirit of life in Christ Jesus has made me free from the law of sin and death."

Thirdly, the guilt, curse, and condemnation of sin, James 2:10. " . . . and offend in one point, is guilty of all," Gal. 3:18. "Cursed is everyone that continues not in all things which are written in the book of the law to do them," Tit. 3:11. " . . . and sins being condemned in himself." But there is no condemnation to them that are in Christ Jesus, Rom. 8:1, for Christ has redeemed us from the curse of the law, Gal. 3:13, and saved us from the wrath of God, Rom. 5:9 and 1 Thes. 1:10, and gives us eternal life and salvation.

Thirdly, how are sinners saved by Jesus Christ? In answer to this query, two things in general must be considered:

1. What Jesus Christ has done for sinners.
2. What he does in them in order unto their everlasting salvation.

[What has Jesus Christ done for sinners] First, Jesus Christ has made full satisfaction unto the divine justice of God for all the transgressions of sinners. Isa. 53:5, 6, 8, 9, 11. "He was wounded for our transgressions," verse 5. "When you shall make his soul an offering for sin," verse 10. "He shall see of the travail of his soul, and shall be satisfied," v. 11. Christ, through the eternal Spirit, offered himself to God, Heb. 9:14 and 1 Pet. 2:24. "Who his own self bore our sins in his own body on the tree. Now once in the end of the world has he appeared to put away sin by the sacrifice of himself," Heb. 9:26. And 1 Tim. 2:6, "Who gave himself a ransom for all, to be testified in due time."

Secondly, Jesus Christ has purchased and obtained for sinners eternal redemption, and everlasting salvation by his own precious blood, Heb.9:12. "By his own blood, he entered in once into the holy place, having obtained eternal redemption for us." Therefore eternal life and glory is called the purchased possession, Eph. 1:14, and an inheritance reserved in heaven for us, 1 Pet. 1:3-5.

Thirdly, Jesus Christ has instituted and ordained the ministry of the gospel, Eph. 4:11, 12, 13, and all gospel-ordinances for the salvation of sinners to the glory of God the Father. And after he was crucified, he rose from the dead, ascended into heaven, and is set down on the right hand of God, where he ever lives to make intercessions for sinners, that they may be saved, Heb. 7:25. The Lord Jesus Christ having done all these things for the salvation of sinners; he does by his Holy Spirit and Word work all his works of grace and salvation in them, Isa. 26:12. "Lord, you have wrought all our works in us." And Phil. 2:12, 13. "It is God that works in you to will and to do according to his good pleasure." Therefore sinners are said to be "God's workmanship," Eph. 2:10. "Created in Christ Jesus unto good works," etc. that thereby it may yet more plainly appear, "that they are his workmanship."

What he does in them in order unto their everlasting salvation. [A.] The first work that God does ordinarily by his Holy Spirit and Word upon a sinful sinner in the ministry and administration of the gospel of his grace is a work of conviction, John 8:9. "Being convicted in their own conscience," Tit. 1:9. "To convince gainsayers," James 2:9. "They are convinced of the law as transgressors." And John 16:8, 9: "He shall reprove the world of sin." The world, that is to say, those sinners that are without Christ, and without God in the world, Eph. 2:12.

Now God reproves the sinner, and sets his sins in order before him, Psal. 50:21, and makes him possess the sins of his youth, Job 13:26. God does by the Scripture (as in a glass) give the sinner a sight of his sinful nature; shows him the sinfulness of his sins, Rom. 7:13. God does by his Spirit and Word convince the sinner's conscience of his transgressions against his holy law, and against the gospel of his grace. The Holy Spirit, ordinarily, by the ministry of the Word, convinces the sinner of his original corruption; tells him that every man is tempted when he is drawn away of his own lust and enticed; Then when lust has conceived, it brings forth sin, and sin when it is finished, brings forth death, James 1:14, 15. "The wages of sin is death," Rom. 6:23. The soul that sins shall die; and also convinces him of his actual transgressions; "that is, " his sins of omission, and his sins of commission, both in doing that which God has forbidden in his holy Word, and in not doing that which he has commanded, or not as he commanded it to be done. God convinces the sinner's conscience of his sinning against light, against checks of conscience, and many good motions of the Holy Spirit; and shows him how he has sinned against the mercies, patience, and long-sufferings of God, and how he has sinned under God's chastisements, corrections, and righteous judgements; and that neither the Word of God, nor his rod, has wrought repentance in him, nor caused him to turn from his sinful courses.

The sinful sinner, being under this great work of conviction of conscience, begins to see and apprehend the vileness of his nature and the sinfulness of his sins to be such, so many, and so great that he trembles and is afraid of death and damnation. He begins to have some sense and feeling in his conscience of the wrath of God, and fears he shall die in his sins, and go to Hell, and be damned to eternity.

Now the terrors of the Almighty are in his conscience, his heart is filled with horror, the sting of sin has wounded his spirit, and "a wounded spirit who can bear?" Prov. 18:14. Being pricked in the heart, he cries out, "What shall I do?" Acts 2:37. "I am a sinful sinner, a vile sinner, a lost undone perishing sinner. Woe is me, that ever I was born! I am a damnable wicked wretch; my heart is deceitful and desperately wicked. Ah my vain thoughts, my vile affections, my evil concupiscence, my sinful lusts! Alas! Alas! My idle words and blasphemies, and my ungodly life and sinful conversation! Woe and alas! The deceitfulness of sin has so hardened my heart that I cannot repent, and I have been so accustomed to do evil, that I know not how to reform and amend my life, and forsake my sins; and if I go on in my former sinful courses, I shall certainly be damned."

At this, the sinful sinner sets upon reformation. He says to his sinful companions, as David did, Psal. 6:8, "Depart from me all you workers of iniquity": and says to his lusts, as Ephraim did to his idols, Hos. 14:8, "What have I to do any more with sinful lusts and pleasures?" Now the convinced sinner resolves to leave his sins that he fears else will damn his soul; and now he begins to perform some holy duties; he will hear sermons, and read the holy scriptures, and good books, and pray. And it may be the convinced sinner will mourn for his sins, and humble himself (as Ahab did) and reform some of his evil courses.

And by this reformation, humiliation, mourning for his sins, and performing some holy duties, the sinner may have some calm, and feel some quiet in his conscience for a season, and begin to hope all will be well with him, until the reigning power of sin, "that has yet the dominion over him" prevails against him; and he, being yet a servant of sin and free from righteousness (as the apostle speaks, Rom. 6:20), yields willing and ready obedience to his own lusts that entice him to sin, and when his lust has conceived and brought forth sin, then his conscience accuses him, and Satan now begins to suggest that there is no hope of pardon nor salvation for him. Now his latter end is worse than his beginning; and therefore the Devil tells him it is vain for him to pray any more, or to hear any more, or to perform any holy duties.

And now the convinced sinful sinner judges his soul's state and condition to be worse than ever it was. He has so many dreadful temptations, he is so filled with blasphemous thoughts, that he begins to be a terror to himself, and is tempted to choose strangling rather than life. He is so tormented in his conscience, and so tempted by Satan, and terrified with fears of Hell. He sees now the law curses him, Gal. 3:10, and the gospel judges him, 2 Thes. 1:9. And he is made to receive the sentence of condemnation in himself and is made to read it in the written Word of God, John 3:18. "He that believes not is condemned already."

Now God goes on with his work of conviction, which he had before begun in the sinful sinner's conscience, and sends his Holy Spirit to convince and reprove him of sin, of righteousness, and of judgment, John 16:8, 9, 10. And the Spirit by that Scripture, John 3:18, or some other Scripture to that purpose, does thoroughly convince the sinner that, although his pride, passion, worldliness, and uncleanness, profanity, lying, stealing, swearing, drinking, whoring, or any one or other of his sins deserves eternal death, Rom. 67:23, yet that sin for which the wrath of God abides on him, and for which he is by the written Word of God condemned already, is his great sin of unbelief, John 3:18, 36, and Heb. 3:11, 18. God has sworn that those who do not believe shall not enter into his rest, that is, into heaven, Heb. 3:18, 19.

Take notice, reader, *that in conviction of sin, because we believe not*, the Holy Spirit does by the Word convince the sinner:

[F]irst, that he is an unbeliever, and has not obtained the precious faith of God's elect, by which the soul is united unto Christ, Eph. 4:13, adopted the child of God, Gal. 3:26, justified, and all its sins pardoned, and at peace with God, Rom. 5:1, and now the convinced sinner sees he is without God, without Christ, and without faith.

Secondly, that he must believe, or he cannot be saved, Mark 16:15, 16. "He that believes not shall be damned." His praying, mourning, reforming, though they are good in themselves, and are his duty, yet the doing these or any other; yea, all other holy duties without this precious faith in Christ, will not, cannot save him; and now the sinner is convinced that there is an indispensible necessity of his believing in Christ for salvation.

Thirdly, that he cannot believe. Faith is not of ourselves, it is not of works, Eph. 2:8, 9. They err, not knowing the Scriptures, nor the holy will of God revealed in it; who say that men may believe, if they will; and they have power in themselves to believe. Ask now the sinner that has been convinced of sin by the Holy Spirit and Word of God, because he believes not (and is commanded to believe, 1 John 3:23). I say, ask that convinced sinner, if it has power of himself to believe; or if faith in Christ be of ourselves, or of our good works, or of holy duties; and he will tell you, "No." Nay, nay, faith in Christ is not of ourselves; Jesus Christ himself is the author and finisher of faith, Heb. 12:2. It is not of our works; but it is the faith of the operation of God, Col. 2:12. It is the exceeding greatness of God's mighty power that does make the soul of a sinful sinner (*convinced of sin because he believes not*) willing and able to believe in Christ, Eph. 1:19, 20.

Now, says this convinced sinner, "I know and am persuaded, that whosoever believes in Christ shall be saved, and I know and am convinced that I ought to believe in Christ, and it is my sin that I do not believe in him. Yea, I am also persuaded (upon Scripture grounds), that if I did believe in Christ, I should not perish, but have everlasting life. But this is my impotency, and here is my misery, I cannot believe in Christ of myself; I know not which way to begin to believe; I could do something *materially* about the works of the law, though but weakly and insufficiently; but I can do nothing about obedience of faith according to the gospel. It is such a mystery as I am very ignorant of. Faith is the gift of God, and unless he give it me, I perish." Now is the sinner convinced of his sin of unbelief. This is God's workmanship upon a sinful sinner's conscience; but this is not the whole work of conviction; therefore God proceeds in this work and convinces the sinner by his Spirit and Word of righteousness, John 16:10, showing the sinner while he goes about to establish his own righteousness by the works of the law, and by performing those duties, that the law requires, he makes void (as much as in him lies) the righteousness of God by faith in the gospel, Rom. 10:3, 4, 5, 6, and thus convinces the sinner,

1. That all his own righteousnesses are as menstruous rags, Isa. 64:6, our most holy duties and performances are polluted and defiled with sin, and God might abhor to accept an offering at our hand. If Christ did not offer up his incense with our sacrifices, they could not come up to God, Rev. 8:3, 4. both our prayers and our persons are accepted only and alone in and through Jesus Christ.

2. That sinners must be covered with the robe of Christ's righteousness and the garments of his salvation, Isa. 61:10. He is the Lord our righteousness, Jer. 23:6. And Christ is made of God unto us wisdom, righteousness, etc., 1 Cor. 1:30. This righteousness of Christ is that skirt, which God casts over the sinner's soul (when he lies in his blood) to cover his nakedness, Ezek. 16:6, 8.

3. That Christ's righteousness is the righteousness of God by faith, Rom. 3:21, 22, which righteousness the apostle Paul did so much prize and desire to be found in, Phil. 3:8, 9. And now the convinced sinner will say with holy Job, chap. 9, v. 21. "If I justify my folly, my own mouth shall condemn me — though I were perfect, yet would I not know my soul."

This is also God's workmanship upon a sinful sinner's conscience: But yet this is not the whole work of conviction; for when God has by his Holy Spirit and Word convinced the sinner of his state of unbelief, and reproved him for sin, because he believes not. And when God has also convinced him that his own righteousness is as filthy rags, and that he must submit to the righteousness of God and take Christ's righteousness by faith unto justification of life, then God proceeds on in the work of conviction, and reproves or convinces the sinner of judgement, John 16:11. And this God does by causing the sinner to know:

1. That there is a day of judgment, called the eternal judgment, Heb. 6:2, and the judgment of the great day of God, Jude verse 6.

2. That all shall appear and stand before the judgment seat of Christ, Rom. 14:10 and 1 Cor. 5:10. And everyone shall then give account of himself unto God, and shall receive a just reward of all that he has done in the flesh, Rom. 2:5-13, Rev. 22:12 and Matth. 16:27.

3. That the prince of this world is judged, and therefore none of the children of disobedience, in whom the God of this world now works, shall escape the righteous judgment of God, Rom. 2:3, 5, 6, for the Lord Jesus Christ ("who shall judge both the quick and the dead at his appearing and his kingdom," 2 Tim. 4:1) shall come from heaven with his mighty angels in flaming fire, taking vengeance on them that know not God, "and that

obey not the gospel, who shall be punished with everlasting destruction," etc. 2 Thes. 1:7, 8, 9. And the Spirit and Word of God does witness and testify to the sinner's conscience, that he must come to judgment, as Solomon told the young man, Eccles. 11:9. "Know you that for all these things, or sins, God will bring you to judgment." And now the sinful sinner is thoroughly convinced, and this is the first part of God's workmanship upon him in order unto his conversion and everlasting salvation.

And I desire the reader to take notice that the lack of a thorough work of conviction is the cause of the lack of a sound and saving work of conversion. One reason why there are so few true converts in this our day and generation is because the ministers of the gospel do not labour in the word and doctrine of a thorough gospel conviction. The reason why so few hearers do believe in Christ is because they were never thoroughly convinced of the sin of unbelief. How many Herod-like hearers are there in and about London? Mark 6:20. How many stony-hearted hearers follow and flock after the preachers of the gospel, "who hear the Word with joy and believe for a time," Luke 8:13. But when the time of the trial of their faith comes, by sufferings and persecutions, then they fall away, Matth. 13:20, 21. And you have the reason of their falling away expressed by both the evangelists. "They had no root in themselves," that is to say, they had not Christ in their souls to be the root of their faith, Col. 2:6, 7. "As you have therefore received, Christ Jesus the Lord, so walk in him, rooted and built up in him, and established in the faith." Faith rooted in Christ will stand out all storms of temptation and persecution; it will endure all fiery trials, but faith without Christ will fall away. And the Spirit tells us expressly, that some ("who made a great and glorious profession of faith") will depart from the faith in the latter days, 1 Tim. 4:1, because they have not possession of Christ, and their faith is not rooted in him. Do but diligently observe and enquire into this matter, and you shall find that those ministers of Christ are most instrumental in converting souls unto God who labour most in the Word and doctrine of the gospel-conviction of sinners. Those ministers that preach Christ and the gospel of free-grace most convincingly and labour in the application of every doctrine to convince the conscience of sinners that they are in danger of the wrath of God and of eternal death for their sins; especially because they believe not in Christ, exhorting them to repent of their sin and believe in the Lord Jesus Christ, that they may be pardoned and saved by him. I say, those ministers have most converts, those are workers together with God, and their convinced, humbled, converted, and sanctified hearers have not received the grace of God in vain, 2 Cor. 6:1.

Some poor souls may haply object, or rather query, "Is there not a sound work of conversion, where there has not been so great a work of conviction and humiliation, nor so great horrors, fears, terrors, and so clear and distinct a work of the Spirit's reproof of sin, righteousness, and judgment, as God works upon some sinners?" I answer; though this is God's workmanship upon some; yea many, if not upon most notorious sinful sinners, yet we may not limit the Holy One of Israel: God is a free agent. And because I would not break the bruised reed nor quench the smoking flax, I know and acknowledge that some sinful sinners have lesser terrors, fewer temptations, fears and horrors than others have; and some are longer under the work of conviction and bondage than others are, though they have been as great and notorious sinners as they that were more and longer exercised with fears and terrors. Yea, and I know both by experience and by Scripture, that some sinners, who have had religious education under godly parents or governors; and have lived (from their youth up) under a godly soul-saving ministry, and have thus been restrained (by the common grace of God) from all gross sins, that have not experienced the said terrors and temptations, nor have they had such horrors of conscience and fears of Hell. Yet this I know, that they have been thoroughly convinced of their sinful natural state, and of their lost and undone condition, being (and seeing themselves to be) without Christ, and without grace; and they have been thoroughly convinced that their own righteousnesses are filthy rags; and that they must have Christ's righteousness to justify them, and his holiness to sanctify them, and his precious blood to redeem them from their iniquity. But as for time, whether longer or shorter; and as for measure, whether greater or lesser, by which God did this work of conviction upon them, who can limit God?

[B.] God having wrought a thorough conviction upon a sinful sinner, the next [second] part and piece of his workmanship upon his soul is spiritual illumination in the saving knowledge of the Lord Jesus Christ, Eph. 1:17, 18, by which the eyes of his understanding is enlightened, that the sinner may know that there is hope of pardon and salvation in Christ for him through faith and holiness.

In the work of spiritual illumination, God does by his Holy Spirit and Word, discover to him, and enlighten the eyes of his understanding first to see the divine beauty and glorious excellency of Jesus Christ above all other persons and things in the world. A poor sinful sinner sees no beauty or comeliness in Christ; why he should desire him? Isa. 53:1, 2, 3. The daughters of Jerusalem said, "What's your beloved (Lord Jesus Christ) more than another's beloved?" Cant. 5:9. "The natural man receives not the things of the Spirit of God — neither can he know them, for they are spiritually discerned," 1 Cor. 2:14, until it please God to make an inward discovery of it by his Holy Spirit and Word in the soul, 1 Cor. 2:9, 10, 11, 12. "But God has revealed them unto us by his Spirit." So 1 John 5:20. "We know that the Son of God is come and has given us an understanding that we may know him," etc. The Psalmist tells the sinner, "that Christ is fairer than the sons of men, full of grace is his lips," Psal. 45:2. The spouse told the daughters of Jerusalem "that her beloved is white and ruddy, the chiefest of ten thousand. He is altogether lovely," Cant. 5:10-6. And the apostle counted all things loss and dung for the excellency of the knowledge of Christ Jesus his Lord, Phil. 3:7, 8.

Secondly, God enlightens the eyes of sinners' understanding to set the worth of Christ in some measure and degree: As poor lost sinners discern not the beauty and excellency of Christ; so they understand not the worth of Christ, until God discover it unto them, and reveal it in them by his Holy Spirit and Word, Gal. 1:15, 16. Now God makes known to the sinner the worth of Christ by showing him in the glass of the gospel,

1. The invaluable preciousness of the blood of Christ that cleanses sinners from all sin and unrighteousness, 1 John 1:8, 9. The precious blood of Christ purges the consciences of sinners from dead works, Heb. 9:14. And Christ both justifies and sanctifies sinners by his precious blood, Rom. 5:9, Heb. 13:12; and 1 Cor. 6:11. This speaks forth the worth of Christ.

2. God shows the sinner in the glass of the gospel the unsearchable riches of Jesus Christ, Eph. 3:8, "the exceeding riches of his grace," Eph. 2:7. And though Christ has freely, richly, and abundantly given forth of his fullness so much grace to so many poor sinners from "the day of Adam's transgression, even to this day"; yet, in that vision of Christ's riches, the poor sinful sinner sees him still as full of grace and truth, as the disciples did, John 1:14.

3. God shows the sinner in the glass of the gospel the glorious liberties of the Spirit of Christ, "Where the Spirit of the Lord is, there is liberty," 2 Cor. 3:17. And the saints are commanded to stand fast in the liberty wherewith Christ has made them free, Gal. 5:1, called the glorious liberties of the sons of God, Rom. 8:21.

This gospel liberty is not a liberty to sin, nor may this liberty be used for an occasion to the flesh, Gal. 5:13, but it is a freedom from sin, Rom. 6:18, 22 in respect of the condemnation due thereunto, Rom. 8:1. "There is no condemnation to them that are in Christ Jesus"; and in respect of the dominion of it, Rom. 6:14. "Sin shall not have dominion over you: for you are not under the law, but under grace."

Thirdly, God shows the convinced sinner in the glass of the gospel his need of Christ, and acquaints him with an indispensible necessity of accepting Christ upon gospel terms of free grace, "without money, and without price," Isa. 55:1, 2, 3, and Rev. 22:17. God does by his Spirit and Word inform the sinner that the Lord Jesus Christ alone is the only saviour of sinners, Acts 4:12. "Neither is there salvation in any other." And hereby the poor lost sinful sinner sees his need of Christ to justify him, and pardon all his sins; also to sanctify him, and save him from his sins and the wrath of God due unto him for his sins; and to save him with an everlasting salvation.

[C.] God, having thoroughly convinced and savingly enlightened the sinner, the third and next part of God's workmanship upon his soul is the work of conversion. Sinners are often called upon to turn unto God, and to turn from their sins, Ezek. 14:6, 18, 30, 32; 33:11, that they may know it is their duty so to do; and that finding by experience it is not in their power, being fallen in Adam, they should pray to God to turn them from their sins unto himself by his Spirit and grace, Jer. 31:18, 19. "Turn you to me and I shall be turned," etc.

Conversion is that part of God's workmanship upon a sinner's soul, in which God does first change the whole man from the sinful similitude of Adam into the image of Jesus Christ, 2 Cor. 3:18. "We are changed into his image," etc. I say, in this work of true conversion, the whole man is changed; the heart is made a new heart, Ezek. 36:26. "A new heart also will I give you, and a new spirit will I put within you. And I will put my Spirit within you, and cause you to walk in my statutes." The man is made a new man, Eph. 4:23, 24. "And that you put on the new man, which after God is created in righteousness and true holiness." And his life, a new life, Rom. 6:4. "Even so, we also should walk in newness of life."

Secondly, God does in the work of conversion, sanctify the converted person wholly and throughout in spirit, soul and body, 1 Thes. 5:23. "The very God of peace sanctify you wholly," etc. Upon (or at the time of) the sinner's conversion, God imparts unto him and implants in him of every grace (that is in Christ) a measure, John 1:14, 16. "And from his fullness have all we received, and grace for grace." Also, Eph. 4:7, "To every one of us is given grace, according to the measure of the gift of Christ," which grace is called the *incorruptible* seed of the new-birth, 1 Pet. 1:23, which seed abides in sanctified believers, 1 John 3:9. It is implanted, and it is inherent grace, which grows like the grain of mustard-seed, Matth. 13:31, 32, unto which spiritual growth every sanctified believer is exhorted, 2 Pet. 3:18. "But grow in grace," etc.

Thirdly, God does in the work of conversion actually and really turn the converted person from darkness to light, from the power of Satan and sin unto God, Acts 26:18. Before conversion, the sinner was under the vassalage of Satan, who had dominion over him and worked in him, Eph. 2:2. And he was then the servant of sin, which had also dominion over him, and reigned in him, Rom. 5:21. And though the sinner was convinced of his sin and troubled in his mind for his sins, yea, and saw the danger that his soul was in by reason of his sins, whereupon the sinner resolved to forsake his initial courses and to commit his sin no more, yet until he was truly converted, he had no power nor strength to overcome them, nor could he pray and perform holy duties with delight and comfort, but as a task and work, that was hard and burdensome, Isa. 43:22, 24, 25. "You have not called upon me, O Jacob, but you have been weary of me, O Israel; but you have made me to serve with your sins, you have wearied me with your iniquities. I, even I, am he that blots out your transgressions for my own sake, and I will not remember your sins." Now that the sinner is converted, he is in the Spirit and grace of God called to repent, and to turn from his sins to God with his whole heart, Jer. 31:18, 19, 20. "Surely after that I was turned, I repented—I was ashamed," etc.

Thus we may see what *work* God does upon sinful sinners, in respect of which they are God's workmanship, created in Christ Jesus.

[D.] Let us in the next place consider what *work* God does upon sanctified believers, in respect of which they also are God's workmanship.

God, having called and convicted sinful sinners unto himself by his Holy Spirit and Word, formed Christ in them and changed them into the image of Christ, giving them his Holy Spirit, and imparted grace unto them, and implanted it in them; and having of his free grace adopted, and justified them through faith in Christ, Gal. 3:26, Gal. 2:16. God is pleased out of the exceeding riches of his free grace to go on with this workmanship gradually, until he has made them complete in Christ, Col. 2:10, whom he has created in Christ Jesus. And in order thereunto, there are diverse other works of God, which he does by his Holy Spirit and Word in and upon the souls of those converts, in respect of which they are his workmanship.

[1.] And the first is the work of faith with power, 2 Thes. 1:11, called the faith of the operation of God, Col. 2:12, in which God demonstrates what is the exceeding greatness of his power toward us who believe according to the working of his mighty power, which he wrought in Christ when he raised him from the dead, Eph. 1:19, 20. And this God does in raising souls from the death of sin to the life of righteousness by Jesus Christ, Eph. 2:5, 6.

This faith Jesus Christ is the author of, and will be the finisher of it, Heb. 12:2, and therefore called the faith of the Son of God, Gal. 2:20, by which faith the soul in its conversion is united unto Christ, and kept through it by the power of God unto salvation. Compare Eph. 4:13 with 1 Pet. 1:3, 4, 5. It's called the precious faith of God's elect, 3 Pet. 1:1, even the same spirit of faith that Abraham had and that all the sons and daughters of Abraham have and do receive, 2 Cor. 4:13. "Now faith is the substance of things hoped for, and the evidence of things not seen," Heb. 11:1.

This faith God works in us ordinarily by his Holy Spirit and Word in the ministry and administrations of the gospel of his grace, Rom. 10:8. "That is the word of faith, which we preach," and verse 17, "so then, faith comes by hearing, and hearing by the Word of God," by which faith we receive Jesus Christ, our Lord, John 1:12. Adhere and cleave to him with purpose of heart, never to forsake him or deny him, Acts 11:23, but to own him for our Head, Lord, and Lawgiver, our King, Priest, and Prophet: And trust and rest upon him alone, *and on him only*, for wisdom, righteousness, sanctification and redemption, Isa. 26:3 with Isa. 50:10. And by this precious faith, believers are justified, Rom. 3:28, adopted, Gal. 3:26, and sanctified, Acts 26:18, through our Lord Jesus Christ. But the converted believer is not yet fully assured Christ will save him: he is fully persuaded that there is not salvation in any other and believes that Christ is able to save to the utmost all that come to God through him. And being drawn to Christ by God the Father, he does by a lively act of faith go to him, and adventure his soul upon him, resolving "If I perish, I will perish here."

This faith is God's workmanship, Eph. 2:8. "By grace are we saved through faith and that not of ourselves, it is the gift of

God." Faith is not of ourselves: for when the poor lost soul sees a necessity of believing, and is willing to believe, he experiences that it is not in his own power to believe, he cannot believe. *Faith is the gift of God*, and the convert lies under doubting until God give him to believe. Though to believe be our duty, yet it is God's grace, gift, and work, 1 Thes. 1:11, called "the work of faith with power, and the faith of the operation of God," Col. 2:12, as before.

[2.] Another part of God's workmanship upon converted believers' mortification of sin; Rom 6:8. "Our old-man is crucified with him, that the body of sin might be destroyed," this is also our duty, Rom. 8:13. "But if you through the Spirit do mortify the deeds of the body (that is, of sin) you shall live." And it is the effect of true faith in Christ, Acts 15:9. Having *purified*, or purged *their hearts by faith*, the Spirit of God by faith works out sin and corruption, both out of the heart, and out of the life gradually, killing and crucifying our Old Man, Gal. 5:24, "that the body of sin might be destroyed. That henceforth we should not serve sin," Rom. 6:6, nor fulfil the lusts of our flesh, and of our carnal mind; "for to be carnally minded is death."

This part of God's workmanship, called mortification, is begun in evangelical repentance, and godly sorrow for sin; by which a sanctified believer is made to loath, abhor and hate his sins, 2 Cor. 7:9, 10, and by the grace of God to deny ungodliness, and worldly lusts: And to live soberly, righteously, and godly in this evil world, Tit. 2:11, 12. Now his heart being out of love with sin, the young convert does, by the assistance of the Holy Spirit and grace of God, labour and endeavour the mortification of every corruption; and the power of the indwelling Spirit in every sanctified believer opposes and subdues the power of indwelling sin that remains in him after regeneration, Gal. 5:17. And the spirit and grace of God in him gets the victory, by which grace reigns, Rom. 5:20, 21. And the law of the spirit of life in Christ Jesus makes him free from the law of sin and death, Rom. 8:2.

Free, first, from the reigning power of sin, Rom. 6:11, 14. Sin has not dominion over a sanctified believer; nor will Christ suffer sin to reign in him, nor suffer him to obey it in the lusts of it. Secondly, from the *captivating* power of sin, which Paul so sadly complained of, Rom. 7:23, 24, 25, and was freed from by the power of the indwelling Spirit of Christ, Rom. 8:2. Thirdly, from the motions of sin in the flesh, Rom. 7:5, 6, so that no lust shall conceive and bring forth sin, James 1:14, 15. And at last Christ will free sanctified believers from the indwelling presence of sin. Death will make a total and final separation between their sins and their souls for eternity.

[3.] Another part of God's workmanship upon converted believers in order to their salvation is sanctification of heart and life. "God has chosen you to salvation, through sanctification of the Spirit," 2 Thes. 2:13. And Jesus Christ sanctifies his people, Heb. 2:11. At the end of our faith is the salvation of our souls, 1 Pet. 1:9, so the way to salvation is sanctification and holiness, Isa. 35:8. And without holiness, no man shall see the Lord to his comfort and salvation, Heb. 12:14. Sanctification consists in the truth of grace, in the growth of grace; and in the perfection of grace. The truth of grace produces the spiritual fruit of the gospel, Col. 1:5, 6. "The word of the truth of the gospel brings forth fruit from the day you heard of it, and knew the grace of God in truth." The growth of grace has a *threefold* gradation; some sanctified believers grow like little children in the grace and knowledge of Jesus Christ, 1 Pet. 2:2, 3. "As newborn babes, desire the sincere milk of the Word that you may grow thereby." Those St. John calls little children, whose sins are forgiven, 1 John 2:12, 13. And St. Paul calls them "babes in Christ," 1 Cor. 3:1 and Heb. 5:13.

"For he is a babe"; one that is weak in faith, Rom. 14:1 and 15:1. Though such have but a little grace, yet it is true grace and does grow. Grace is of a growing nature, like a grain of mustard seed, Matth. 13:31. Other sanctified believers grow like young men; they are strong in faith and overcome the wicked one, 1 John 2:13, 14. Their faith is great, their love is fervent, and their patience has its perfect work that they may be entirely lacking nothing, 1 Thes. 1:3. And some sanctified believers are compared to fathers, that is to say, gracious, grave, grown, and experienced Christians, 1 John 2:13, 14. Such were some of the saints in the church at Thessalonica, 2 Thes. 1:3, 4. "Your faith grows exceedingly, and the charity of every one of you all toward each other abounds." The perfection of grace is the state of sanctified believers in heaven; there are the spirits (that is, the souls) of just men made perfect, Heb. 12:23. Sanctified believers ought to go on to perfection, Heb. 6:1. And they that have received the promises ought to cleanse themselves from all filthiness of flesh; and filthiness of Spirit perfecting holiness in the fear of God, 2 Cor. 7:1, 2. And God has ordained the ministry of the gospel for the perfecting of the saints, Eph. 4:11, 12, 13. "Until we all come in the unity of truth unto a perfect man." And though the apostle was not perfect (as he confessed) yet he pressed toward the mark for the prize of the high calling of God in Christ Jesus,

Phil. 3:12, 14. So ought all the saints to do until they are translated from earth to heaven, and from grace to glory, and shall be set down in the Father's house among the spirits of just men made perfect. This Jesus Christ (*who came into the world to save sinners*) brings them to salvation.

[II.] The next particular in our general position to be explained is that Jesus Christ came into this world to build up his own house, *the church of God*. As Moses was faithful in the house of God as a *servant* who did all things about the tabernacle according to the pattern showed unto him by God in the mountain, Exod. 25:4, Acts 7:44, and Heb. 8:5, so Jesus Christ was faithful unto God that appointed him as a son over his own house, the true tabernacle, which the Lord pitched, and not man, Heb. 3:2, 3, 5, 6, and Heb. 8:2, called "the church of the Living God," 1 Tim. 3:15.

The Lord Jesus Christ, in order unto the building up his house, *the church of God*, did ordain a gospel-ministry, Eph. 4:11, 12, 13. "He gave some apostles, and some prophets, and some evangelists, and some pastors and teachers," etc. And set them in his church, 1 Cor. 12:28. "And God has set some in the church, first apostles, secondarily prophets, thirdly teachers," etc.

The apostles, as wise master builders, did prepare fit materials for to build the house of God, and to that purpose, they, having received commission and command from the Lord Jesus Christ, Mark 16:15, went out into the world and preached the gospel, beginning at Jerusalem. And when they had made and baptised many disciples, they planted those churches that we read of in the Holy Scriptures, which were built upon the foundation of the apostles and prophets, Jesus Christ himself being the chief cornerstone, in whom all the building fitly framed together was built together a habitation of God through the Spirit, Eph. 2:19-22. The church at Jerusalem was the first of all those gospel-churches, Acts 2:47. "And the Lord added to the church daily such as should be saved." Which church was at its first constitution a particular congregation of sanctified believers baptized in the water in the name of the Father, and of the Son, and of the Holy Spirit, Matth. 28:19. And separated from the synagogues of the unbelieving Jews to worship God in spirit and in truth, John 4:21, 23, 24, according to the sacred institution of Christ and his apostles, *even the ordinances of God delivered unto his churches of saints*, 1 Cor. 11:1, 2 . And although the number of the disciples were multiplied from one hundred and twenty, Acts 1:15, to three thousand, Acts 2:41, yea to five thousand, Acts 4:4 and Acts 5:14, "and believers were the more added to the Lord, multitudes both of men and women." So that the apostles had their own distinct companies, societies, or congregations in Jerusalem (Acts 4:13, 19, 23). "And Peter and John being let go, they went to their own company." Yet they all being of one heart, and of one soul, were but one church, and are so denominated, Acts 15:4. "And when they were come to Jerusalem, they were received of the church," etc., Acts 15:22, "*The whole church.*" And so were all the particular congregations in every city denominated and called, namely, the church of God at Corinth, 1 Cor. 1:2. And so our Lord and Saviour denominated all the churches of God in Asia by the particular cities in which they were first planted and assembled to worship God, Rev. 2:1, 8, 12, 18 and Rev. 3:1, 7, 14. Read those verses.

I entreat the reader to consider,

1., that our Lord Jesus Christ, in building up his own house, *the church of God*, ordained and appointed a preceding ministry to be workers together with him in building his house, Heb. 3:4, 1 Cor. 3:9, 10, 11. "We are labourers together with God—you are God's building," etc.

2. That the churches of God under the gospel are not *national*, but *political*, and *congregational*.

3. That a particular visible true constituted gospel church of God does consist of fit matter and due form. Jesus Christ, the chief cornerstone, is a lively stone, and the materials of the church ought to be living stones, 1 Pet. 2:4, 5. Sanctified believers, 1 Cor. 1:2, 6. And Christ himself was baptized with water and with the Holy Spirit; everyone in his visible churches of saints ought to be baptized with water and with the Holy Spirit (John 5:5). 2. Those sanctified believers ought to be fitly framed together and orderly compacted, joined, and built together, an habitation of God through the Spirit, Eph. 2:19, 20, 21, 22 and chap. 4:15, 16, which is the form of the house of God, the church of the Living God, 1 Tim. 3:15.

God commanded his prophet Ezekiel, chap. 43:10, 11, saying, "You son of man, show the house to the house of Israel. And let them measure the pattern—Show them the form of the house—And write it in their sight." A wise master builder will take care to prepare fit materials in every respect answerable and suitable unto the house he is about to build; and so get the ministers of Christ, who are coworkers with God in building his house (*which is his church*) to take heed both *what* and *how* they build, 1 Cor. 3:9-14. "Every man's work shall be made manifest, for the Day shall declare it. And the fire shall try every man's work, of what sort it is," etc. Young converts, new born babes in Christ, may be added to the church of God, Acts 2:41, 47. But they are not *fit* materials to be laid next unto the cornerstone of that spiritual building. I say again, they are not fit for the foundation work of God's building, nor are they fit for pillars in the house of God. Consider what St. Paul, *that wise master builder*, says of such young converts, 1 Cor. 3:1, 2, 3 and Heb. 5:12, 13. Read the words: these and such as these are not fit matter for the foundation, nor for pillars, nor for beams in the house of God, at the first beginning, painting, and building or gathering of a church of God. But rather fathers, that is, grave, gracious, holy, wise and experienced believers. Also some young men, that is, such Christians that are strong in faith and have in *some measure* overcome the world, the Devil, and their own corruptions, who are full of the Holy Spirit, rich in grace, and zealous for the house of God, and the purity of his worship. I say a competent number of such Christians, being found in the faith, holy in their life, and fitly qualified with diversity of spiritual gifts, knowledge and grace, are (in my opinion) most meet to be (by their own mutual free consent and agreement) joined together to become a particular church of saints by the help of some wise master builders and faithful ministers of Jesus Christ, 1 Cor. 3:9-11.

The gospel form of a *particular* church of God consists (as we said) in the fitly framing, compacting, and joining those sanctified believers together into ONE fellowship, society, and gospel brotherhood in a solemn day of prayer with fasting. In this day, some able ministers of the gospel, having, by preaching the word unto them, showed them their respective duties in a church relation. The elders and chief brethren of some particular churches of saints being present and assisting in the work of the day (if they may be obtained) may, in the name and authority of the Lord Jesus Christ (by virtue of this commission given to him), constitute and make them a particular visible church of God. They giving up themselves *professedly* first to the Lord, and then one to another, mutually and solemnly with one accord engaging themselves to come together in ONE congregation and to assemble themselves together in some one place every first day of the week to worship God publicly in all his holy ordinances, with their mutual professed subjection unto the laws of God's house, and with a professed resolution to continue in the apostles' doctrine, and in fellowship, and in breaking of bread and prayer, through the help of God. All which being done, the same minister ought to declare them to be a church of saints, and the ministers and brethren of other churches being also present ought to own and acknowledge them to be a sister church by giving them the right hand of fellowship, and so to commend them by prayer unto God and to the Word of his grace, who is able to build them up and to give them an inheritance among all them which are sanctified.

The well-being of a *particular* church of saints does principally consist in three things, namely oneness, order, and government. That gospel oneness, which makes very much for the well being of a particular church, is threefold:

[Oneness] First, that there be but ONE church in one city; and that all the congregations of saints in that city (called churches) bear but one name, that is, the church of God in that city, as in the apostles' days, Acts 15:4, 22; 1 Cor. 1:2. That so there may be no schism, divisions, nor sinful separations from the church of God; but that the whole church may be perfectly joined together in ONE. As a city that is compact together, Psal. 122:3, as a house or building fitly joined together, Eph. 2:21, 22, and as a body fitly joined and compacted by every joint of supply, Eph. 4:16.

Secondly, that this church be of one heart, and of one soul, Acts 4:32, being perfectly joined together in the same mind, and in the same judgment, 1 Cor. 1:2, 9, 10, that so they may all with one mind and one mouth, glorify God, even the Father of our Lord Jesus Christ, Rom. 15:6, having the same love one to another, Phil 2:1, 2, 3, and the same care one for another, 1 Cor. 12:25, 26, 27, each one endeavouring to keep the unity of the Spirit in the bond of peace, Eph. 4:3-6. This oneness will make the communion of saints very comfortable, Col. 2:2-5. And hereby they will enjoy fellowship with the Father, Son, and Spirit in all God's holy gospel ordinances, to the glory of God and their own edification.

Thirdly, that this one church, and all the congregations of saints that are members of it, walk by one and the same rule *of the written Word of God*, being ordered and guided by their bishops, pastors, teachers, presbyters, or elders, according to the royal laws of God's house (called the "perfect law of liberty," James 1:25) submitting themselves unto those guides, whom God has made their overseers, who watch for their souls, as they that must give an account, Heb. 13:7, 17.

[Order] Gospel-order is a great beauty and ornament to the church, Col. 2:5, and order makes very much for the well being of the church. And gospel-order consists in these things; first, that the bishop and presbyters set in order the things which are wanting in the church, Titus 1:5 and 1 Cor. 11:34. Secondly, that all

things in the church be done decently, and in order, *which Christ has commanded to be done.* And for which his apostles and disciples have given us example. Thirdly, that the order of the gospel be carefully observed, and kept in the administration of God's sacred ordinances, in the admission of members, in the ordination of church-officers, and in withdrawing from every brother that walks disorderly. God was offended with his church under the law, because they sought him not in due order, 2 Chron. 15:11, 12, 13. And God has committed the government of his gospel church and kingdom unto Christ, to order it, etc., Isa. 9:6, 7, and God is not the author of confusion.

[Government] Gospel-government is ordained and appointed of God for the well-being of his church: the church of God cannot have a well-being without Christ's instituted gospel-government. And to that end, God the Father has laid the government of his church upon his Son Jesus Christ, Isa. 9:6, 7, to whom he gave all power in heaven and earth, Matth. 28:18. And he has made Christ head of his house and king of his church, Heb. 3:1-6 and Psal. 149:2. The Lord Jesus Christ delegated this his ecclesiastical government of the church unto his holy apostles, prophets, evangelists, pastors, and teachers, called bishops, presbyters or elders, who were "allowed of God to be put in trust with the gospel," 1 Thes. 2:4. And the apostles and evangelists did commit the same unto faithful men, 2 Tim. 2:12, whom they ordained bishops, presbyters or elders in the churches of saints, Titus 1:5, 7; Acts 14:23, which gospel-government (as we said before) is not a coercive-power over men's consciences; nor is it a dominion over their faith; neither is it a lordship over God's clergy or heritage; but it is a stewardship of the mysteries of God, 1 Cor. 4:1, 2, 3, 4. "Let a man so account of us, as of the ministers of Christ, and stewards of the mysteries of God." And Titus 1:7. "For a bishop must be blameless, as the steward of God." Unto this gospel-government appertains church censures of admonition, 2 Thes. 3:15 and Titus 3:10, suspension (or withdrawing from a brother or member, that had and does walk disorderly), 2 Thes. 3:6, and excommunication of those members that live in gross and scandalous sins, 1 Cor. 5:1, 4, 5, 13.

CHAP. II.

Of gospel ministry.

Section 1

The Lord Jesus Christ is the chief minister of God's sanctuary and of the true tabernacle (Heb. 8:1, 2), which the Lord pitched and not man. He is the chief pastor of God's little flock (1 Pet. 5:4), the bishop of our souls, 1 Pet. 2:25 & Heb. 13:20. The great shepherd of the sheep, who in all things has the pre-eminence or supremacy.

Section 2

He gave apostles, prophets, evangelists, pastors and teachers for the work of the ministry, Eph. 4:11, 12, 13, and 1 Cor. 12:28. The apostles, prophets, and evangelists were appointed by Christ to preach the gospel to the world, Mark 16:15, and for the gathering of the saints, framing, and perfectly joining them together (Eph. 4:11, 12, 13) the pastors and teachers were set by Christ in the churches, as fixed officers, for the edifying of the body, "until we all meet together in the unity of faith," etc.

Section 3

Those pastors and teachers are called elders, 1 Pet. 5:1. Elder is a name of office in the church of God. Elders are indeed fixed officers for rule and government who are to be counted worthy of double honour, 1 Tim. 5:17. They are also called bishops, Phil. 1:1. And the elders of the church of Ephesus, Acts 20:17, were called bishops, Acts 20:28, "over which the Holy Spirit has made you overseers, or bishops." The office of a pastor, bishop, and presbyter, or elder in the church of God is to take the charge, oversight, and care of those souls which the Lord Jesus Christ has committed to them; to feed the flock of God; to watch for their souls (Acts 20:28, Heb. 13:17, 1 Tim. 5:17, 1 Tim. 3:15, Isa. 33:22) ; and to rule, guide, and govern them (by virtue of their commission and authority received from Christ, Matth. 28:18, 19, 20 and Titus 2:15) according to the laws, constitutions, and ordinances of the gospel.

Section 4

The office of episcopacy and presbytery or eldership in the church of God is divine and sacred, but not lordly; 1 Pet. 5:1, 2, 3, *neither over-ruling the clergy*: No bishop, pastor, or presbyter is the master of the house of God, which is the church of the Living God, but a steward (or dispenser) of the mysteries of God, 1 Cor. 4:1, 2. The apostles, bishops, pastors and teachers were fellow elders, 1 Pet. 5:1. "The elders which are among you I exhort, who am a fellow-elder": But they were not all of equal dignity and authority.

Section 5

It does appear (at least I think so, and indeed it is my opinion) that there was (even from the beginning of the gospel of the grace of God) a priority and pre-eminence among the ministers of Christ, approved of God, yea, and appointed by himself in the church, 1 Cor. 12:28, 29. "And God has set some in the church, first apostles, secondarily prophets, thirdly teachers, after that miracles, then gifts of healings, helps, governments, diversities of tongues. Are all apostles? Are all prophets? Are all teachers? Are all workers of miracles?" Christ gave priority, and pre-eminence unto his apostles above the ordinary prophets and evangelists, pastors, and teachers, and all other ministers, Eph. 4:11, 2 Cor. 2:9 and 11:28, 2 Thes. 3:6, The evangelists Timothy and Titus (called bishops in the subscriptions of St. Paul's epistles to them, both in our English Bibles and in the Greek Testament) had authority and pre-eminence above other pastors, teachers, and elders in the Ephesian church and in Crete, 1 Tim. 1:3. "As I besought you to abide still at Ephesus, when I went into Macedonia, that you might charge some that they teach no other doctrine," Titus 1:5, 10, 11, 13 and 2:15 and 3:10, 11. "For this cause left I you in Crete, that you should set in order the things that are wanting, and ordain elders in every city, as I had appointed you. For there are many unruly and vain talkers and deceivers, especially they of the circumcision, whose mouths must be stopped; who subvert whole houses, teaching things which they ought not, for filthy lucre's sake. This witness is true; therefore rebuke them sharply; that they may be found in the faith. These things speak and exhort, and rebuke with all authority. Let no man despise thee. A man that is a heretic, after the first and second admonition, reject; knowing that he that is such is subverted, and sins, being condemned of himself."

Section 6

And the consonant testimonies of the authors, with the general consent of modern divines and Protestant writers of good esteem and approbation, do assent and acknowledge that Timothy and Titus were not only evangelists, but bishops set and fixed by some of the apostles to oversee, order, and govern churches, ordain bishops and presbyters, and to exercise authority over them according to the law, canons, and constitutions of Christ and his apostles given unto them. Walo, called Samasius[5], who

---

5. A learned Protestant who died in 1654.

professedly pleaded for the identity of bishops and presbyters, confessed concerning the Ancients that Chrysostome, Epiphanius, Theophylact, Theodoret[6], and other Greek Commentators have collected out of the words of St. Paul that Titus was verily the bishop of Crete. Jerome has recorded both Timothy and Titus bishops, the one of Ephesus, and the other of Crete, to whom Ambrose, Primasius and Gregory the Great do consent; so do Reverend Beza[7], learned Scultetus[8], Luther, Master Moulin[9], Tossanus[10], Zuinglius[11], Calvin, Dr. Gerard[12], Dr. Reynolds[13], and several others assert and acknowledge that the presbytery had their presbyter (or president) over them in the Apostolical Age, when the community of names of presbyters and bishops remained among them. Such were Timothy and Titus, whom the apostles ordained bishops, 1 Tim. 4:14, 2 Tim. 1:6, and Titus 1:5.... Luther, tom. 1, fol. 309, conclus 13. "As I have ordained you," Calvinus in Titum 1:5.

Section 7

Jesus Christ commanded his servant John the apostle to write a book and send it to the seven churches in Asia, Rev. 1:11. He directed his seven several epistles to the seven several angels of the seven churches beginning thus: "Unto the angel of the church of Ephesus," and so the rest, Chap. 2:1, 8, 12, 18, and chapters 3, 1, 7, 14. And those seven epistles were by those seven angels to be communicated to all the Asian churches, and everyone was called upon (in that epiphonema, at the end of every several epistle): "He that has an ear, let him hear," etc., Rev. 2:7, 11, 17,

---

6. These were early church fathers.

7. He served with Calvin at his Academy in Geneva and when Calvin died he became Geneva's chief pastor and the Academy's leader.

8. a Protestant minister born in Selesia in 1556. He became pastor of the church in Heidelberg in 1598 and attended the Synod of Dort in 1618 defending the reformed faith against the Armenians.

9. Pierre Du Moulin was born in Buhy in 1568. He trained for the ministry in London and Cambridge. In 1592 he moved to the University of Leiden and then in 1598 he returned to France and became a minister of the Huguenot church in Paris and Charenton. He returned to England in 1615 remaining there till 1625.

10. Likely Daniel Tossanus 1541-1602. He helped reestablish reformed protestantism under Frederick III as his court preacher.

11. Zwingli was the leader of the reform movement in Zurich. He died in 1531.

12. Likely the early English Reformer, Thomas Gerrard, who died at the hand of Henry VIII in 1540.

13. John Rainolds (or Reynolds) born in 1549 and died in 1607) was an English academic and churchman who held Puritan views.

29, and 3:6, 13, 22. That is, to hearken, attend, and observe what the Lord Jesus Christ by his Spirit says unto the churches, not to this or that *particular* church *only*, Rev. 2:1, 7, nor to these seven churches *exclusively*, but unto all the churches of saints in all other countries, cities, and places in all the future ages and the world. Dr. Scultetus[14] said, "All the most learned interpreters by angels expound the bishops of the churches, nor can it be otherwise interpreted without violence to the text." As punctually and pertinently speaks Marlorat[15], "Some things (says he) were to be corrected as well in the people, as in the clergy; yet does not Saint John write unto the people, nor yet to the clergy, but to the chief of them, which is the bishop." Dr. Reynolds, in his conference with Hart. chap. 2, devisio 3, said, "Although in the church of Ephesus, there were sundry elders and pastors to guide us, yet among these sundry pastors was there one chief, whom our Saviour called the angel of that church," Apoc. 2:1. And the said doctor telling us of that very time when St. Paul assembled the elders of Ephesus at Miletum, Acts 20:17, 28, chapter 8 distinct 3 said, "One was chosen as chief"—called bishop.

Section 9[16]

Smectym[17], etc., assert that the word "angel," Rev. 2:1, etc. does signify only the presbytery, or the college of elders, pastors, and not the church. And they draw argument from the epistle of Christ to the church in Thyatira, Rev. 2:18, 20, 24. Upon which place Beza thus paraphrased, "Unto you, that is (says he) unto the angel as president; and unto the rest (of the elders, namely the college of presbyters) in Thyatira." And as many as have not the doctrine, that is, have not received this doctrine of Jezebel. But why would Christ have the angel or chief bishop of the church of Thyatira blamed for suffering false teachers in that church to teach and seduce his servants if he was not their president or superintendent who had priority, pre-eminency, and authority above other pastors, teachers, presbyters, or

---

14. Abraham Scultetus was born in 1566 and died 1625. He was a German professor of theology, and the court preacher for the Elector Frederick V of the Palatinate.

15. Augustin Marlorat du Pasquier was born in 1506. He was a French Protestant reformer, who was executed on a treason charge in 1562.

16. There is no section 8. This was probably a mistake made by the printer.

17. Properly Smectymnws. This was the compilation of the first letters of the names of those who wrote a treatise against episcopacy in the seventeenth century. They were Stephen Marshall, Edmund Calamy, Thomas Young, Matthew Newcomen, and William Spurston.

elders called bishops in that church? Consult Beza, Gualter[18], especially Ignatius[19], that holy martyr (who is said to have lived in the days of the apostles, who wrote an epistle to the Ephesians; in which he has plainly and fully distinguished between bishops and presbyters, and towards the end of that epistle, he does exhort them to obey both the bishop and the presbytery with an undivided mind).

Section 10

Polycarp was bishop of Smyrna when St. John wrote that epistle, Rev. 2:8. "Unto the angel of the church of the Smyrnians," said Irenaeus. And who can better inform us than they that lived in the days of the apostles? "Polycarp" (said Irenaeus) "was not only taught by the apostles, and conversed with many that had seen Christ, but also was by the apostles constituted in Asia bishop of the church, which is in Smyrna; Whom we ourselves also did see in our younger age; for he continued long. And being very aged, he most gloriously and nobly suffering martyrdom, departed this life." To this, let me add the testimony, which those brethren of the church of Smyrna who were present at the martyrdom of their bishop Polycarp gave him, as Eusebius, l. 4. Hist. [head] 15. "He was (said his brethren) the most admirable man of our times, an apostolical and prophetical doctor, and bishop of the whole church in Smyrna." Famous and certain is the testimony of Hegesippus[20], in his history of the church, as Eusebius noted to the same purpose. The next and last I shall cite is the testimony of Clement[21], whom St. Paul mentioned among other [of] his fellow labourers, Phil. 4:3.

Section 11

Clement is said by the Ancients to have written an epistle to the church and saints at Corinth, which epistle has the attestation of Irenaeus, who calls it a most substantial epistle to the Corinthians, and of Photius, that styles it an eloquent (or a worthy spoken) epistle. It is also highly commended by Origin, Cyril,

---

18. This is likely Rudolf Gwalther (1519–1586) who was a Reformed pastor who succeeded Heinrich Bullinger as the leader of the Zurich church.

19. Very early church father who was martyred for the faith around 110-15 AD.

20. Hegesippus was born circa 110 and died around 180. He was a historian of the early church who also wrote against the heretical teachings of the Gnostics and Marcion.

21. Polycarp, Clement and Irenaeus were three of the earliest of the early church fathers.

Justin Martyr, St. Jerome[22], and other godly and learned men. Which epistle Mr. Patrick Young says is extant in the King's Library at Oxford.[23] His words in that his epistle are these, "Our apostles knew (said he) by our Lord Jesus Christ that there will be contention about the name of episcopacy; and therefore for this very same cause, having received perfect knowledge, they appointed the foresaid degrees, and gave thereupon a designed order, and list of offices, etc. And it would be no small sin in us (said he) if we should refuse or reject them who have sacredly, and without reproof, undergone the offices of episcopacy," etc. The Magd. Cent. 1, 2, 3 do make mention of such bishops in the churches of God. And all ecclesiastical historians (that I have read) do testify the priority and pre-eminence of bishops.

Section 12

I would not be misunderstood, therefore I will take liberty to tell the reader that this priority, presidence, and pre-eminence of any one bishop above other bishops, pastors, teachers, presbyters, or elders, and ministers of Christ is not any lordly prelacy with coercive power over the conscience or dominion over the faith of God's clergy. For the holy apostles did approve themselves to every man's conscience in the sight of God, 2 Cor. 4:1, 2, not having dominion over their faith, 2 Cor. 1:24. Neither as being lord over God's clergy or heritage, 1 Pet. 5:1, 2, 3. But I mean and intend any one of the bishops, pastors, teachers, presbyters, or elders, who are, or shall by the consent, approbation and choice of the rest be appointed, ordained, and set over them as chief bishop or presbyter of the church in any city and villages adjacent, who for order sake in gospel-government, has priority, pre-eminence, and authority above the rest of the presbyters or bishops of the same church, not alone, *nor without them*, but when convened with them, to act, rule, guide, order and govern with their consent, suffrage, and assistance according to the laws of the Lord Jesus Christ, the constitutions and commandments, the practice and example of his holy apostles, Acts 15:2, 6, 19. 22. Nor should the ministers of Christ strive which of them should be greatest, Luke 22:24, 25, 26. Neither ought any of them to love (and affect) to have pre-eminence among them, as Diotrephes did. 3. Epistle of John, v. 9 (1 Tim. 3:1, 2, 3, 4, Tit. 1:7, 8, 9, 2 Tim. 4:1, 2, 3). But a bishop must be blameless, an example to the flock, vigilant, patient, apt to teach; not covetous,

---

22. All early church Fathers.
23. Patrick Young was a Librarian to King James I for at least the years 1622-23.

not greedy of filthy lucre, and one that rules well in his own house, that he may take care of the church of God; holding fast the faithful Word, etc.

CHAP. III.

[III]. The third work that our Lord Jesus Christ came into this world to do was to institute those gospel-ordinances, in which his churches of saints must worship God in spirit and in truth. When the church is assembled on the first day of the week in some convenient place to worship God, Christ has appointed that first of all prayers, supplications, and thanksgivings be made, 1 Tim. 2:1, 2, 3. "For this is good and acceptable in the sight of God our Saviour." Men having their heads uncovered and women having their faces veiled or covered, 1 Cor. 11:4, 5, 7, 10, 13, reverently kneeling, Psal. 95:6 and Acts 21:5, or decently standing, Luke 18:11, 13. They ought not to sit in prayer-time unless some weakness of body or some bodily infirmity does constrain them. This part of the worship of God ought to be administered by one of the elders of that church, who ought to pray in the Spirit, and to pray with the understanding also, 1 Cor. 14:15.

To pray with the spirit implies two things: First, that the minister has a spiritual gift to pray, Zech. 12:10. Secondly, that he has the Spirit's assistance in praying, Rom. 8:26.

To pray with the understanding is to pray with such words as all the congregation does hear and understand, that they may say "Amen," 1 Cor. 4:16.

After prayer, the teacher ought to read the written Word of God distinctly and give the sense of it by expounding and interpreting the words of that Scripture, that so the people may understand and be instructed or taught to know the will and mind of God in it revealed for their learning and edification as they did, Neh. 8:4, 5, 6, 7, 8. And as Christ himself, and his apostles also did, Luke 4:16, 17, 21, 22 and Acts 28:23. Reading the Holy Scripture is an ordinance of God unto which Christ has promised a gospel blessing, Rev. 1:3 and Col. 4:16.

And then the pastor ought to preach the gospel, and to exhort the people to repent and believe the gospel; to be holy, and to walk in all the commandments and ordinances of the Lord blamelessly; labouring in the Word and doctrine to convert sinners, to edify believers, to convince gainsayers, and to comfort, strengthen, and establish them that believe in Christ. Also, let the prophets speak two or three, and let the rest judge, 1 Cor.

14:29, 31 and Rom. 12:6, 7, 8. "Having then gifts differing according to the grace that is given unto us: Whether prophesy, let us prophesy according to the analogy of faith: or ministry, let us wait on our ministering; or he that teaches, on teaching; or he that exhorts, on exhortation; and he that rules with diligence." The apostles so preached that many believed, Acts 14:1. And it pleased God by the foolishness of preaching to save them that believe, 1 Cor. 1:21.

Our Lord Jesus Christ did command his ministers also to baptize them that do believe in him with water in the name of the Father, Son, and Holy Spirit, Matth. 28:19, 20, Mark 16:15, 16, and John 1:33. Our Lord himself was baptized by John in the river Jordan, Matth. 3:13. "Then came Jesus from Galilee to Jordan unto John, to be baptized of him." Verse 16, "And Jesus, when he was baptized, went up straightaway out of the water." Mark 1:5, 9: "And were all dipped of him in the river Jordan, confessing their sins." We read that both men and women were baptized (when they believed), Acts 8:12. (But we read not in the Holy Scripture of truth that any infants were baptized). They that had received the Holy Spirit were commanded to be baptized with water in the name of the Lord, Acts 10:47, 48. Those men and women are fit subjects of baptism that have received the Spirit of Christ, do believe in Christ, confess their sins, and repent, Acts 2:37-41. The manner of the administration of this gospel-ordinance of baptism was thus practiced in the days of Christ, and of his apostles, that is, the person baptizing and the persons baptized went into the water, Acts 8:38, 39. "And they went down both into the water, both Philip and the eunuch; and he baptized him": that is, Philip dipped the eunuch into the water, and then they came out of the water, v. 39. The Spirit of God has inspired the apostles in writing the Holy Scriptures to use one Greek word for dipping and another for sprinkling. So that if to dip in water be to baptize, to sprinkle with water is to rantize. And the manner of baptizing in water is represented in the Holy Scripture by burying in water and raising up out of the water, Col. 2:12 and Rom. 6:4. By which is also figured forth the believer's fellowship with Jesus Christ in his death and resurrection, Col. 2:12.

Jesus Christ also, before his death, did institute his own supper, Matth. 26:26, 27, 28, and 1 Cor. 11:23, 24, 25, and commanded his disciples to do so, and to do so often in remembrance of him, 1 Cor. 11:25, 26, and as a memorial of his death until he come again, verse 26. In administering this sacred ordinance of the Lord's Supper according to the example of Christ and his disciples, these particular things ought to be observed:

1. The time: the Lord's Supper ought to be administered *ordinarily* on the Lord's Day, that is, the first day of the week, Acts 20:7. On the only day of Sabbaths (it is a Hebraism) and upon the first day of the week, the disciples came together to break bread, etc. And the time of the day was at evening; then Christ administered his supper, Mark 14:17, 22.

2. The minister ought to take the bread, and consecrate it by the Word and prayer, with thanksgiving; and after the bread is so consecrated, he ought to break it in pieces, and give it unto the communicants, expressing the words of Jesus Christ, saying, "Take, eat, this is my body." And after the communicants have eaten the bread, the minister ought to take the cup with wine in it, and in like manner consecrate it by prayer and thanksgiving, and then give it [to] all the communicants, expressing the words of Christ, saying, "Drink you all of this, for this is my blood of the New Testament, which is shed for you, and for many, for the remission of sins," Luke 22:20 and Matth. 26:27, 28. And the minister also having received with them;

3. They all ought to praise God together in singing and hymns; as Christ and his disciples did, Matth. 26:30; Mark 14:26.

Singing is also a gospel ordinance, which ought to be performed by the church as a part of God's public worship, Isa. 52:8. "With the voice together shall they sing." The matter that we are to sing is the Word of God, namely, the psalms, hymns, and spiritual songs contained in the Holy Scriptures, the written Word of God, Col. 3:16. "Let the Word of Christ dwell in you richly in all wisdom," etc. The manner of singing psalms, hymns, and spiritual songs is to sing in meter and measure, with audible voice, as our English manner is.

The psalms, hymns, and spiritual songs in the Book of Psalms were sung in meter and measure [as they that understand the Hebrew tongue know well].

The end of singing is to make melody in your heart to the Lord, Eph. 5:19. Singing with a tunable voice makes melody in our ears and stirs up our pure minds to rejoice in the Lord; but singing with grace in our hearts does make melody to the Lord. Though the voice of the church (espoused to Christ) was sweet and pleasant unto him in the Song of Songs, Cant. 2:14, yet the Spirit acting grace (namely faith, love, and joy) in the hearts of the saints is much more sweet, well-pleasing, and acceptable unto God than their voice in singing psalms, hymns, and spiritual songs to the Lord, Col. 3:16. "Singing with grace in your hearts to the Lord."

Query. Did not some of the saints in the church at Corinth sing other psalms, hymns, and spiritual songs, which they themselves indicted and sang alone by the Spirit with grace in their hearts to the Lord?

Answer. I think some members of that church did compose a psalm upon occasion, 1 Cor. 14:26. And it is my opinion that a minister or member of the church (if he has received a gift of the Spirit to sing) may sing in the church to edification, 1 Cor. 14, 15, yea and ought so to do, 1 Pet. 4:10, 11. But this I say,

First, that those hymns and spiritual songs, which ministers or members of the church do indict and sing, are not psalms; and we are commanded to interact and exhort one another in psalms, and to sing psalms as well as hymns and spiritual songs, Eph. 5:19 and Col. 3:16. And I know that the word "psalms" is interpreted "David's Psalms", the Book of Psalms, and the Psalms of David, Asaph, etc. Search these Scriptures: Acts 1:20; Acts 13:33, 35; Luke 20:42 and 24:44.

Secondly, that those ministers and members of the church cannot affirm, will not assert, that their hymns or spiritual songs are materially the inspiration of the Holy Spirit as the Book of Psalms were; they may sing with the Spirit, and with understanding, unto edification; but the Psalms of David, and of Asaph, and the Song of Songs, which is Solomon, and the hymns of Jesus Christ and his apostles must have the pre-eminence.

Thirdly, although I have also, *through the riches of free grace*, received the Holy Spirit, and have learned in some measure what it is to pray in the Spirit and to pray with understanding; also to sing in the Spirit, and to sing with understanding, yet I rather choose to sing in the church those psalms, hymns, and spiritual songs, which are contained in the Holy Scripture, than any of my own inditing; for these reasons, because,

First, although I should be assisted by the Holy Spirit of God to indite an hymn, or a spiritual song, and sing it in the church with grace in my heart, and so make melody to the Lord and edify the church, yet some matter of it may be doubtful to some persons that hear me sing it; if that matter be prophetical, or mysterious, and they understand it not; or if there should be any words or sentences in it expressed, which are not sound words. (For I pretend not to sing by the Spirit, otherwise than to pray by the Spirit, that is, as the Spirit helps my infirmities) which I may be subject to, and so through my infirmity, may err, or utter some unsound words.

Secondly, when I sing a psalm, hymn, or spiritual song, which is written in the Holy Scripture of truth, none but an atheist or an atheistical spirit will object against the matter of it, for those psalms, hymns, and spiritual songs were given by inspiration of God and revelation of the Holy Spirit, and I do only translate them into English meter and measure out of the Hebrew text that the church may sing them together with their voice making melody to the Lord by singing praises to the Lord with grace in their hearts.

Thirdly, the church cannot practise the Lord's command given by the apostles to those two churches, and all other churches of saints, though they sing hymns and spiritual songs, unless they also sing psalms, which are by the same Holy Spirit that inspired David to indite them expounded and interpreted, The Book of Psalms and The Psalms of David, etc., as has been proved by those Scriptures aforecited, which the reader is humbly deferred to search.

CHAP. IV.

Lastly, the Lord Jesus Christ having finished the work for which he came into this world, being to leave the world and return to heaven whence he came, Eph. 4:9, 10, did, at the request of his disciples, Matth. 24:3, 4, foretell them the signs of his second coming and of the end of this world. The ending time of this world, and the second coming of Christ, have some evident signs set upon them. And God has caused those signs to be recorded and written in the Holy Scripture of truth. First, to strengthen the faith of his people, that they might upon Scripture ground believe that this world shall have an end, and that the Lord Jesus Christ will come again from heaven in power and great glory; and secondly, to leave all unbelievers without excuse.

One sign of the ending time of this world is the last and greatest apostasy of professors and the Laodicean lukewarmness of ministers and members in the churches of Christ.

The first and great apostasy, which the apostle foretold, was a departing from the faith of the gospel, which Christ and his apostles had preached, and which the churches, their ministers and members embraced and professed, I Tim. 4:1, 3. "Now the Spirit speaks expressly that, in the latter times, some shall depart from the faith, giving heed to seducing spirits, and doctrines of devils; Forbidding to marry, and commanding to abstain from meats, which God has created to be received with thanksgiving of them which believe and know the truth." Which apostasy happened in the fourth century (as ecclesiastical historians tell us) when the church at Rome and other churches, their bishops, presbyters, and members departed from the faith and fell away from the sound doctrine, pure worship, and true discipline of the gospel. And then the apocalyptical Beast, the pope, and the great whore, Mystery Babylon the Great, that mother of harlots, and the false prophets, those Roman croaking frogs, did begin to rise, who afterwards greatly increased in the ten European kingdoms. See my book entitled *Mystery Babylon Unveiled*, printed 1679.

But the last and greatest apostasy noted in the Holy Scripture of truth is both in faith and manners by men of corrupt minds and carnal principles, having the form of godliness, but denying the power of it, 2 Tim. 3:1, 2, 3, 4, 5. "This know also, that in the last days, perilous times shall come. For men shall be lovers of their own selves, covetous, boasters, proud, blasphemers, disobedient to parents, unthankful, unholy, without natural affections, truce breakers, false accusers, incontinent, fierce despisers of those that are good, traitors, heady, high minded, lovers of pleasures more than lovers of God, having a form of godliness, but denying the power of it; from such turn away." The particle in v. 1, which is "likewise" or "besides," directs us to look back to the former epistle, chapter 4, v. 1, 2, 3, before-mentioned, which is the time of the first apostasy in the latter days, v. 1. But here the apostle speaks of the times of the last apostasy, v. 1. "That in the last days," etc. The great inquiry now will be, "What days the apostles meant here?" I answer: my opinion concerning this is, that, by the last days here, we are to understand those three prophetical days and a half of the 1260 days that Christ's two witnesses shall prophesy in sackcloth, Rev. 11:3, 7-12; "And I will give power unto my two witnesses, and they shall prophesy a thousand two hundred and threescore days clothed in sackcloth. And when they shall have finished their testimony, the Beast that ascended out of the bottomless pit shall make war against them, and shall overcome them, and kill them: And their dead bodies shall lie in the street of the great city, which spiritually is called Sodom and Egypt, where also our Lord was crucified. And they of the people and kindreds, and tongues, and nations, shall see their dead bodies three days and a half, and shall not suffer their dead bodies to be put in graves. And they that dwell upon the earth shall rejoice over them, and make merry, and shall send gifts one to another, because these two prophets tormented them that dwelt on the earth. And after three days and a half, the spirit of life from God entered into them. And they stood upon their feet, and great fear fell upon them which saw them." Read my exposition of the eleventh chapter of the Revelation, published in 1679. These days of slaying the witnesses (are those last days) and will be perilous times: for

1. The Roman Beast will make war against the witnesses, and overcome them, and kill them, Rev. 11:7.

2. They will be perilous, hard, difficult, dangerous, grievous, and troublesome times or days, because the rights, liberties, and freedoms of the people will be infringed, and taken from them; and such temptations and snares will be laid by which men's liberties, lives, and estates shall be in great hazard and danger, Matth. 24:21 and Luke 21:22, 26, 27.

3. These last days will be so full of amazing distractions, disturbances, and tribulations, that wise men shall be at their wits' end, not knowing what to do nor what course to take for their own safety. And many eminent professors of religion will fall off from their former principles and practice, and be drawn aside to follow the pernicious ways of ungodly men, and so fall in with the sins of those last days here mentioned, 2 Tim. 3:1, 2, 3, 4, "Lovers of their own selves." Self-love is the root of apostasy, both political and ecclesiastical. When men of name began to love themselves more than their most solemn oaths, vows, and covenants, more than truth and righteousness, more than the good laws of the nations, and the just liberties and rights of the people, then began the last and greatest political apostasy. And when men of eminency for religion began to love themselves more than the ways and worship of God, more than the churches and saints of God, more than Jesus Christ the only begotten Son of God, then began the ecclesiastical apostasy of those last days. This is one sign that Christ gave his disciples of the ending time of this world, Matth. 24:3, 4, 12. "And as he sat upon the Mount of Olives, the disciples came unto him privately, saying, 'Tell us how shall these things be, and what shall be the sign of your coming, and of the end of this world.' And Jesus answered, and said unto them, 'Take heed that no man deceive you. And because iniquity shall abound, the love of many shall wax cold.'" Covetous, Danaeus[24] in loc. said, *hic a Paulo dicitur, qui five aurum, five argenium, five agros-five quaslibet alias opes ardenter expetit and vitiose.* The Greek word is often rendered *studium pecuniae,* the desire of money. And "the love of money," says the apostle, 1 Tim. 6:10, "is the root of all evil, which while some

---

24. Unknown.

have coveted after, they have erred from the faith," etc. How much of the Spirit of the world and of the things of this world is crept into the hearts of many professors and church members in these last days, who consider not the testimony of the apostle against them, 1 John 2:15. "If any man love the world, the love of the Father is not in him." Covetousness is idolatry, Col. 3:5. Another character of those apostates of the last days is pride. Proud so are those covetous self-loving professors and church members in these evil days: witness the periwigs and petticoats of London professors and sermon hearers in the city. "Does not even nature itself teach you, that if a man have long hair, it is a shame unto him," 1 Cor. 11:14. Yea, it is a shame *indeed* for men professing godliness to wear such long periwigs of women's hair, as some men do. What an abomination is it unto the Lord, to see a hoary head covered with long hair (that has been cut off from a whores' head) when he is praying to God and worshipping the all-seeing God, Heb. 4:13. "All things are naked and opened unto the eyes of him with whom we have to do." And does not the Holy Scripture teach women professing godliness, when they come to pray and worship God, to adorn themselves in modest apparel with shamefacedness and sobriety, not with broidered hair or costly array? 1 Tim. 2:8, 9, 10, 11, 12 and 1 Pet. 3:3, 4, 5, 6. And more especially in days of humiliation and tribulation (even at such a time as this, which is indeed a perilous time. Read Exod. 33:4, 5, 6, 7 and Isa. 3:16-24). Another character of those apostasies of the last days is truce-breakers, covenant-breakers, such as do break their oaths, vows, promises, and engagements. Oh, how guilty have some courtiers, counsellors, soldiers, mariners, citizens, professors, and church-members been of those heinous sins! Read the *Army Remonstrance 1648* and that book entitled *A Looking Glass for the Army*, in which book you may find collected the vows, promises, and covenants that those sword-bearing professors made and several of them broke. To say nothing of the Scots and English covenants so solemnly taken in their parish churches. Many professors have broken God's covenant, as Israel did, Jer. 31:23. "Which my covenant they broke." Another character of the apostasies of the last days is false accusers, calumniators, devils incarnate; such are those false witnesses that rise up against men and do falsely accuse them, Psal. 35:11. And when many false witnesses do not agree in their testimony, *which men suborned*, at last comes other false witnesses, and then the sentence of death is given and afterwards executed. Thus they dealt with the Lord of life, and put him to death, Matth. 26:59, 60, and with Stephen, Acts 6:11,

12, 13, and stoned him to death. Another character of the apostasies of the last days is this: lovers of pleasures more than lovers of God. Who does this apply to more than rich professors for fine clothes, sumptuous houses, delicate fare, costly furniture, and court fashions, in which they have exceeded since the burning of the city[25]; besides other vain pleasures in which they have delighted themselves more than in the ways of God and godliness? Amos 6:1. "Woe to them that are secure in Zion," verse 3. "You that put far away the evil day," verse 4. "That lie upon beds of ivory," verse 5. "That chant to the sound of the viol," verse 6. "That drink wine in bowls—but they are not grieved for the affliction of Joseph." The last character of these apostates in the last days, which is a sign of the ending time of this evil world, is this, namely, *having a form of godliness, but denying the power of it*. To have a form of godliness is to hold on in religious duties, and gospel ordinances, as praying in their families, often hearing sermons, attending days of public fasting and of thanksgiving; also frequently assembling with the separated congregations of saints, and in them partake of all gospel-administrations; such are sinners in Zion and hypocrites (like them, Isa. 33:14) yet are lovers of themselves and lovers of pleasures more than God, Christ, godliness, and the poor afflicted children of God: proud professors, covetous church-members, covenant-breakers, and false accusers, denying the power of godliness. For though these apostates profess they know God, yet in works they deny him, Tit. 1:16. Read Isa. 1:11, 12, 13, 14, 15, and Isa. 6:2, 3, 4. I am not against the true form of godliness, that is to say, church-fellowship, and gospel order, and the worship of God in Spirit and in truth, according to the contributions of Jesus Christ and his apostles. But I thus speak and write to open and expound the words of this prophecy.

Another sign of the ending time of this world is the abounding of iniquity among the profane persons of the world, Matth. 24:3, 12, "'Tell us what shall be the sign of your coming, and of the end of the world?' and Jesus answered and said unto them, 'Iniquity shall abound.'" The apostle also tells us, 1 John 5:19, "The whole world lies in wickedness." Ungodliness was the destruction of the old world, Gen. 6:5, 6, 7. "And God saw that the wickedness of man was great in the earth," verse 5. "And the Lord said, 'I will destroy man—from the face of the earth,'" verse 7. The destruction of the old world was by the flood, but the desolation of the world that now is shall be by fire, 2 Pet.

---

25. The Great Fire of London in 1666.

3:6, 7. "The earth also, and the works that are in it shall be burnt up." By iniquity we are to understand those immoralities and abominable wickednesses that are committed and practised by ungodly men, who declare their sins as Sodom and boast of their abominations. Now, reader, consider how does iniquity abound, that is, adultery, that has gotten a whore's forehead, which is not ashamed of that abomination. Also, profane and false swearing, which is an abomination to the Lord, who hates profane and false oaths: and drunkenness, which so unmans men and so effeminates them that they are thus fit for nothing but sinfulness, wantonness, lasciviousness, and all manner of wickedness. Likewise oppression, violence, robbery, injustice, bribery, and all sorts of unrighteousness. Lastly, persecution, imprisonment, and banishment for preaching the Lord Jesus Christ and practicing the ordinances of the gospel. Do not these iniquities abound in our days? I think that the inhabitants of this nation do abound in these iniquities, much more than in former ages.

Another sign of the ending time of this world is that great tribulation, which our blessed Saviour spoke of, Matth. 24:21, 29, 30. This is that hour of temptation, which Christ said shall come upon all the world, Rev. 3:10, 11. This day of tribulation will be a time of trouble; such as never was since there was a nation, even to that same time, Dan. 12:1-4. "Shut up the words, and seal the book even to the time of the end." The tribulation of the people of God will be the war that the Roman Beast will make against Christ's two prophetical witnesses, in which he shall overcome them and kill them, Rev. 11:7. See my exposition of that chapter and verse, printed 1679. And the tribulation of the Roman Beast, the great whore, and the false prophet, will be the seven vials of the last plagues of God Almighty, which shall be poured forth upon Mystery Babylon the great, Rev. 16:17, 18, 29, 21, 21. "And the seventh angel poured out his vial into the air, and there came a great voice out of the temple of heaven from the throne, saying, 'It is done.' And there were voices, and thunders, and lightnings. And there was a great earthquake, such as was not since men were upon the earth, so mighty an earthquake, and so great. And the great city was divided into three parts, and the cities of the nations fell, and great Babylon came in remembrance before God, to give unto her the cup of the wine of the fierceness of his wrath. And every island fled away, and the mountains were not found. And there fell upon men a great hail out of heaven, every stone about the weight of a talent, and men blasphemed God because of the plague of the hail, for the plague of it was exceeding great." And immediately after the tribulation of these days, they shall see the Son of Man coming in the clouds of heaven with power and great glory, Matth. 24:29, 30. Then will Christ take unto him his great power and reign; he will create new heavens and a new earth, in which dwells righteousness, Isa. 65:17 and 66:22, 2 Pet. 3:13, and Rev. 21:2-5. "And he that sat upon the throne said, 'Behold, I make all things new.'" Now this new creation is the world to come.

CHAP. V.

Of Separation

Section 1

God did separate his ancient people the Jews from all other people in the world to be his peculiar people, to worship him according to his institutions and commandments, Levit. 20:24, 26. And God has commanded the believing Gentiles to be separated from idolaters, and unbelievers, or infidels, and to have no communion or fellowship with them in any false worship, 2 Cor. 6:14-18.

Section 2

But though believers may be and ought to abide separated from the worship and worshippers of idols in their temples (2 Cor. 6:16,17), and from the worship of the unbelieving Jews in their synagogues (Acts 19:8, 9); and also from the worship and worshippers of the Beast or his image (Rev. 14:9,10, & 20, 4), and from the assemblies of all false worshippers (Rev. 14:9, 10 and 20:4), and from all false worship, yet sanctified believers ought not to separate themselves from the true churches of God, and of his saints, that worship him in spirit and in truth, and walk in the faith and order of the gospel, according to the rule of the written Word of God, so far as they have attained.

Section 3

The most pure churches of saints on earth are subject to mixture. Some false brethren may creep into a church of Christ unawares (Gal. 2:4), and some false teachers, too (2 Tim. 3:1, 2, 3, 4, 5, 8). Men of corrupt minds and corrupt manners also (2 Cor. 2:17). And there may be some errors in doctrine, and some evils in conversation among them; as there was among some of the churches of Christ in Asia, in the apostles' time (Rev. 2:14, 15, 20, 24). But yet believers ought not to separate themselves from those churches of saints, of which they are members, for those errors in doctrine, or evils in conversations, until they have first, faithfully and orderly, born their testimony against them. Secondly, until they have humbly entreated the church, and the ministers of it, to reform those things that are amiss among them, and thirdly, until the church, and the ministers in it, do utterly refuse to reform those errors in doctrines, and those evils in conversation among them.

Section 4

The minsters and members of the churches of God ought to imitate Christ in this matter and to follow his steps. Our Lord Jesus Christ did see many things amiss in some of the churches in Asia, namely, unsound doctrines and corrupt manners; that is, the doctrine and deeds of the Nicolaitans, which Christ hated, etc. But notwithstanding, Christ did not presently forsake those churches, nor did he command any of the ministers or members of it to separate themselves from them; neither did Christ blame any believers that were found in their judgements and holy in their conversations for holding communion with those churches. But Jesus Christ did, first, bear his testimony against those errors in doctrines, and corruptions in conversation. Secondly, Christ called upon the church and angel to repent, and reform what was amiss. And thirdly, Christ gave them space to repent, and waited for their amendment before he did forsake them. Read the second and third chapters of the Revelation. And therefore I conclude that none of the ministers nor members of any true church of God ought to separate themselves from the church nor ought they to forsake the assembling of themselves with the church, nor absent themselves from any part of the true worship of God, nor turn their back on any gospel ordinance of Christ in the church, because of offence against any member or minister in the church. But they ought to bear, and have patience, and to wait upon Christ and his church, until such offenders are *orderly* proceeded against, and those offences are reformed or removed by the laws of God's house. Or else, until the candlestick be removed out of its place for suffering those errors in doctrine, or corruptions in manners and conversation; and for adding impenitency unto such impiety and iniquity suffered and indulged in the church by the ministers in it, and by the members of it, to the dishonour of God, the scandal of the gospel, and the great offence and grief of the godly who have walked orderly, and have not defiled their garments, but have watched and kept themselves unspotted of the world, and uncorrupted with those evils in the church; which would not be healed, and therefore ought to be forsaken and separated from by the faithful ministers of Christ, and all the holy people of God. Seeing, then, that the ending time of this evil world will be so perilous, and a day of so great tribulation, I do entreat both unconverted sinners and sanctified believers to suffer a word of exhortation. I do therefore exhort unconverted sinners, upon whom the end of this world is coming by death or dissolution, that you would come to Christ. Believe in Jesus Christ, and repent of your sins.

First, I exhort you to come to Christ, for there is not salvation in any other, Acts 4:12. If you will not come to Christ while you live, you will certainly go to Hell when you die, Psal. 9:17.

Some poor sinner haply will say, "Alas! I am a vile sinful sinner; I am unworthy, may I presume to come unto Christ?" Yes, Jesus Christ who came into the world to save the chiefest of sinners does invite all that will to come unto him, Isa. 55:1, 2, 3, and Rev. 22:17. "But if I do come unto Christ, will he not refuse me, and reject me and cast me off?" No! John 6:37. "Him that comes unto me, I will in no wise cast out." Some poor lost sinner may haply say, "Indeed, I see a great need of Christ to justify me, and to sanctify me, and to save me, but I know not how to come to Christ, I cannot come to Christ, what shall I do?" I answer, "It is true, no man can come to Christ, except the Father draw him, John 6:44, but God the Father does draw sinners unto Christ with his cords of love," Jer. 31:3. "Yea, I have loved you with an everlasting love; therefore, with lovingkindness have I drawn you." Though you cannot come to Christ, yet know that the Lord Jesus Christ can, and will come to you, and teach you to go to him, as he did Ephraim, Hos. 11:3, 4. The danger is not in your own inability, that you cannot come to Christ, accept of Christ, and take Christ upon gospel-terms of free grace; but your soul's danger lies in your own unwillingness. You will not come to Christ; this Jesus Christ complained of, John 5:40. "But you will not come to me, that you might have life." "Ah! Woe is me," says the poor lost sinner, "If I were so deeply humbled for my sin; if I had a soft, broken, penitent heart; if I could get victory over my corruptions, then I should be willing to come to Christ for pardon, and for salvation, but these things hinder me, and discourage me from coming to Christ; I am ashamed to come; I am afraid to come; I confess I am unwilling to come." Yet know, God and Christ is willing that you should come, Matth. 11:28. And ere long, the day of God's power will come upon you;

and then you will be willing, Psal. 110:3. "Your people shall be willing in the day of your power."

Secondly, I exhort you to believe in Christ. When the jailor asked Paul and Silas, and said, "Sirs, what must I do to be saved?" They said, "Believe on the Lord Jesus Christ, and you shall be saved," Acts 16:30, 31. This is that glad tidings of the gospel, which Christ has commanded and commissioned his ministers to preach unto every creature, Mark 16:15, 16. "He that believes shall be saved, but he that believes not shall be damned." There is an absolute necessity of believing in Jesus Christ unto salvation; for "without faith it is impossible to please God," Heb. 11:6. "Alas!" says a poor sinner, I cannot believe, I know not how to believe; what shall I do to believe? I answer, "Faith is not of ourselves, it is not of works, but it is the gift of God," Eph. 2:8, 9, 10. The faith of the operation of God, Col. 2:12. It is the exceeding greatness of his mighty power, Eph. 1:19, 20. The same almighty power of God, that raised Jesus Christ from the dead, must raise the soul of a sinner from the death of sin unto the life of righteousness. The soul being dead in trespasses and sins must be quickened together with Christ and raised together with Christ, Eph. 2:5, 6.

Thirdly, I exhort you to repent of your sins. Repentance is also the gift of God, Acts 11:18. "Then has God also to the Gentiles granted repentance unto life." Evangelical repentance is a godly sorrow for sin, or a sorrowing for sin after a godly manner, 2 Cor. 7:9, 10. "For godly sorrow works repentance to salvation," etc., which gospel repentances consists of confession of sin to God, contrition, and mourning for sins before God, and turning from sins unto God with our whole heart, and with our whole man, in spirit, soul, and body.

And I do exhort sanctified believers to prepare themselves to leave the world and to enjoy the world to come. Noah did prepare himself, all the time he was building the ark, by being a just and perfect man, and walking with God, Gen. 6:9, for the ending time of this world draws near. And the end of our natural life is to us the end of this world. And that we may be prepared, we ought to die daily to sin, to self, and to this evil world; And we must live to God, live God in Christ Jesus, Titus 2:11, 12, 13, 14. "For the grace of God that brings salvation has appeared to all men, teaching us that denying ungodliness, and worldly lusts, we should live soberly, righteously, and godly in this present world; looking for that blessed hope, and the glorious appearing of the great God, and our Saviour Jesus Christ, who gave himself for us, that he might redeem us from all iniquity, and purify unto himself a peculiar people, zealous of good works."

The World to Come
CHAP. I.

In which the general position is propounded, proved, and explained.

1. The Position Propounded.

There is a world to come, in which will be the new heavens, a new earth, and the new Jerusalem; also the kingdom of Christ and his saints; the resurrection of the dead, and the eternal judgement, which the world to come will begin when the Lord Jesus Christ shall come again from heaven.

2. The Position Proved.

The Holy Scripture of truth does testify,

1. That there is a world to come, Matth. 12:32—"But whoever speaks against the Holy Spirit, it shall not be forgiven him, neither in this world, neither in the world to come," Eph. 1:20, 21. "Not only in this world, but also in that which is to come." And Heb. 2:5. "For unto the angels has he not put in subjection that world, even that to come?"

2. That then the Lord Jesus Christ will come again from heaven, Phil. 3:20. "For our conversation is in heaven, from whence also we look for the Saviour, the Lord Jesus Christ," Heb. 9:28. "And to them that look for him shall he appear the second time," etc., 1 Thes. 3:13, "At the coming of our Lord Jesus Christ with all his saints."

3. That then there will be the new heavens, and a new earth, and the new Jerusalem, yea, and all things new, Isa. 65:17. "I create new heavens and a new earth," 2 Pet. 3:13. "We, according to his promise, look for new heavens, and a new earth," etc. Rev. 21:1, 2. "And I saw a new heaven, and a new earth"; "And I, John, saw the holy city, the new Jerusalem coming down from God, out of heaven," etc. And Heb. 12:22, 23, 24—the heavenly Jerusalem. [26]

4. That the Lord Jesus Christ and his saints shall have a kingdom and shall reign on earth. Dan. 7:13, 14, and 27. "And there was given to him a kingdom," Zech. 14:9. "And the Lord shall be king of all the earth," Dan. 7:27. "And the kingdom, and dominion, and the greatness of the kingdom under the whole heaven shall be

---

[26]. Notice that the new heavens and earth and the reign of Christ and his saints precedes the resurrection of the dead and the day of judgment. This is his in agreement with his teaching in *The Parable of the Kingdom of Heaven expounded* written seven years earlier. See final chapter for Knollys's eschatology.

given to the people of the saints of the Most High," etc. Rev. 5:9, 10. "And you have made us unto our God kings and priests, and we shall reign on earth." Also Rev. 11:15 and 20:4. "And they lived and reigned with Christ a thousand years."

5. That then there shall be a resurrection from the dead, 1 Thes. 4:16. "And the dead in Christ shall rise first," Rev. 20:5, 6. "And the rest of the dead lived not again until the thousand years were finished," 1 Cor. 15:21, 22, 23, 51, 52. "And the dead shall be raised incorruptible," etc.

6. That then shall be the last and eternal judgement, Rom. 14:10 and 2 Cor. 5:10. "For we must all appear before the judgment seat of Christ." And Acts 17:31, Rom. 2:16, and 2 Tim. 4:1. "Who shall judge the quick and the dead at his appearing, and his kingdom," 1 Pet. 4:5. "Ready to judge the quick and the dead," Eccles. 12:14. "God shall bring every work into judgement, with every secret thing," etc., Rom. 2:16 and Matth. 12:36, called the eternal judgement, Heb. 6:2.

So then, without all controversy, or any modest contradiction, we have the testimony of Christ, his apostles, and his prophets recorded in the Holy Scripture of truth for the full confirmation of our general position.

3. The Position Explained.

[A.] In explaining our general position, I shall begin with the first branch of it already proved; namely

"That there is a world to come," in which will be the new heavens, and a new earth, and the new Jerusalem. By the world to come, we are to understand that which the apostle calls "That uninhabited world, [even] that to come," Heb. 2:5. The apostle Peter tells us that the old world being overflowed with water, perished, and the world that now is (even this present evil world) is received unto fire against the day of judgement, etc., 2 Pet. 3:6, 7. But there will come another world after the world that now is, called the world to come, in contradistinction unto this world, Eph. 1:21. This world is distinguished from that world by Christ himself, Luke 20:34, 35, 36, 37. The world to come will be a new creation, "then Christ will make all things new," Rev. 21:5. He will create new heavens, and a new earth, and a new Jerusalem, Isa. 65:17. When St. John had seen [in his vision] the new heaven and a new earth, Rev. 21:1, 2, he saw the new Jerusalem coming down from God out of heaven; and verse 5, "He that sate upon the throne said, 'Behold, I make all things new.'" This new creation will bear some resemblance unto the first creation; in respect of matter, manner, parts, and end of it.

The matter out of which the Lord Jesus Christ will create the world to come, of which we treat, is a mere chaos, namely the confusion and desolation of this present evil world. All things will be in a confused and desolate condition; toward the end of this world will be perilous times, 2 Tim. 3:1. "In the last days, perilous times shall come." And great tribulation, such as never was, Matth. 24:21. Yea, and most wicked abomination; the whole world lying in wickedness, 1 John 5:19, and behold then (*even then*) will the Lord Jesus Christ appear, Matth. 24:29, 30. And he will come, and restore all things. "For then will be the times of the restitution of all things," Acts 3:21, and then will Christ restore our judges as at the first, Isa. 1:26, 27. He will make our oppressors peace, and our exactors righteousness, Isa. 60:17. "Then the wolf and the lamb shall feed together. 'They shall not hurt nor destroy in all my holy mountain,'" says the Lord, Isa. 65:25.

The manner of the new creation will be in an instant, as the first creation was: God spoke the word, and it was done; "He commanded, and they were created," Psal. 148:5. "God said, 'Let there be light,' and there was light," Gen 1:3 and Isa. 66:8. "Who has heard such a thing? Who has seen such things? Shall the earth be made to bring forth in one day?" (They are created now, and not from the beginning, Isa. 48:6, 7). "Or shall a nation be born at once? For as soon as Zion travailed, she brought forth her children." And so will the whole new creation, there will be a restitution of all things and all things will be all of a sudden made new, Rev. 21:5.

The parts of the new creation of the world to come, are,

[F]irst, the new heavens and the new earth, in which dwells righteousness, 2 Pet. 3:13, by which we are to understand that new state and frame of government here on earth, which the Lord Jesus Christ, the King of Kings, and King of Nations, will constitute and command his saints to execute in all his dominions and kingdoms under the whole heaven, Dan. 7:13, 14, 27 and Isa. 9:6, 7.

Secondly, the new Jerusalem, that heavenly Jerusalem, Heb. 12:22, 23, 24, called the general assembly, and the church of the firstborn, written in heaven, etc., by which we are to understand that glorious state of the church of God on earth, which will be in that day when God will glorify the house of his glory, Isa. 60:1, 2, 7, 13, 19, 24, which Christ shall present unto himself a glorious church, not having spot or wrinkle nor any such thing, Eph.

5:27, but "holy and without blemish," called the Lamb's wife, Rev. 21:9, 10, 11, "prepared as a bride adorned for her husband," v. 2. In this holy city, the heavenly new Jerusalem, shall the pure worship of God be celebrated, and his sacred ordinances shall be administered according to his divine institutions; and his spiritual gifts shall again be given unto his saints for the glory of his holy name and for the conversion of the nations that shall be saved, Isa. 60:1, 2, 3, 4, 5. The Gentiles shall come to your light; "The abundance of the sea shall be converted unto you." And Rev. 21:10, 23, 24. "And the nations of them which are saved, shall walk in the light of it," etc.

Thirdly, the renewed creatures, whose earnest expectation waits for the manifestation of the sons of God, Rom. 8:23. "And not only they, but ourselves also, which have the first fruits of the Spirit, even we ourselves groan within ourselves, waiting for the adoption, that is, the redemption of our body."

The end of the new creation in the world to come is,

[F]irst, to make all things very good, as God did in the first creation, Gen. 1:31. "And God saw everything that he had made, and behold it was very good." So the Lord Jesus Christ will create all things new and make everything very good in the world to come. In which will be the times of the restitution of all things, which God has spoken by the mouth of all his holy prophets since the world began, Acts 3:19, 20, 21.

Secondly, to glorify himself and to make his church glorious, Isa. 28:5 and 62:3. "In that day shall the Lord of hosts be for a crown of glory, and for a diadem of beauty unto the residue of his people. You shall also be a crown of glory in the hand of the Lord and a royal diadem in the hand of your God," Isa. 60:1, 2, 3, 7, 9, 13, 19, 22. "I, the Lord, will hasten it in his time."

[B.] The second branch of our general position, which has also been proved, is this: that the Lord Jesus Christ shall appear the second time; which is now to be explained.[27] The second coming of Christ from heaven is often asserted by the prophets and apostles, and confirmed by the testimony of Christ himself, Rev. 22:7. "I come quickly," verse 12, "Behold, I come quickly," and verse 26, "Surely I come quickly." "Amen, even so, come Lord Jesus," Zech. 14:5. "And the Lord my God shall come, and all the

---

27. This is to be understood as his second coming at the beginning of the 1000 year reign when he comes personally in his saints. Not his coming at the end of the 1000 years when he comes personally and visibly and the general resurrection of the saints and judgment day follow.

saints with him." Also 1 Thes. 3:13, "At the coming of our Lord Jesus Christ, with all his saints." These Scriptures, and those also beforementioned for proof of this branch of our position, namely Phil. 3:20 and Heb. 9:28, do testify that our Lord Jesus Christ will certainly, suddenly, and visibly appear the second time, and come from heaven upon the earth in his own person. This Job believed, and therefore did he speak, Job 19:25, "For I know that my Redeemer lives. And he shall stand in the last of time or day upon the earth." Read verses 26, 27, Heb. 10:37. "Yet a little while and he that shall come, will come, and will not tarry." Acts 1:11, "This self same Jesus, which is taken up from you into heaven, shall so come in like manner, as you have seen him go into heaven." As Christ ascended into heaven in his own person; so he shall likewise descend from heaven in his own person, Matth. 24:27. "As the lightning comes out of the east, and shines unto the west, so shall also the coming of the Son of Man be, so visible," Rev. 1:7. "Behold he comes with clouds, and every eye shall see him." And 1 Thes. 4:13, 14-18. "The Lord himself shall descend from heaven," etc. "To them that look for him, he shall appear the second time without sin unto salvation."

Now the principal things to be explained in this branch or part of our general position are three: namely, 1. the manner, 2. the time, and 3. the ends of Christ's coming.

First, touching the manner of Christ's second personal coming from heaven, it is testified, Matth. 16:27, "that the Son of Man shall come in the glory of his Father." The glory of the Father is the highest and most heavenly glory, called the excellent glory, 2 Pet. 1:16, 17, 18. "When we made known unto you the power and coming of the Lord Jesus Christ. For he received from God the Father, honour and glory—from the excellent glory," which was but a glimpse of that excellent glory of the Father, which Christ shall come in, attended with all his holy angels and glorified saints from heaven, and met in the air by all the changed saints then living on earth, Jude v. 14. "Behold, the Lord comes with ten thousand of his saints, and ten thousand times ten thousand, and thousands of thousands of angels, saying with a loud voice, 'Worthy is the Lamb (that was slain) to receive power, and honour, and glory,'" Rev. 5:11, 12, and 2 Thes. 1:7-10. "When the Lord Jesus Christ shall be revealed from heaven with his mighty angels at the coming of our Lord Jesus Christ with all his saints," 1 Thes. 3:16 and 1 Thes. 4:17, 18, "Then we which are alive and remain (unto the coming of the Lord, verse 5) shall be caught up together with them in the clouds, to meet the Lord in the air, and so shall we ever be with the Lord." Read Luke 21:17, Mark 13:16, and Matth. 24:30.

Secondly, touching the time of Christ's second personal coming from heaven. Though of that day and that hour (when Christ shall come) knows no man, no not the angels of heaven, nor the Son of Man, but the Father only, Mark 13:26, 32. Yet there are some signs of Christ's second coming recorded in the Scripture of truth; by which we may know that it is near, even at the door. The disciples of Christ asked him, "What shall be the sign of Your coming?" Matth. 24:3, to whom Christ gave this for a sign; verse 37, 38, 39. "But as the days of Noah were, so shall also the coming of the Son of Man be." And Luke 17:28, 29, 30. "Likewise also as it was in the days of Lot, even thus shall it be in the day when the Son of Man is revealed."

It will be so with the men of this world as it was with the men of the old world, which God destroyed with water. Then the wicked ones of that generation were very ungodly, Gen. 6:5. "And God saw that the wickedness of man was great in the earth," etc. And Christ told his disciples, Matth. 24:12, "that iniquity shall abound," a little before his second coming, verse 30. And it will be so with the men and women of these cities as it was with those citizens of Sodom and Gomorrah, whose cities were burned.

Another sign of Christ's second coming is a great apostate both in the doctrine and worship of the gospel. This sign of Christ's second coming, the apostle Paul foretold, 2 Thes. 2:1, 2, 3. "Now we beseech you, brethren, by the coming of our Lord Jesus Christ,—Let no man deceive you; for that day shall not come, except there come a falling away first." An apostate first from the doctrine of the gospel, especially faith and love, 1 Tim. 4:1, 2, 3. "Now the Spirit speaks expressly, that in the latter days some shall depart from the faith," etc. And Christ says, Matth. 24:3, 12, "The love of many shall wax cold" before his second coming from heaven, verse 30. Some teachers made the law of the Ten Commandments a doctrine of faith in Christ, affirming that those ten words are a covenant of grace. Other preachers make the gospel of the grace of God a doctrine and covenant of works, teaching justification by works, and salvation by works, holding freewill, and falling away. And many there are of whom the apostle Peter prophesied, 2 Pet. 2:1, 2, "False teachers, who privily shall bring in damnable heresies, even denying the Lord that bought them," etc. And 2 Pet. 3:3, 4, "That there shall come in the last days, scoffers, walking after their own lusts, and saying, 'Where is the promise of his coming?'" etc. Insomuch that our Saviour said, Luke 18:8, "When the Son of Man comes, shall he find faith on earth?" And many professors will fall from their first love, as the Ephesians did, Rev. 2:4. The faith and love of the primitive saints in the churches of Christ continued and increased, 2 Thes. 1:1, 2, 3. "Your faith grew exceedingly, and the love of every one of you all towards each other abounded." But in these last days, many depart from the faith, and many cool in their spiritual affections to Christ; there are great decays of grace, and many flourishing professors experience great withering, fading, and decaying in the spiritual gifts and graces; their backslidings are increased.

As the apostasy in doctrine, so in worship, is a sign of the last days and of the second coming of Christ, the apostle Paul foretold of it, 1 Thes. 2:3, 4 and 2 Tim. 3:1, 5. "This know also, that in the last days—men shall be lovers of their own selves, etc. more than lovers of God, having a form of godliness, but denying the power of it." In those last days, even a little before the second coming of Christ, the Laodicean churches will be lukewarm, neither cold nor hot; formal, not fervent in spirit serving the Lord, Rev. 3:15, 16. And then the national churches will be papal, superstitious, and willworshippers, Col. 2:16, 18–22, 23. "Which things have indeed a show of wisdom in will-worship," etc. Then Mystery Babylon will say, "I sit a Queen," etc. Rev. 18:7, 8. "Therefore shall her plagues come in one day," that is, the seven vials of the last plagues, for in them is filled up the wrath of God, Rev. 15:1, 7. And then our Lord Jesus Christ will come in power and great glory and shall utterly destroy the antichrist, 2 Thes. 2:8. "Whom the Lord shall destroy with the brightness of his coming."

When those Virgin-Professors, who have highly pretended to be upon their watch waiting for the coming of the Bridegroom Christ Jesus, shall grow secure, careless, invigilant, and all slumber and sleep, it is a sign that the second coming of Christ is near, Matth. 25:5, 6. "While the Bridegroom (Jesus Christ) tarried, they all slumbered and slept. And at midnight there was a cry made, 'Behold, the Bridegroom comes.'" And verse 10. "The Bridegroom came," called the Son of Man, verse 13. See my exposition upon the *Parable of the Ten Virgins* printed in 1667[28]. David prophesied in Psalm 145:10, 11, 12, 13 that the latter day saints shall bless the Lord, saying, "They shall speak of the glory of your kingdom, and talk of your power, to make known to the sons of men-the glorious majesty of his kingdom."

---

28. This is a printer's mistake. This work was written in 1674.

But when the wise virgins begin to be sinfully silent, and dare not bear their testimony boldly and publicly for Christ against Antichrist; when they cease to teach, and preach the doctrine of Christ's second coming, and of the glorious majesty of his Davidical kingdom; then they begin to grow carnal, worldly, careless and secure, formal, and lukewarm. But there will then come a midnight dispensation that will awaken all virgin professors, and then Christ will come.

Another sign of Christ's second coming from heaven is that great tribulation, which our Saviour foretold his disciples would be immediately before his second coming and appearance, Matth. 24:21, 29, 30. "For then shall be great tribulation-and immediately after the tribulation of those days-they shall see the Son of Man coming in the clouds of heaven," etc. This great tribulation will cause distress of nations with great perplexities, "Men's hearts fading them for fear, and for looking after these things which are coming upon the earth," Luke 21:25, 26, 27. Read Dan. 12:1, 2, 3, 4, 8, 9, 13, etc. This great tribulation will be such as never was since the world began, Matth. 24:21. "WOE, WOE, WOE to the inhabitants of the earth," Rev. 8:13, and of the sea, Rev. 12:12. And the people of God (especially his two prophetical witnesses, that is, the separated churches and their faithful ministers) shall not be exempted from the tribulation of these days; for they shall suffer persecution, 2 Tim. 3:1, 12. "This know also, that in the last days, perilous times shall come. Yea and all that will live godly in Christ Jesus shall suffer persecution." And when the two prophetical witnesses of Christ shall have finished their testimony (that is to say, have preached the gospel of the Kingdom of Christ, King of Nations, Jer. 7:10 and Matth. 24:14), the Beast that ascended out of the bottomless pit shall make war against them, and shall overcome them, and kill them," Rev. 11:7. See my exposition of the 11th chapter of the revelation where I have proved that, before the second woe is past, Rev. 11:14, the papal Beast shall ascend, that is, rise and reign; and he shall overcome, that is, the Papists will prevail against the Protestants, and will kill the two witnesses, that is, they will persecute the separated churches of saints and their ministers; scatter their assemblies, disperse their congregations, break their meeting-places, imprison some, banish others, and condemn some to death, and will burn them, kill, and slay them. And the second woe being past, the third woe will come quickly, Rev. 11:14, that is, the seven vials of the last plagues of God Almighty shall then be poured out upon the Papal antichristian Beast, the great whore, and the false prophet, whose name is

Mystery-Babylon, Rev. 17:5. See my book entitled *Mystical-Babylon Unveiled.*

Thirdly, touching the ends of Christ's second coming, that is, what Christ will do when he comes again from heaven.

First, when Christ comes from heaven with his holy angels, he will send them to gather together his elect from one end of heaven to the other, Matth. 24:30, 31. Then shall the dispersed of Judah be gathered, and the outcasts of Israel with them, as was foretold in Isa. 11:12, 16. "And he shall set up an ensign for the nations, and shall assemble the outcasts of Israel; and gather together the dispersed of Judah from the four corners of the earth." In that day, God will pour upon the house of David, and upon the inhabitants of Jerusalem, the spirit of grace and supplication; and they shall look upon Christ whom they have pierced and they shall mourn for him, Zech. 12:10 and Rev. 1:7. "Behold he comes with clouds, and every eye shall see him, and they also that pierced him." Then shall come to pass that wonderful work of the Jews' conversion prophesied, Isa. 66:6, 8. "Who has heard such a thing? Who has seen such things? Shall the earth be made to bring forth in one day? Shall a nation be born at once?" And so all Israel shall be saved (as it is written), the Redeemer shall come to Zion, Isa. 59:20. And shall turn away ungodliness from Jacob, Rom. 11:26, 27. "For this is my covenant unto them, when I shall take away their sins." And all the tribes of Judah and Israel being gathered, they shall all be reunited into one nation; which the prophet Ezekiel showed them by the parable of two sticks made one stick in his hand, Ezek. 37:15-22. "And I will make them one nation; and one king shall be king to them," verse 24. "And they shall have one shepherd," verse 27. "My tabernacle also shall be with them: Yea, I will be their God, and they shall be my people," verse 28. "My sanctuary shall be in the midst of them for evermore." Then shall also the fullness of the Gentiles be converted unto them, Isa. 6:1, 2, 3, 5. "And the Gentiles shall come to your light, and the abundance of the sea shall be converted unto you," Rom. 11:25. "Until the fullness of the Gentiles is come in. And the nations of those which are saved, shall walk in the light of it, and the kings of the earth do bring their glory and honour unto it," Rev. 21:24. This will be a glorious day, and a glorious work; and then will the Lord be for a crown of glory and for a diadem of beauty unto the residue of his people, Isa. 28:5, 6. Then shall they be also a crown of glory in the hand of the Lord and a royal diadem in the hand of their God, Isa. 62:3. And this is one end of our Saviour's second coming from heaven, Isa. 49:6. To gather his people together unto himself, Psal. 50:5, "Gather my saints together unto me," Matth. 24:27, 28.

Secondly, another end of Christ's coming from heaven and another work that he will do when he comes again is this: namely he will put down all rule, all authority, and all power that are his enemies who would not have him to reign, Luke 19:27. "For he must reign until he has put all his enemies under his feet," 1 Cor. 15:24, 25, as was prophesied, Psal. 110:1 and Luke 20:42, 43. The external enemies of Christ are principally three:

First, Ezekiel's' Gog and Magog who are prophesied of in Ezek. 38 and 39. "Thus says the Lord, 'I am against you, O Gog,'" Ezek. 38:2, 3, 8, 11, 16. "And you shall come up against my people Israel; It shall be in the latter days," and verse 23. "Thus will I magnify myself, and sanctify myself," etc. Ezek. 39:1, 8-13, 21, 25, 29.

Secondly, Mystery Babylon and the kings of the earth who have given their power and strength unto the Beast, Rev. 19:19, 20, 21.

Thirdly, John's Mystical Gog and Magog, and all their multitude, Rev. 20:8, 9. "Who will compass the camp of the saints about, and the beloved city: And fire will come down from God out of heaven and devour them."

Thirdly, another end of Christ's coming from heaven, and another work that he will do when he comes again, is this: namely, he will set up his Davidical kingdom on earth, Dan. 2:44. "And in the days of these kings, shall the God of heaven set up a kingdom that shall never be destroyed;" Luke 1:31, 32, 33. "And the Lord shall give unto him the throne of his Father David." And Isa. 9:6, 7.

The next particular in our general position is touching the kingdom of Christ and his saints. The Holy Scriptures of truth do in several places plainly affirm that the kingdom of this world shall become the kingdom of Christ and his saints, Dan. 7:13, 14, 27. Verse 14. "And there was given him dominion, glory, and a kingdom. His dominion is an everlasting dominion, which shall not pass away. And his kingdom that, which shall not be destroyed." Verse 27, "And the kingdom and dominion, and the greatness of the kingdom under the whole heaven shall be given to the people, even to the saints of the Most High." And Rev.

11:15—"The kingdoms of this world are become the kingdom of our Lord, and of his Christ," etc. By the kingdoms of this world, we may understand universally, all the kingdoms in the whole world; "for Christ shall be king of all the earth," Zech. 14:9. "In that day shall there be one Lord, and his name one:" Particularly, the kingdom of David, that is, Judah and Israel, Luke 1:31, 32, 33. "And the Lord God shall give unto him the throne of his father David. And of his kingdom there shall be no end," Isa. 9:6, 7, Micah 4:8. "And you, O tower of the flock, the strong hold of the daughter of Zion, unto you shall it come; Even the first dominion, the kingdom shall come to the daughter of Jerusalem." And verse 7. All those prophecies shall be fulfilled, Dan. 2:37-43, 44. When the stone has broken all those kingdoms in pieces, verses 34, 35, 45 (which stone is Christ, Luke 20:17, 18, and his Jerusalem, Zech. 12:3 compared with Matth. 21:44 and Jerem. 51:19, 24. "And with you will I destroy kingdoms"), then that stone will become a great mountain and fill the whole earth, Dan. 2:35, that is to say, Christ will be king of all the earth, Zech. 14:9. And the kingdom of Christ will be enlarged:

By the extraordinary conversion of sinners, both Jews and Gentiles, Isa. 60:3, 5, 8, 10-15 and Rom. 11:25, 26, 27.

By the pouring out of the Spirit upon all flesh, Joel 2:28. Isa. 44:3, 4, 5, by which "the earth shall be filled with the knowledge of the Lord, as the waters cover the sea," Joel 2:29 and Hab. 2:14. Then the nations shall know "that the Lord Jesus Christ is king of nations," Jer. 10:7. "The king of kings and the only potentate," 1 Tim. 6:15. "And he shall put down all rule, and all authority and power," 1 Cor. 15:24, 25. "For he must reign until he has put all enemies under his feet." And the saints shall know "that the kingdom of Christ is not of this world," John 18:36, that is to say, Christ's kingdom is not of a worldly constitution, but it is a spiritual and heavenly kingdom, 2 Tim. 4:18, and called the kingdom of heaven, Matth. 25:1, 2, though it will be a glorious kingdom, Psal. 145:10, 11, 12, 13, yet it is not that kingdom of glory where Jesus Christ, his holy angels, and the spirits of just men made perfect now are, for there are no foolish virgins in that kingdom of heaven. See more of this matter in my exposition of *The Parable of the Kingdom of Heaven* printed in 1674. And also in the third part of my *Apocalyptical Mysteries* printed in 1667. Likewise, in my *Exposition of the 11th Chapter of the Revelation* printed in 1679.[29] This kingdom of our Lord Jesus Christ will begin in the days of their kings, Dan. 2:44. That is to say, the

---

29. See my essay in the final chapter.

ten kings of the fourth kingdom: the Roman monarchy. Then the dominion shall be given unto the saints, Dan. 7:27. "And the saints of the most high shall take the kingdom, and possess the kingdom forever and ever," Dan. 7:18, 22. And they "shall reign on earth," Rev. 5:9, 10. Then the saints shall be rarely qualified and spirited for government; for "they shall be all righteous," Isa. 60:1, 2, 3, 20, 21. "They shall do no iniquity," Zeph. 3:13. And "they shall be without fault before the throne of God," Rev. 14:5. They shall be endued with courage, clad with zeal, and girded with strength to bind kings in chains, and nobles in fetters of iron, and execute upon them the judgment written (Luke 19:27). "This honour have all his saints," Psal. 149:1, 2, 6, 7, 8, 9 and Zech. 12:5, 6, 7, 8, 9 and Isa. 60:12. "For the nation and kingdom that will not serve thee, shall perish, yea those nations shall be utterly wasted." And when the kingdom of our Lord Jesus Christ is established on earth, and all the kingdoms of this world are become his; the thousand years of the reign of Christ and his saints being ended (Rev. 20:4, 5, 6, 7), then Christ will raise the dead, and he will judge the quick and the dead; which being done, he will deliver up the kingdom to God, even the Father "that God may be all in all," 1 Cor. 15:24-28.

The next particular in our general position to be explained is the resurrection of the body at the second coming of Jesus Christ.[30] Compare 1 Cor. 15:20, 22, 23 with 1 Thes. 4:16. "The Lord himself shall descend from heaven — and the dead in Christ shall rise first." The dead bodies of the saints shall then be raised from the dead that shall yet remain in their graves. They that sleep in Jesus will God raise up; them will Jesus Christ awaken with the trump of God, 1 Thes. 4:14. The resurrection of the dead has this order and is described by the apostle in this manner, that is, Christ first, 1 Cor. 15:22, 23, 24, *afterwards* they that are Christ's at his coming. But the rest of the dead lived not again until the thousand years were finished, Rev. 20:5, 6. "This is the first resurrection. Blessed and holy is he that has part in the first resurrection." They shall reign with Christ a thousand years, and that on earth, Rev. 5:9, 10. These kings and priests are the children of the resurrection, Luke 20:35, 36, being the children of God. Whose vile bodies shall be changed and fashioned like unto Christ's glorious body. The saints' raised bodies will be perfect, no defect, no deformity, but spiritual, and glorious, 1

---

30. This is the resurrection of the saints at the beginning of the 1000 year reign, not to be confused with the general resurrection of the dead at the end of the 1000 years.

Cor. 15:42, 43, 44. So is the resurrection of the dead; it is sown a natural body, it is raised a spiritual body. It is sown in dishonour, it is raised in glory. After the saints deceased are raised and have lived and reigned with Christ a thousand years, there shall be the general resurrection, Rev. 20:12, 13. "And I saw the dead small and great stand before God."[31]

The last particular in our general position to be explained is the eternal judgement. So it is called, Heb. 6:2. There are several days of judgement as that of the old world, and that of Sodom and Gomorrah, etc., but the eternal judgement is that last sentence which our Lord Jesus Christ shall pronounce upon and unto the righteous and the wicked, Matth. 25:34 and 41. "Come you blessed of my Father, inherit the kingdom prepared for you from the foundation of the world." And verse 41. "Depart from me you cursed, into everlasting fire, prepared for the Devil and his angels." And verse 46. "These shall go away into everlasting punishment, but the righteous into eternal life," which is the execution of God's eternal judgement.

CHAP. II.

Our general position being proved and explained, it ought to be improved and fitly applied to the inhabitants of this world, and more especially to the men and women of this generation, whether they are unconverted sinners or sanctified believers. The unconverted sinners of this world and of this generation are either sinners in Zion, Isa. 33:14, that is to say, sinful professors who seem to be religious (whose religion will prove in vain, James 1:26) and who have a form of godliness, but deny the power of it, 2 Tim. 3:1-5. Those are foolish virgins, that having gotten their lamps lighted, wait (a while) for the coming of the Bridegroom; but while the Bridegroom tarries, they slumber and sleep till their lamplight goes out, Matth. 25:1-13. See my exposition on that parable printed in 1674. Or else, those that are sinfully profane, who make no resolution to godliness, called ungodly sinners, Jude, v. 15, unrighteous, 1 Cor. 6:9, and wicked persons, Psal. 9:17.

O you unconverted professors! Consider, I beseech you, there is a world to come, and Christ will come, and then everyone shall give account of himself to God, Rom. 14:10, 11. What account will you give to God for your formality, lukewarmness, hypocrisy, and unprofitableness under the means

---

31. Knollys mentions the general resurrection here before he goes on to the last particular, day of judgment, which occurs at the end of the 1000 year reign.

of grace, you sinful professors, that have refused the offer of Christ, and despised the goodness of God, which should lead you to repentance; you that have sinned against gospel-light and knowledge, quenched the Spirit, resisted the Spirit, and grieved the Holy Spirit. It will be more tolerable for Tyre and Zion than for you in the day of judgement, except you repent and believe in Christ. And you unconverted ungodly wicked sinners, what account will you give to Christ, in the world to come, for all your unrighteousness, and all the wickedness that you have done, and still do in this world? Read Jude verse 15. It will be more tolerable for Sodom and Gomorrah in the day of judgement than for you, Jude verse 7, which cities are set forth for an example, suffering the vengeance of eternal fire.

O you unconverted sinners, both professors and profane, will you now accept of and receive a word in season of spiritual counsel? Then I will instruct you how you that are miserable may become happy; and you that are in a damnable state may get into the state of salvation before Christ comes from heaven to judge the quick and the dead and before you die. That you may obtain eternal life and glory, my counsel to you is as follows:

1. Consider, you are *dead* in sins and trespasses, and you are without Christ, Eph. 2:1, 5, 12. You have no saving sanctifying grace; you are not holy; and if you die in this your sinful state and condition, you will be damned to eternity; Psal. 9:17. "The wicked shall be turned into Hell."

2. Consider your *need* of Jesus Christ: There is not salvation in any other, Acts 4:12, no Christ, no salvation. He is that one thing necessary; without him you can do nothing, John 15:5, to please God or to glorify God, Heb. 11:6. Without faith in Christ, it is impossible to please God. Without being and abiding in Christ, you cannot bring forth fruit, nor do anything by which God is glorified, John 15:5-8. You stand in need of Christ to justify you, to sanctify you, and to save you from sin and from Hell.

3. Consider, God offers Jesus Christ to poor, lost, miserable sinners, Rev. 3:17, 18, yea to the chief of sinners, 1 Tim. 1:12-15, upon gospel-terms of free grace, Isa. 55:1-7, without exception of person, and without respect of price, Rev. 22:17. "The Spirit and the Bride say 'Come,' and let him that hears say 'Come,' and let him that is thirsty come, and whosoever will, let him take the water of life freely," that is to say, anyone, everyone that is *willing* may come to Christ, and receive Christ, and have Christ freely, for he is the free gift of God to sinners who are without Christ in the world, John 3:16. Be but willing to take Christ, and the work

is done. Christ complained of them that would not come to him, that they might have life, John 5:39, 45.

When you have seriously considered those three particulars, then I counsel you poor, lost, perishing sinners,

[F]irst, suffer the Lord Jesus Christ to come by his Spirit and Word into your hearts, and set up the kingdom of his grace in your souls; that where sin has abounded, grace may much more abound; and where sin has reigned unto death, there grace might reign through righteousness unto eternal life by Jesus Christ our Lord, Rom. 5:20, 21. Do not resist the Holy Spirit, as they did. Zech. 7:7, 8, 9, 11, 12, 13, and their children after them, Acts 7:51.

Secondly, open your hearts to Christ when he knocks at the door of your souls and calls you to come to him, to receive him, and let him come into your hearts, and dwell in your hearts by his Holy Spirit and sanctifying grace, Rev. 3:20. "Behold I stand at the door and knock, if any man hears my voice, and will open the door, I will come in to him, and will sup with him, and he with me." If the sinner be willing to open the door of his heart, Christ will come in by his Holy Spirit, and he will communicate of his grace to his soul.

Thirdly, let the Lord Jesus Christ have the throne, and be exalted above all in your souls, Isa. 2:17. "And the Lord alone shall be exalted in that day." Let your own imaginations be cast down, and every high thing that exalts itself against the knowledge of God, that every thought may be brought into captivity to the obedience of Christ. Be willing to resign your whole man, spirit, soul and body, unto the government of Christ, as Lord and King, to reign and rule, guide and govern you by his Holy Spirit and written Word.

Not that you can do those things of yourselves; I have told you, without Christ you can do nothing, John 15:5. But it is your duty to do them, and it is the free grace of God to work in you to will and to do according to his good pleasure, Phil. 2:12, 13, that he so working in you, you may work out your own salvation with fear and trembling.

I would, through the divine assistance of the Spirit and grace of God, make some application of this our general position unto the churches of saints for their edification.

First, I most humbly beseech all the churches of saints to receive this doctrine of Christ's second personal coming from heaven, and to believe,

1. That when he comes, he will glorify the house of his glory, Isa. 60:1, 2, 7, and will make Zion an eternal excellency, verses 14, 15, 22. God will build up Zion, and then he shall appear in his glory, Psal. 102:13, 16. Then shall Zion be the perfection of beauty, Psal. 50:2. Out of which God shall shine. In that day, God shall be his church's everlasting light and glory, Isa. 60:19 and Rev. 21:23. Then shall Christ and his church be each other's crown and glory, Isa. 28:5. "In that day shall the Lord of Hosts be for a crown of glory, and for a diadem of beauty unto the residue of his people," Isa. 62:3. "You shall also be a crown of glory in the hand of the Lord, and a royal diadem in the hand of your God." Read Zech. 9:16 and Isa. 60:13.

2. That when Christ comes, he will restore all his holy ordinances unto their primitive power and purity; yea, unto a higher and greater degree of excellency than in the apostles' days. God will not only give his churches of saints pastors according to his own heart, which shall feed them with knowledge and understanding, Jer. 3:14, 15; but he will also pour out his Spirit upon sons and daughters, and upon the servants and upon the handmaids. Also God will pour out his Spirit, Joel 2:28, 31, 32. "Before the great and terrible day of the Lord come." The Lord will vouchsafe unto his churches such anointing of his Holy Spirit, as the apostle John witnessed and recorded, 1 John 2:20, 27. "But you have an unction from the Holy One, and you know all things," etc. Read verse 27 and John 6:45 and Isa. 54:13 and Jer. 31:34. "It is written in the prophets, and they shall be all taught of God." And not only be instructed and led by the holy eternal Spirit into the sound and saving knowledge of all the truths in God's written Word, as the truth is in Jesus, but they shall see with their eyes those things fulfilled, which they have read and heard out of the written Word of God, Matth. 24:33, 34, 35. That gospel ordinance of praising God will then be with greater spiritualness and with more heavenly mindedness performed in the general assembly and church of the firstborn, where all the sons of God shall sing together, even all the saints and angels shall celebrate the high praises of God together. Read Rev. 5:11, 12, 13; Rev. 11:15, 16, 17; Rev. 14:1, 2, 3; Rev. 15:2, 3, 4; Rev. 19:1, 4, 5, 6, 7, 8, 9. The whole worship of God shall then be performed by the true worshippers in spirit and in truth according to Christ's Word, John 4:23, 24, for God will then give all his people one heart and one way, Jer. 32:38, 39, 40, to worship him with one consent, Zeph. 3:9, 14, 16, 17, 18. "In that day shall there be one Lord, and his name one," Zech. 14:9. A restitution of all things, Acts 3:21.

3. That when Christ comes, his glorious personal and spiritual presence with his church, Heb. 12:21, 23, 24 and Rev. 22:2, 3, will occasion a confluence of all comforts, Isa. 51:3, 12 and 66:13 and Zech. 1:13, 17. Then Zion shall be adorned with spiritual and glorious beauty, Isa. 52:1, 9, 10, and compassed about with peace and safety. God will be as a wall of fire round about Zion, Zech. 2:5, 10. "'Sing and rejoice, O daughter of Zion, for lo, I come, and I will dwell in the midst of you,' says the Lord." Read Ezek. 34:23, 24, 25, 28, 29, 30, 31. No Canaanite in the land of Israel, nor none that shall hurt or destroy in all God's holy mountains, Zech. 2:4. Jerusalem "shall be inhabited as towns without walls"; for God's salvation shall be her walls and bulwarks, Isa. 26:1, 2, 3. Then the state of the church of God will bear some proportional resemblance to the kingdom of heaven, for it will then be a sinless state, Isa. 60:1, 21; Zeph. 3:13, and Rev. 14:1, 5, and a sorrowless state, Rev. 21:1, 2, 3, 4, 5, and a timeless state, Rev. 10:6. "Time shall be no more." For the thousand years times of the church's glory being fulfilled (and all the time of Satan and his instruments ended, who are the abusers of time), time shall pass into eternity of glory and beatifical vision and eternal life.

Secondly, I would also humbly entreat my reverend brethren to declare to the ministers of Christ, churches of saints, what is noted in the Holy Scripture of truth concerning the world to come, the new heavens and a new earth, and the new Jerusalem. Also the second personal coming of our Lord Jesus Christ from heaven. You are commissioned and commanded to declare unto the people the whole counsel of God, revealed in his written Word, and this gospel of the kingdom and coming of Christ must be preached in all the inhabited world towards the latter end of it, Matth. 24:14, as a witness unto all nations, and then shall the end come. This is the generation truth, which ought to be preached and testified by the ministers and churches of Christ in these latter days, though they are killed for bearing this testimony, Rev. 11:3, 4, 7. "Be faithful to death, and Christ will give you a crown of life," Rev. 2:10 and 12:11.

Lastly, a word of consolation to those who do believe, pray and wait for the world to come, and the spiritual glory of it.

1. In general, for then the "ransomed of the Lord shall return and come to Zion with songs, and everlasting joy," etc. Isa. 35:10. Then shall be the confluence of all spiritual comforts to the church and people of God, Isa. 60:1, 2, 3, 7, 13, 19-22.

"The Lord shall be your everlasting light, and your God your glory," verse 19. All the promises of grace and glory shall then be performed, which are in Christ, yea, and in Christ, amen, to the praise and glory of God, 2 Cor. 1:20. And then all the prophecies relating to the churches' spiritual glory shall be fulfilled, Acts 3:19-21, "which God has spoken by the mouth of his holy prophets." Then will be a superabundant pouring out of the Spirit, Joel 2:28. "And it shall come to pass afterwards that I will pour out my Spirit upon all flesh, and your sons and your daughters shall prophesy, your old men shall dream dreams, your young men shall receive visions." And God will graciously prevent the prayers of his saints, Isa. 65:17, 24. "It shall come to pass, that when they call, I will answer, and while they are yet speaking, I will hear." All the sons and daughters of God will then be of one heart and of one mind, Jer. 32:39, 40. Then all sanctified believers will come in the unity of the Spirit to a perfect man, Eph. 4:13. And in that day there shall be one Lord, and his name one in all the earth, Zech. 14:9 and Zeph. 3:9. And "they shall serve the Lord with one consent." And then honour, dignity, and renown shall be given to the church of God, to religion, to religious persons, and to all holy things, Zech. 9:16. "The church shall then be as the stones of a crown lifted up." Those living stones, in that spiritual building, will then be a crown of glory and a royal diadem in the hand of the Lord, Isa. 62:1, 2, 3, and 28:5.

2. In particular,

1. To the seed of Abraham; the Jews. They shall be called, gathered, united into one nation, and the Davidical kingdom of Jesus Christ shall be given to them, Micah 4:8, which they shall take and possess forever and ever, Dan. 7:14, 18, 27, 28. They shall be all holy, Isa. 60, and so all Israel shall be saved, Rom. 11:26, 27.

2. To the offspring of Japheth, the Gentiles, whom God shall persuade to dwell in the tents of Shem. Even all the nations of them that are saved, who shall then walk in the light of the new Jerusalem, Rev. 21:24, and shall also enjoy the spiritual glory and blessings of the world to come, of which we speak.

A word of counsel to virgin professors in this generation:

1. Take heed you do not fall asleep while the Bridegroom tarries (or rather only seems to delay his coming), as they did, Matth. 25:5, 6. "They all slumbered and slept" until a midnight dispensation, a cry did awaken them out of their carnal security.

When being at ease in Zion, they became formal, lukewarm, and worldly, minding earthly things more than heavenly, and seeking their own things more than the things of Christ.

2\. Prepare yourselves for that time of tribulation, which shall come before Christ comes, Matth. 24:21, 39, 30. It's called an hour of temptation, which shall come upon all the world to try them that dwell upon the earth, Rev. 3. It will come upon the Jews, Dan. 12:1, 2, 3, and upon the Gentiles, Rev. 11:7, but more especially upon the inhabiters of the earth, Rev. 8:13 and 12:12 and Rev. 19:19, 20, namely, upon the Beast and the false prophet, and upon the kings of the earth, and their armies. Prepare for that midnight dispensation of darkness, distress, and temptation, which is coming upon nations, cities, and churches to try them.

3\. Consider what manner of persons you ought to be in all holy conversation and godliness that look and wait for the glory of Christ, his church and saints in the world to come, 2 Pet. 3:11, 13, 14.

Lastly, a word of instruction to the king, the nobles, the judges, and all the magistrates in this island, and in this city[32]: the kingly prophet David gave the instruction I intend, Psal. 2, in which by the spirit of prophecy he foretold,

1\. That the kings of the earth will set themselves and the rulers take counsel together against the Lord and against his anointed, verses 2, 3.

2\. That God speaks to them in his wrath and vexes them in his hot displeasure, verse 5.

3\. That the Lord Jesus Christ will break them with a rod of iron and dash them in pieces like a potter's vessel.

4\. That God will set his king (namely King Jesus, upon his holy hill of Zion, verses 6, 7).

5\. That God will give the Lord Jesus Christ the heathen for his inheritance, and the utmost part of the earth for his possession, and his dominion shall be from sea to sea, even unto the ends of the earth, verse 8. And then the holy prophet exhorts those kings and judges to be wise and to be instructed, verses 10, 11, 12. "Be wise now, therefore, O you kings; be instructed you judges of the earth; kiss the Son lest he be angry, and you perish." This phrase of kissing the Son implies:

1\. A declaration or testimony of love and peace between Christ and them, Cant. 1:2. Christ who is the prince of the kings

---

32. Britain and London.

of the earth, Rev. 1:5, is the Prince of Peace, Isa. 9:6, and it concerns all kings to be at peace with Jesus Christ. And the Lord Jesus Christ is the judge of the quick and dead, and he sits among the judges (called gods) of the earth, and they also must stand before the judgement seat of Christ; therefore it concerns all judges to kiss the Son, that is, to make their peace with Christ.

2. To kiss the Son implies to worship Jesus Christ. And if God commanded the holy angels to worship him, Heb. 1:6, then kings and judges are not exempted from worshipping Jesus Christ, Phil. 2:9, 11. "Every knee shall bow to him, and confess that he is Lord": Because God has exalted Christ above all, and given him a name above every name, etc. Eph. 1:20, 21, and set him far above all principalities and powers in this world, etc.

3. By kissing the Son is intended the submitting to his dominion and government, Isa. 9:6, 7. God the Father has laid the government of saints upon Christ, for he is king of saints, Rev. 15:3, and the government of Zion (his church) upon Christ, for he is King of Zion, Psal. 149:1, 2, and the government of the nations upon Christ, for he is king of nations, Jer. 16:7, 10. By him, kings reign and princes decree judgement. He puts down one and set up another, Jesus Christ is king of kings, and judge of judges; therefore be wise, O kings, and be instructed you judges of the land.

Now I will conclude with a word of exhortation to the magistrates and inhabitants of this city; Consider God has visited this city with the pestilence, and with a fire[33], and yet the inhabitants of it have not returned to the Lord. Now God threatens a famine of bread, if he shut up heaven, that it rain not; and a famine of the Word, if he suffer the papists to prevail; O repent and amend! Administer justice and righteousness. Plead the cause of the widow and fatherless; relieve the oppressed, and acquit the innocent. Let the grace of God that brings salvation teach you citizens of London to deny all ungodliness, and worldly lusts, and to live soberly, righteously, and godly in this present evil world, that in the world to come you may have life everlasting. Amen.

Finis.

---

33. The plague of 1665 and great fire of 1666 in London. Just over fifteen years earlier.

5

The Eschatology of Hanserd Knollys with Special Reference to His Commentary on the Book of Revelation

Introduction

THE SEVENTEENTH CENTURY WAS an interesting and fascinating period of time politically, sociologically, economically, ecclesiastically, theologically and in particular, eschatologically. Many Englishmen anticipated the final Coming of Christ to consummate His work and usher in the kingdom of God, with many of them reading the Book of Revelation and confidently predicting the time, place and signs of the end. Hanserd Knollys was one of those people caught up in all the excitement of the end times. Knollys wrote six books over a thirty year period addressing the subject of the Second Coming of Christ.[1] What is interesting about Knollys's work is not that he wrote on the subject, for many learned men were writing on it, but that all of his eschatological works were written during the Restoration period. Most of the important English eschatological works were written before the Interregnum by such men as John Napier, Thomas Brightman, Arthur Dent, Joseph Mede, Thomas Goodwin, Nathaniel Homes, and John Archer. But during the Revolution period there was a ballooning of eschatological works because the end-time predictions of men like those of Mede appeared to be coming true.

---

1. *Apocalyptical Mysteries* (1667), *The Parable of the Kingdom of Heaven Expounded* (1674), *Mystical Babylon Unveiled* (1679), *An Exposition of the Eleventh Chapter of the Revelation* (1679), *The World that now is, and the World that is to Come* (1681), and *An Exposition of the Whole Book of the Revelation* (1689).

In addition, Knollys' work is not only interesting for its timing in history but its timing in his life. These six works only began to be published when he was sixty-nine years of age. From these facts certain questions concerning Knollys' eschatology emerge. For example, why did he not publish his eschatological views earlier in life? And why did he not publish them during the height of the 1640s and 50s eschatological frenzy? And again why did he only begin to publish and continue to publish during the Restoration period? These are interesting questions that beg for answers.[2]

2. There is no evidence that explicitly tells us why he did. We can only surmise an answer to this question from the external and internal evidence we have. From the political/historical context Knollys wrote these works during the return of the monarchy under the reign of the seemingly pro-catholic Charles II called the restoration. With the ejection of the dissenting ministers (pro-protestant/anti-Catholic) in 1662, the various Parlimentary Acts enacted against them, leading to persecution, and incidents like the Popish Plot, Knollys believed that the beast and whore were waging their final war against God's true church.. There were also ssigns of the end with the great plague (1665) and the great Fire (1667) in London (See Bustin, *Paradox and Perseverance*). In addition, from our study one obvious theological reason he wrote these works is that he believed the end was near. In several of his works he taught that the end would occur around 1688. His first work was written in 1667 only twenty-one years prior to 1688 and only a year after Goodwin's eschatological date of 1666. He probably felt compelled to warn people about the imminent coming of Christ at this crucial time. Writing "To all the Saints" in 1667 he states, "They that would serve God in their Generation . . . ought to inquire diligently into the particular Truths of the Age they live in . . . The days wherein we live, being . . . the last dayes of those perilous Times mentioned by him [Apostle Paul], 2 Tim. 3. 1,5." He went on to state his purpose for writing this treatise, "The late Apostacy of some, who have fallen in with the corrupt self-seeking interests of this sinful generation; and the Zeal of others, who have separated themselves from their Brethren, judging them to be defiled with the sins of the times, and therefore dare not have and hold Communion with them, though they hope they are Saints, and the dear Children of God, hath given me occasion to publish my testimony at this time for the Kingdom of Christ, and against the Kingdom of Antichrist, wherein I have said some things that may, by the blessing of God, tend unto the recovery of backsliders, and to the rectifying of the Judgments of my zealous Brethren, and to the reducing of those Saints unto repentance, who have been defiled with any sins of this Age or Generation."

Moreover, with the passing of the important date of 1666 Knollys may have felt people would either think Christ was not coming at all or not for along time, and so not be prepared. And so he wrote that they might be prepared. So that people might be prepared he wrote *The Parable of the Kingdom of Heaven Expounded* in 1674 warning professors of the faith about lukewarmness because he believed they were not ready for Christ's coming. Again in 1681 in *The World that now is and the World that is* to Come he gave words of counsel to virgin professors of the faith, and instructions to kings, nobles, magistrates, etc. in light of the coming of the Christ. There is also another reason Knollys may have felt compelled to write at this time. Christopher Hill has rightly taught that the discussion of a specific Antichrist had diminished after 1660. But this was not so for Knollys. He believed that the Antichristian beast was the papacy. For this reason he felt it was necessary to warn England and its people of their danger at this time. In 1679 in the aftermath of the Popish Plot affair he wrote *Mystical Babylon Unvailed* to

This essay, however, will primarily be a descriptive study of Knollys's eschatology with a special focus on his exposition of the Book of Revelation. From it we will draw some lessons for the church presently.

This analysis of Knollys's eschatology will fall into two parts. The first will be to survey his eschatology using his six eschatological works but with special reference to his exposition of Revelation.[3] The second part will be to

---

warn England against the Papists who Knollys believed were seeking in *"their Plots and Conspiracies," "the* utter *destruction of the Protestants . . . and the* Protestant-Religion *in* England *especially, and the* Re-establishment *of the Popish-Religion of the Church of* Rome *in this Kingdom; which End the Popish-Recusants in* England (in this Bloody and Traiterous design, that Damnable and Hellish Plot contrived and carried on by them for Assassinating and Murdering the King, Subverting the government, and Rooting out and Destroying the Protestant-Religion, as the King and Parliament have voted and declared) *are still endeavouring to effect, and bring to pass."*

In addition, Knollys ended this *work* and his commentary on *Revelation* with a call to those in Babylon to come out. Commenting on the words from *Revelation* 18:1, "Come out of her my people," he explains, "This *Call* is the Call of God our *Saviour* unto all his People in Mystical *Babylon (Papal Rome)* to come out of HER . . . To come out of HER, is to Separate themselves from the Church of *Rome*, which is now a *false* Church, called *the great Whore, and Mother of Harlots . . . Wherefore come out from among them, and be ye separate, saith the Lord."*

We must also remember that Knollys considered all national churches as daughters of the whore, the Roman papal church. He could say in 1688, "And *is not England* like *Egypt* for oppression, exaction, and other cruelties against the *Israel* of God?" And when commenting on the second vial of the wrath of God he believed that it would be poured out on "the See of *Rome*, the See of *Canterbury*, the See of *York* and all other *Ecclesiastical, Metropolitan*, and *Diocesan Sees."* And again after the seventh vial was poured out in *Revelation* 16:19 where it is written, "the great city was divided into three parts. And the cities of the nations fell," Knollys interpreted the cities as National churches, and the three parts as "the National churches of the Papists, of the Lord Bishops [England], and of the Presbyterians." Remember that Knollys considered the true church to be that of congregational churches. Remember also that he saw a significant future for England and London in the end as well as Scotland and Ireland. In preparation for the end Knollys believed the British kingdom must be warned in these last days to choose Christ and so fulfill its destiny. These are some of the reasons Knollys wrote so much at this time. Maybe he also felt that many were not addressing this subject which was so important for his generation. Therefore, he had to take up the task. Maybe he felt his eschatological efforts unnecessary prior to 1667 (there was enough preaching and writing to encourage English people to be prepared for Christ's coming, and enough hopeful expectation of the end among the people). But maybe he felt this was not so after 1666 when the date passed and the heavy persecution of the 1660s ended. But for Knollys His coming was just around the corner; England needed to be warned and English people needed to be ready. And so for the last twenty-five years of his life Knollys preached and wrote about the coming of Christ, concerned for his fellow Christians, countrymen, and country.

3. Because of the scope of this paper we will not be able to compare Knollys's eschatology with others of his time. For that comparison see Howson, *Erroneous and Schismatical Opinions*, chapter 6. For works that compare and examine the eschatology

examine the purpose, outline, and method of interpretation of his exposition of Revelation.

General Survey

Knollys, like most preachers of his time believed that Christ's Second Coming was imminent, and that the book of Revelation should be interpreted in an historical manner.[4] The 1260 prophetic days which signify 1260 years of our time were almost at an end. These days began between 407 and 428 AD. This was when the beast arose out of the bottomless pit[5] and the beginning of Mystical Babylon, Papal Rome.[6] This beast according to Knollys was the beast of the eighth head, the Popes of Rome.[7] The Pope is the man of

---

of various writers of the sixteenth and seventeenth centuries: Ball, *A Great Expectation*. This work addresses the subject from a theological point of view. Other works that deal with the same subject and time period but from a different point of view include: from a political view point, Christianson, *Reformers and Babylon*; from an intellectual historical point of view, Firth, *The Apocalyptic Tradition in Reformation Britain, 1530–1645*; from an intellectual historical viewpoint, Hill, *Antichrist in Seventeenth-Century England*; and from a intellectual historical viewpoint, Toon, *Puritans, the Millenium and the Future of Israel*. Some more specific focused works on the subject include Capp, *The Fifth Monarchy Men*; Toon, "A Message of Hope for the Rump Parliament"; Korshin, "Queuing and Waiting," 240–65; Murrin, "Revelation and Two Seventeenth-Century Commentators," 125–46; Clouse, "The Apocalyptic Interpretation of Thomas Brightman and Joseph Mede," 181–93; Brady, "The Number of the Beast," 219–40; Cooper, "The Academic Re-Discovery of Apocalyptic Ideas in the 17th Century," 351–62; Clouse, "John Napier and Apocalyptic Thought," 101–14; Cameron, "The Commentary on the Book of Revelation," 123–29; Hutton, "Henry More and the Apocalypse," 131–40; Dawson, "The Apocalyptic Thinking of the Marian Exiles," 75–91; Solt, "The Fifth Monarchy Men," 314–24; Cohen, "Two Roads to the Puritan Millenium," 322–38; Lamont, "Richard Baxter, The Apocalypse and the Mad Major," 68–90; Brown, *The Political Activities of the Baptists and the Fifth Monarchy Men*; Murray, *The Puritan Hope*; Rogers, *The Fifth Monarchy Men*; and White, "John Pendarves, the Calvinistic Baptists and the Fifth Monarchy," 251–71. For general and specific histories of eschatology see: Froom, *The Prophetic Faith of our Fathers*; Torrance and Reid, *Eschatology*; Lea, "A Survey of the Doctrine of the Return of Christ in the Ante-Nicene Fathers," 163–77; Tuveson, *Millenium and Utopia*; Cohn, *The Pursuit of the Millenium*; Emmerson and McGinn, *The Apocalypse in the Middle Ages*; Cohn, "Medieval Millenarism," 31–43; Reeves, *The Influence of Prophecy in the Later Middle Ages*; and Reeves, "The Development of Apocalyptic Thought," 40–72.

4. Knollys, *Revelation* (1688), 61.

5. Knollys, *Revelation* (1688), 130; *An Exposition of the Eleventh Chapter of the Revelation* (1679), 13.

6. Knollys, *Revelation*, 137; *Mystical Babylon Unveiled* (1679), 1–4.

7. Knollys, *Revelation*, 137; *Babylon*, 5–13. Henceforth, all footnote titles where no author is given are Knollys's books.

sin, the Antichrist[8] who became universal bishop and head of the church in 428 AD, though he was not pronounced as such until 607 AD by Emperor Phocas. Later the Pope obtained temporal sovereignty in the days of Henry V (1387–1422).[9] According to Knollys the Church of Rome is the Great Whore because it leads people into spiritual adultery with its false worship and idolatry.[10] And the Roman Priests are the false prophet because of the false doctrines they teach and believe.[11]

During the 1260 year period of Papal Rome's rule the two witnesses of Revelation chapter eleven prophesy.[12] The two witnesses are the ministers and saints of Christ, the true church. In these days the two witnesses are to preach true doctrine, worship, and to proclaim Jesus as King. In addition, they are to preach against Papal Rome and its false teachings, its false worship, and its exaltation of the Pope.[13] Their preaching will continue until the gospel is preached in all the world.[14] Again during these 1260 years the woman clothed with the sun and travailing in childbirth (Revelation 12:1) flees into the wilderness.[15] This woman signifies the true church of Jesus Christ.[16] In these days the true church is persecuted by Papal Rome.[17] This persecution prior to the seventeenth century had been experienced by the true church represented by the Waldensians[18], the Wycliffites, Hussites, and Lollards, and was now being experienced by the true church in England during the Restoration.[19] Knollys believed the beast would rage more fiercely at the end of the 1260 days and make war against the witnesses because the witnesses opposition would be more open and visible at this time.[20] According to Knollys this raging of the beast had already been fulfilled in the past and was being fulfilled in his day. This war had been experienced in the days of Charles V in the countries of Germany, France and Scotland (Reformation times of the 16th century), and in the days of Mary in England when

8. *Revelation*, 178.
9. *Babylon*, 6–7; *Revelation*, 175.
10. *Babylon*, 14–19.
11. *Babylon*, 22–24.
12. *Revelation*, 126.
13. *Revelation*, 136.
14. *Revelation*, 135.
15. *Revelation*, 126, 162.
16. *Revelation*, 159.
17. *Revelation*, 162
18. Pope Alexander persecuted them. *Revelation*, 138.
19. *Revelation*, 138.
20. *Apocalyptical*, Pt. 1, 18–19.

the saints and ministers were persecuted.[21] And it was being experienced in Knollys's time during the Restoration period as the Beast raged against dissenting conventicles.[22]

Knollys believed when he wrote *Apocalyptical Mysteries* in 1667 that the end of the 1260 years was near[23]; they were living under the sixth trumpet.[24] In fact, he believed that the end would be in 1688 or thereabouts.[25] But according to Knollys before the end of the 1260 years there must be the fulfillment of *Revelation* chapter eleven's 3 1/2 year period. At the beginning of this period the witnesses will be put to death by the beast of Rome. These witnesses will lie dead in the street of the great city of Babylon which according to Knollys was England and London.[26] Knollys saw a special place for England and London in the plan of God. He believed that later when the witnesses were raised the tenth part of the city, represented by England, Scotland and Ireland, would break away from Papal Rome and follow Christ.[27]

During the 3 1/2 years the two witnesses who were dead and who represented the church would be deprived of civil liberty, the exercise of religion and even life. As a result the church would be diminished in various ways and become spiritually weak.[28] Knollys believed that during these 3 1/2 years there would be great tribulation for all[29], a great apostasy from the true faith, and the church would be lukewarm and worldly.[30] At the end of the 3 1/2 years the witnesses would be raised and so the testimony of the Church restored. Knollys believed that the witnesses had not yet died, and so the 3 1/2 year period had not yet begun when he published his final eschatological work in 1688 but that it was close to fulfillment. When the witnesses are restored the seventh trumpet is sounded and the end begins. The seven vials of God's wrath begin to be poured out on Mystical Babylon (Papal Rome) and

---

21. *Apocalyptical*, Pt. 1, 19.
22. *Apocalyptical*, Pt. 1, 19–20; *Eleventh*, 22.
23. *Apocalyptical*, Pt. 1, 28.
24. *Eleventh*, 39. This work was published in 1679.
25. *Revelation*, 130.
26. *Revelation*, 140. Commenting on Revelation 16:18–19 Knollys interpreted the "cities of the nations" as the daughters of the great Whore, all national churches; and the "three parts of Mystical Babylon" as the national churches of the Papists, of the Lord Bishops, and of the Presbyterians (*Revelation*, 200).
27. *Revelation*, 148.
28. *Revelation*, 138–39; *Apocalyptical* Pt. 1, 20.
29. *Eleventh*, 30.
30. *Apocalyptical*, Pt. 1 28–29; *Revelation*, 144–45.

all those nations who align themselves against Christ.[31] During the pouring out of these vials the Islamic Turkish dominion will be destroyed[32] and the Jews will return to their own land.[33] This is also the time of the Battle of Armageddon when Christ and His saints tread on Mystical Babylon, the beast and the false prophet and the Kings of the earth who follow the beast;[34] and where the Jews defeat the Pope and the Turk.[35]

At the end of the seventh vial Christ's kingdom shall be set up in the new heavens and new earth and in the New Jerusalem; thus begins the latter day glory.[36] The false prophet and the beast are cast into the lake of fire, and the serpent, the devil, is bound for 1000 years.[37] This is the beginning of the literal 1000 year reign of Christ with His saints on earth.[38] It is important to note that in most of Knollys's writings he believed in a spiritual return of Christ at this time.[39] It takes place after the seventh trumpet and prior to the millennial reign, and it is a virtual, spiritual, powerful, and glorious coming to earth but not a physical or visible one.[40] During the reign of the 1000 years Christ is not physically present but reigns spiritually in and through His saints. In addition, the saints are given perfect bodies[41]; there will be no sufferings, sins, persecutions or pains;[42] and the saints will be kings and priests unto God. During this time the kingdoms of this world successively become the kingdoms of Christ.[43] This is accomplished by the preaching of the Gospel, by the pouring out of the Spirit, and by the breaking to pieces of the kingdoms of this world who oppose Christ.[44]

In this millennial kingdom of Christ and His saints, spiritual worship takes place in the New Jerusalem and the nations are converted by it.[45] The kingdom of Christ in the millennium is enlarged by the extraordinary

---

31. *Apocalyptical*, Pt. 3, 2–3.
32. *Apocalyptical*, Pt. 2, 27.
33. *Apocalyptical*, Pt. 2,, 27.
34. *Apocalyptical*, Pt. 2, 39.
35. *Revelation*, 198–99.
36. *Apocalyptical*, Pt. 2, 31; *Revelation*, 232.
37. *Revelation*, 230.
38. *World*, Pt. 2, 31; *Apocalyptical*, Pt. 3, 15–16; *Eleventh*, 44.
39. See footnote 123 [x-ref].
40. *Parable*, 78–79.
41. *World*, Pt. 2, 28–29.
42. *Revelation*, 229–30.
43. *Apocalyptical*, Pt. 3, 16–18; *Eleventh*, 14; *World*, Pt. 2, 28.
44. *Eleventh*, 41–42.
45. *World*, Pt. 2, 8.

conversion of Jews and Gentiles and by the pouring out of the Spirit on all flesh.[46] Those nations that do submit to Christ and His saints become the kingdom of Christ but those that do not are destroyed.[47] During this millennium the saints will be given the dominion and government of the kingdom of Christ; and they will rule by the laws of Christ.[48] They will be qualified for this work by being righteous, being spirited for government, and being clothed with humility. In addition, to being clothed with humility they will be endued with courage, clad with zeal, and girded with strength and truth so that they may be able to bind kings in chains, and nobles in fetters of iron, and execute judgment upon them.[49]

Once the kingdom is established and the 1000 years are over, Satan is loosed and defeated[50]; Christ returns and appears personally, certainly, suddenly, visibly and gloriously[51]; the dead will be raised; all people, righteous and wicked, will be judged; and the kingdom of Christ will be handed over to the Father.[52] Then the eternal kingdom will be ushered in.

Commentary on Revelation

Now that we have examined Knollys' eschatology generally we will examine more precisely his commentary on Revelation under several headings: purpose, outline, and method, concluding with his interpretation of chapters 6-22.

Purpose

Knollys clearly states his purpose for publishing this exposition of the Book of Revelation in his "Epistle to the Reader". He gives two reasons: "First, Those learned and godly Men [those past commentators who have exposited Revelation] have improved their five talents of knowledge and wisdom, in their studies and labours published for the benefit of others, in preaching, expounding, and writing their understanding of the Revelations of Jesus Christ to his servant John (written in this Book) And I dare not hide my talent, knowing that my Lord and Master will shortly call me to give an account of my Stewardship.

---

46. *World*, Pt. 2, 26.
47. *World*, Pt. 2, 28; *Apocalyptical*, Pt. 3, 16-18.
48. *Apocalyptical*, Pt. 3, 16.
49. *Apocalyptical*, Pt. 3, 16.
50. *Revelation*, 225.
51. *World*, Pt. 2, 10-12.
52. *World*, Pt. 2, 28-30.

Secondly, That promised blessing, Rev. 1. Vers. 3. did incourage [sic] me to read, study, and expound this part of holy Scripture, publickly [sic] in the course of my ministry: And now (being aged) I have adventured to publish this my Exposition thereof (such as it is) for the benefit of them that shall read it, that they also may be partakers of that blessing."

Regarding his second reason, it is important to note that Knollys did not publish any of his eschatological works for speculative reasons but for pastoral purposes. His was a pastor's heart to encourage and instruct professors of Christ to live a life of godliness and look for the blessed hope of Christ's return, and to exhort sinners regarding the day of the coming of the Lord. For example, Knollys ended his commentary on Revelation with a call to those in Babylon to come out. Commenting on the words from *Revelation* 18:1, "Come out of her my people", he explains, "This *Call* is the Call of God our *Saviour* unto all his People in Mystical *Babylon (Papal Rome)* to come out of HER ... To come out of HER, is to Separate themselves from the Church of *Rome,* which is now a *false* Church, called *the great Whore, and Mother of Harlots, ... Wherefore come out from among them, and be ye separate, saith the Lord".

Knollys pastorally calls believers who are ready for Christ's coming to be "watching." [53] This watching means that the believer be awake, be in continual expectation of Christ's glorious appearance, and be looking out desirous of and longing for the coming and kingdom of Christ.[54] Moreover, since Christ was coming soon, Knollys out of concern not only for the common reader but also for the rulers of England and London exhorted the King, Nobles, Judges, and all magistrates to Kiss the Son.[55]

Moreover, for Knollys the truth of the coming of Christ not only called for preparation but also provide encouragement. For the saints the coming of the Lord gives them great hope.2 Therefore, according to Knollys the coming of Christ, this Generation Truth, ought to be preached for a warning to professors and profane, and for encouragement to the saints.[56]

In addition, although not explicit in the text, we must remember the context into which Knollys writes. The time that he publishes is the date of 1688, around which he believes the end will come, that is, the events that

---

53. *World*, Pt. 2, 130–32. Knollys explains what it means to watch. At the time of publication he believed they were under the second of three watches which would end in about fifteen years. The third watch would begin with death of the two witnesses. He also explains how to be ready in *World*, Pt. 2, 82–83, 89, 93, 96, 120–21.

54. *World*, Pt. 2, 131–32.

55. *World*, Pt. 2, 45–46. He exhorts the profane in *Parable*, 47.

56. *World*, Pt. 2, 42–43. Though written in *Parable*, certainly applies to his *Exposition of Revelation*.

inaugurate the millennial reign of Christ. The signs of the time pointed to it: James II was on the throne, moving England back to its catholic roots; the dissenters were under much persecution from 1682–88; and James had produced an heir to ensure a catholic future.

Outline

According to Knollys the Book can be divided into three parts or three principal visions: 1) the seven candlesticks (Rev. 1-3); 2) the seven seals, seven trumpets and seven vials (Rev. 6-19); and 3) the new heavens and earth (Rev. 20-22).[57] The seventh seal contains the seven trumpets and vials and the seventh trumpet contains the seven vials. This is called the telescoping of these three visions that make up the bulk of Revelation.

Knollys, as many other expositors, sees chapter 1 verse 19 as significant to the outline of the book. "The things which are" are the first three chapters dealing with the historical Asia Minor churches of the time of John's writing during the persecution of Domitan. Chapters four to six deal with "the things which thou hast seen," that is, the condition of the church under the Roman Pagan state. And "the things which shall be hereafter", given in chapters seven to twenty-two refer to the condition of the church under the Antichristian Roman, Arian and Papal state, and its victory in the millennial state.[58]

Method of Interpretation

Two things stand out in Knollys'method of interpretation of the Book: one, he was a historicist, maintaining that most of the Book was to be interpreted historically; and two; he used the figurative-symbolic principle of interpretation freely.

Concerning the figurative-symbolic principle Knollys agreed with many interpreters of his time. For example, with John Napier he maintained that the prophetical day of *Revelation* equaled a year of our time;[59] with Arthur Dent and Thomas Brightman that "the great Monarchs and Monarchies of this WORLD, have been figured forth by wild beasts";[60] with Dent that the heads and horns symbolize kinds of government;[61]

---

57. *Eleventh*, preface.
58. *Eleventh*, 15.
59. *Eleventh*, 163
60. *Apocalyptical*, Pt. 1, 11; *Revelation*, 169.
61. *Revelation*, 206–7.

with Bernard and John Cotton that the "waters" and "sea" symbolize people and nations;[62] with Joeseph Mede that the woman harlot riding the scarlet beast is the false church of Rome and that the "woman clothed with the sun" *is* the true church;[63] and with Pareus that the "angels" are the "ministers and messengers of truth."[64] His whole commentary is replete with this interpretative principle.

Concerning the historicist interpretation of the *Revelation* he writes,

> *The* Historical *matter of this Book concerns the state of the Church of God, from the days of the Apostle* John *in the Isle of Patmos (about the year 96.) in the Reign of* Domitian *the Emperor unto the end of this World. And therefore, I would advise the* Reader *diligently to observe what is already past and fulfilled, what is now fulfilling in our days, and what is hereafter to be fulfilled. And to that end search the Scriptures, read Ecclesiastical Histories, and other* Expositions *of this Book, together with this* Exposition.[65]

Therefore, the Book dealt with the state of the church from the time of the reign of the Roman Emperor Domitan to the end of the world.[66] Consequently, the visions of the seals, the trumpets, and the vials were to be interpreted historically. According to Knollys the seven seals (Rev. 6:4-17) contained the judgments of God upon the Roman Pagan Idolators (the years prior to Constantine), the trumpets (Rev. 8:7-13; 9:1-21) contained the woes of God executed on the Arian apostate persecutors (the years prior to the fall of Rome) and Papal Rome, and the seven vials (Rev. 16; 18:8-21; 19:19) contained the last plagues of God in judgment against the Roman Antichristian Papal beast, whore and false prophet (the time of the destruction of Mystical Babylon).[67]

Knollys's Interpretation of Chapters 6-22 of the Book of Revelation

Now we will take a closer look at Knollys's historicist interpretation of chapters 6-22. The first principal vision of the seven seals primarily signified the sufferings of God's people under the Roman Pagan Emperors and

---

62. *Revelation*, 169.
63. *Revelation*, 203, 159.
64. *Revelation*, 19, 105.
65. *Revelation*, preface.
66. *Revelation*, preface.
67. *Revelation*, preface.

the judgment of God on the European empire.[68] This judgment took place through Constantine the Great with the destruction of Paganism and the setting up of the worship of Christ throughout the empire (opening of the sixth seal bringing salvation and judgment).[69] This great day of God's wrath took place in the days of the 10th persecution of the Christians during Diocletian's reign.[70]

Beginning in chapter eight through to chapter thirteen is the seventh seal which begins the sounding of the seven trumpets.[71] But before the trumpets begin in verse eight there is peace in the church for half the reign of Constantine, fifteen years.[72] After this peace the great Arian heresy began in which the orthodox bishops, ministers and Christians were persecuted by the Arians.[73] The first angel who sounded the first trumpet represented the faithful ministers of Christ such as Athanasius and Hilary of Poitiers; and it also included the kings of the Goths and Vandals. This angel sounded against the Roman Empire and Arianism.[74]

The second angel represented the faithful ministers of the fourth century in the Western church; he sounded the second trumpet concerning the preeminence of the Pope of Rome and the corruption of the worship and ordinances by the clergy.[75] The third angel represented the ministers of the fifth century such as Augustine and Jerome who sounded the third trumpet concerning Nestorius' corruption of worship and teachings (the star that fell from heaven); this is also when popery's teachings began (extreme unction, procession of the image of Mary, use of chancel).[76] The fourth angel represented Gregory the Great who opposed John, Bishop of Constantinople, Boniface III, who took the name of universal bishop pronounced by Emperor Phocas in 607 AD. It also includes all the faithful ministers who opposed innovations in worship and doctrine. This angel also sounded the fourth trumpet concerning the corruption of the ministers.[77] After this the three woes against the Roman Papal church which is Mystical Babylon begin. The first woe takes place at the time of the sounding of the fifth trumpet

---

68. *Revelation*, 79ff.
69. *Revelation*, 87.
70. *Revelation*, 88.
71. *Revelation*, 97.
72. *Revelation*, 97.
73. *Revelation*, 98.
74. *Revelation*, 100.
75. *Revelation*, 101.
76. *Revelation*, 102–3.
77. *Revelation*, 103.

(7th century). This trumpet sounds the judgment of God upon the apostates which include an eminent apostate churchman (the man of sin) and those who follow after him. This is the beginning of Popedom and of the Antichristian Papal power, and the opening of the bottomless pit of idolatry.[78] This Antichristian Papal power will continue for 1260 years.[79]

The sixth angel and the second woe now follow. The sixth angel represents the orthodox ministers who sounded against Popish idolatry, image worship, and other superstitions of the Roman clergy. This angel also loosed the four angels of the river Euphrates representing the commanders of the armies of the Turkish Emperor who will judge the Roman empire for their idolatrous worship and departure from true worship.[80] Knollys cautiously suggests this takes place for some 390 years.

We are told in the tenth chapter that when the seventh angel sounds two things will happen: the reign of the beast, whore, false prophet and all those kings that follow the beast will come to an end; and the mystery of God will be finished, that is, the conversion of the Jews to Christ and the restoring of the church to its primitive purity of worship and ordinances.[81]

Chapter 11 is a recapitulation of the time of the rise and reign of Anti-Christian Papal Rome which began around 428 AD. In chapter eleven John is told that the church will be tread under foot for 42 months (1260 prophetic years) by false Christians who are atheists, Papists, all profane and ungodly persons, and unbelieving Jews.[82] This period of time coincides with the prophecy of the two witnesses (11:3–13), the woman in the wilderness (12:1–17), and the beast's presence out of the bottomless pit (13:1–5).[83]

The focus of chapter eleven is the two witnesses. This passage is important for Knollys's interpretation of Revelation in the late seventeenth century. According to him they are the ministers and true constituted gospel churches who are given prophetical power from God to preach the Word

---

78. *Revelation*, 105–6. This anti-Christian papal power is putting into practice false doctrine and practice. See 106f for a list.

79. *Revelation*, 108.

80. *Revelation*, 112–13. In this section Knollys lists numerous examples of idolatrous worship, e.g. their adoration of images, crosses, crucifixes; and their worship of the image of the virgin Mary and image of Christ upon a cross. In addition, they murder the souls of people who follow their false doctrines and worship; they worship their breaden God in the Mass; and they steal by getting money for the Roman church under pretence and pretext of giving pardons, indulgences and dispensations (*Revelation*, 115–16).

81. *Revelation*, 118.

82. *Revelation*, 125.

83. *Revelation*, 126.

of God and to pray.[84] These witnesses are to prophecy 1260 prophetic years which began about 407, 409, 410 or before 428 AD. Therefore, these 1260 years will end somewhere around 1688, although, according to Knollys, these are uncertain conjectures.[85]

84. *Revelation*, 126–28. They are not given magisterial power and, therefore, they are not to use the sword (*Revelation*, 128, 129).

85. *Revelation*, 130. Setting a date for the end of the last times was not simply a phenomenon of the fringe expositors of the seventeenth century but also a practice of the mainstream. Most if not all believed that only the Father knew the specific day of the end of the last times; but they also believed that certain signs could tell us approximately when the end would be. Moreover, the prophetic numbers given in the Book of Revelation when placed in their proper historical context could yield an approximate date for the end. As a result there was a tremendous propensity among seventeenth-century English expositors to set dates for the end. For example, in 1593 John Napier calculated that the 1335 years of Daniel 12:12 were to commence from the time of Julian the Apostate in AD 363. This calculation yielded a final date of AD 1700. In addition, he believed the vision of the seven angels pouring out the vials of God's wrath began in 1541. The first three bowls were poured out consecutively, forty-nine years each, bringing the time to 1688. The last four bowls will be poured out simultaneously at the end of this time. So Napier concluded from these calculations, "Wherefore, appearinglie betwixt this 1688 yeare, according to the Reuelation, and the 1700 yeare, according to Daniel, the said latter day should fall." Thomas Brightman not too long after Napier calculated a similar date. He believed the 1260 years of Revelation chapter 13 related to the time of papal supremacy. This commenced around the time of Constantine plus the 140 years approximately that the beast was wounded by the Goth's kingdom. So he concludes, "The last ende of Antichrist shall expire at the yeare 1686, or thereabouts." A generation after Napier, Joseph Mede made his own calculations. For him the key was to get the right starting date from which to commence them. He had to find the right date from which to calculate the 1260 years, that is, the point of time from whence Antichrist first appeared. He had three options: the death of Julian the Apostate in AD 365; the sack of Rome by Alaric in AD 410; or the death of Valentinian in AD 455. He believed, therefore, that the end would come sometime between the years 1625 and 1715. During the Interregnum Thomas Goodwin attempted to calculate the date of the end. He cautiously came up with several possible dates which were dependent on his starting point. He came up with the dates 1666/70, 1653/56, and 1690/1700. His 1666 date was taken from AD 406 which was around the time the Goths took over the kingdom (410), the time of the succession of Innocent the bishop of Rome (404/6), and the excommunication of the eastern Emperor Arcadius (407). Others who set dates include Johan Alsted (1694), Ephriam Huit (1695), Edmund Hall (1650), Thomas Parker (1649), and Nathaniel Homes (1670) (Ball, *Great Expectation*, 116ff.). When Knollys believed that the day for the latter day glory would be 1688 or thereabouts, he wasn't speaking from the fringes but along with the mainstream expositors. Knollys believed along with Napier, Mede, et al. that the 1260 prophetic years of *Revelation* were significant. He also maintained with them that the commencing of the 1260 years was to be marked from somewhere between AD 407–428. He writes, "But yet I may say, that the best Ecclesiastical Historians, and the later Expositors of this Book of the *Revelation*, *affirm*, That these [*thousand two hundred* and *threescore days*] began about the Year of our Lord 407, 409, 410. or before 428 . . . And if these [*thousand two hundred* and *threescore days*] did begin about 428, then they will end about 1688, which a short time will manifest more certainly" (*Revelation*, 130; *Eleventh*, 13; *Apocalyptical*, Pt. 1, 10). He also agreed with those expositors like Goodwin who looked for historical events that

Knollys believed that in 1688 when he published this commentary the witnesses were still suffering under the Roman Papal Beast, and that the end of their prophesying would come when the gospel is preached to the whole world.[86] This was a novel interpretation for his time. Here he explains that the testimony of the witnesses is: proclamation of true doctrine, true worship, the kingship of Jesus, and condemnation of Papal false teaching and worship.[87] These witnesses will be killed near the end of the 1260 years by the beast out of the bottomless pit. This beast is Mystical Babylon who is also the beast of the eighth head (Rev. 17:8-11) who is also the Pope of Rome.

This war with the two witnesses has recently been taking place; for example, the Popes and Emperors against the German Protestants, the edicts of the Papists in the days of Mary in England, Pope Alexander III against the Waldensians, and in 1464 the Roman persecution of the Lollards.[88] The witnesses eventually suffer a civil and ecclesiatical death which includes deprivation of livelihood, life, civil and ecclesiatical rights and liberties, estates, and imprisonment. They will also lose their spiritual vigour against the Antichrist, be deprived of the Spirit of Life, become lukewarm, and some will fall into the great apostasy; all of this is a kind of spiritual death that the church will experience during the days the witnesses are dead.[89] Their death takes place in "the street of the great city." This city is the whole Anitchristian kingdom of the beast; and according to Knollys the street is England and, in particular, London.[90]

These witnesses will lie dead for 3 1/2 years. At the end of these years the two witnesses will be raised which means the testimony and witness of the church is restored. At this time the 1260 year period is completed and the end has come. As mentioned above, Knollys believed, contrary to most expositions of his time, that the witnesses had not yet been killed. He gave his reasons which included his conviction that the two witnesses likely began their prophesying in 428 so ending their prophetic ministry about 1688.[91]

---

signalled the rise to power of the papacy. For this reason he was particularly drawn to the year AD 428 because, "The tyrannical power of the Papal Beast, according to the accompt of the best Ecclesiastick Historians, began about the year of our Lord 428. in the reign of the Emperor *Theodosius* the Second, when Pope *Sixtus* the III. a *Roman*, who at the instance of the Empress *Eudoxias,* made a holy day for St. Peter's Church" (*Revelation*, 143-42). Even though Knollys and his fellow expositors of the seventeenth century worked out and published their calculations they also believed that "these ... [were] uncertain Conjectures" (*Revelation*, 130; *Eleventh*, 13).

86. *Revelation*, 131, 135.
87. *Revelation*, 136.
88. *Revelation*, 135-39.
89. *Revelation*, 138-39.
90. *Revelation*, 139-41.
91. *Revelation*, 143-46.

According to Knollys when the witnesses ascend, a tenth part of the city will fall. He believed this to mean that England, Scotland and Ireland would break away from following Papal Rome.[92]

The sixth trumpet and the second woe have now ended. The seventh angel sounds forth the seventh trumpet which signals the third woe when the Roman Antichristian beast will be destroyed. This will be accomplished by the seven vials of the wrath of God, which are the seven last plagues. Knollys believed, contrary to many expositors, that none of the seven vials had been poured yet (1688).[93] When the vials are poured out the kingdoms of the world become the kingdom of our Lord and of His Christ. The kingdoms of this world are the kingdom of David (Judah and Israel), the kingdoms of the Roman Caesars (the fourth monarchy), and all the kingdoms of the earth. These kingdoms will become the kingdom of Christ by the preaching of the gospel, by the pouring out of the Spirit, and by the breaking to pieces of these kingdoms.[94]

Chapters twelve and thirteen are also recapitulations of the time from the beginning of the church in the apostles' day through to the present day. The "woman clothed with the sun" is the true visible constituted church, and the child is the many converts in the days of the apostles. The "great red dragon" is the Roman Pagan government that persecuted the saints from the time of Tiberius to Diocletian.[95] The "man-child" of verse five is Christ and His saints as well as, possibly, Constantine who ruled in those days of the early fourth century. The "war in heaven" of verse seven took place when the Christian emperors, kings and governors (especially Constantine) defeated the Roman Pagan empire with its idolatry.[96] Then according to verse 13 the dragon began to persecute the true church through Arianism after the death of Constantine. The church at this time was preserved by the "two wings of a great eagle," that is, by Arcadius and Honorius, the two sons of Theodosius between whom the Roman empire was divided. Yet still the dragon tried to corrupt and destroy the church by means of the heresies of Arianism and Pelagianism.[97]

According to chapter thirteen, verse one, the sea represents the barbarian nations under Alaric which invaded the Roman Empire and sacked Rome in 410 AD. And the beast who rose up out of the sea is the Popedom

92. *Revelation*, 148.
93. *Revelation*, 149–52.
94. *Revelation*, 151–54.
95. *Revelation*, 159–61.
96. *Revelation*, 161–62, 164.
97. *Revelation*, 157–58.

of Papal Rome with its ten crowned horns that is the ten Roman provinces. The rising of this beast is between 410 and 428 AD.[98] The power of the beast comes from the devil, and this power is his Poli-Ecclesiastical jurisdiction in all causes and over all persons, civil, military, maritime and ecclesiastical. The Roman Pope was wounded when Rome was sacked again by the Barbarian armies (mid-fifth century). He was then healed by the Dragon and the world submitted to the Pope.[99] Then in verse eleven we are told of another beast who rose out of the earth. According to Knollys this was the same beast as the one who rose up out of the sea. The healing of his wound took place when the Pope (Boniface III) returned to Italy and Emperor Phocas made him universal bishop and head of the Catholic church about the year 606 AD. This coincides with the number of the beast which is 666, that is, the beast begins his reign 666 years after the Roman Empire began.[100] The woman, the true church, at that time fled into the wilderness for 1260 years. This wilderness signifies the persecution of the church by the Roman Papal powers.[101]

Now Knollys sees the visions in chapters fourteen to nineteen as those events that will take place after the 1260 year period, even after the two witnesses have been raised.[102] At this time the judgment of God is announced against Papal Rome, the beast of the eighth head, the pope, the false prophet, the great whore, mystery Babylon and all the national, synodal and parochial false churches. This judgment is described as the wine of the wrath of God which is the seven vials of the seven last plagues. The winepress is Armageddon where the saints trod on Babylon.[103]

Chapter fifteen and following give us the third principal vision of this prophecy which is the seven vials of the seven last plagues and the third woe. These judgments will be the means of the conversion of Jews and Gentiles.[104] The seven angels are to pour out the vials on all the earth, that is, upon the whole Roman Papal state, both political and ecclesiastical. The vials are poured out: first, against the earthly state of the Roman Papal kingdom; second, against all ecclesiastical, metropolitan and diocesian Sees; third, against all the political rulers under the Papal kingdom; fourth, against the

98. *Revelation*, 169. This is the same interpretation as that of Joseph Mede. The ten crowned horns are the Britains, Saxons, Franks, Burgundians, Wisigothes, Swedes, Vandals, Alemans, Ostrogoths, and Grecians.
99. *Revelation*, 170–71.
100. *Revelation*, 174–75, 179.
101. *Revelation*, 161–63.
102. *Revelation*, 181.
103. *Revelation*, 184–88.
104. *Revelation*, 191.

Emperor of Germany, the French King, and the Pope of Rome; fifth, against the city of Rome; sixth, against the Turkish kingdom and power; and seventh, against all Satan's kingdom, and all kingdoms of Antichrist, both of Turk and Pope. At this time Mystical Babylon, the Roman Papal empire and power, and her daughters, the National churches of the Papists, of the Lord Bishops and of the Presbyterians are destroyed.[105] Between the sixth and seventh vial there was an interval in which the pope, the cardinals, etc. and the devil gather forces to make war against Christ. This is the great battle of Armageddon where the Turks will be utterly destroyed.[106] The Jews will be involved in this battle.[107]

In chapters seventeen to nineteen Knollys focuses on the fifth angel of chapter 16, verse 10, who declares God's judgment upon Mystical Babylon. In chapter seventeen she is described as a great whore riding on a scarlet coloured beast. The beast is the Roman Papal Emperor with the kings of the earth who give their strength and power to the beast.[108] The seven kings of the fourth kingdom mentioned in verse eleven are the successive governments of the Roman empire. The first five that were before John's time were kings, consuls, decemvers, tribunes, and dictators. The "one that is" is the Roman Caesars of John's time, and the "one that is to come" is the Pope of Rome. This is the "beast that was, and is not," who is also the eighth head, the man of sin who reigns for forty-two months or 1260 years.[109] He has ten kingdoms and kings under him. These ten kings shall in the end turn against the church of Rome.[110] Once Babylon has fallen, that is, the church of Rome is ruined, then praise and rejoicing in heaven takes place as recorded in chapter nineteen; and the church is made ready for the marriage of the Lamb. Verses eleven to the end of this chapter describe the battle of Armageddon, which is the same battle as Ezekiel's Gog and Magog. Christ and the armies of heaven which include the angels and saints, war against the beast, the kings of the earth. Christ is victorious fighting this battle with two weapons, the Word of God (his word of threatened vengeance) and his rod of iron.[111] At that time the beast and the false prophet are cast into the lake of fire.

105. *Revelation*, 193–201.
106. *Revelation*, 197–99.
107. *Revelation*, 197, 198–99.
108. *Revelation*, 201–2.
109. *Revelation*, 206.
110. *Revelation*, 207, 208.
111. *Revelation*, 216–21.

After the destruction of Papal Rome according to Revelation 20, Satan is bound for a literal thousand years where he is kept from tempting and deceiving the nations by himself or his instruments i.e. Pagan, Papal or Mahometan false teaching.[112] Then Christ reigns with His suffering, overcoming saints. Those who had worshipped the beast were not raised until the thousand years were over. The first resurrection of verse five is the raising of the two witnesses, that is, those Christians who are alive at Christ's coming; they shall reign with Christ for a thousand years.[113] Satan is then released at the end of the thousand years at which time he deceives the nations, Gog and Magog, gathering them together to war against the New Jerusalem and the Church. Then God destroys Satan, and he is cast into the lake of fire forever.[114] At this time Christ Second Coming occurs and all stand before His judgment-seat. Here the wicked and righteous, both dead and alive, are judged.[115] They are judged out of the things written in those books which were opened, the Old and New Testaments, and the Book of life. The wicked are then cast into the lake of fire.[116]

The last two chapters are concerned with the millennial period. Chapter twenty-one gives us a vision of the world to come, that is, the world as it is during the thousand years on earth. This world to come is the newly created heavens and earth, and where the New Jerusalem, the church in her latter-day glory, is located.[117] The description of the New Jerusalem during these thousand years is given in the rest of the chapter and in the first five verses of chapter twenty-two. The rest of the last chapter looks to Christ's Second Coming which will be personal, visible and with all His saints.[118] This will occur at the end of the thousand years.[119] During

---

112. *Revelation*, 222–23. Knollys states that this literal thousand years was held by Pareus and other expositors.

113. *Revelation*, 223–24.

114. *Revelation*, 224–25.

115. *Revelation*, 225–26.

116. *Revelation*, 225–26.

117. *Revelation*, 227–28.

118. *Revelation*, 239.

119. The meaning of the "thousand years" of chapter 20 of John's *Revelation* has been debated throughout the history of the church (Kromminga, *The* Millennium *in the Church*). The debate also continued in seventeenth-century England. As we noted earlier most expositors were neither preterist or futurist but historicist in their interpretation of *Revelation*. And of those who were historicist each one interpreted the thousand years essentially in one of three ways. The first and probably the largest group were amillennialists or modified Augustinians. Many expositors including Hugh Broughton, Arthur Dent, David Pareus and Christopher Love fell into this group. They taught that the millennium encompassed the whole period between the two comings of Christ.

When Christ comes a second time the resurrection of the dead, the eternal judgment, and the eternal kingdom will all occur quickly. Some expositors in this category like William Guild and Thomas Hall even believed that the millennium had already been fulfilled. A second group of expositors were premillenialists. This group fell into two categories: some premillenialists like Goodwin, Mede, Alsted, Homes, and Archer believed that Christ would personally return at the beginning of the millennium, set up his kingdom, return to heaven, and reign spiritually for the thousand years through the saints; other premillennialists including John Durant, William Hicks, John Tillinghast, and George Hammon taught that Christ would personally return to earth, set up his kingdom, and personally reign on earth for a thousand years. Some of the premillennialists, like Nathaniel Homes, believed that the last two chapters of Revelation which contained the vision of the new heavens, the new earth, and the new Jerusalem, depicted the millennial state and not the eternal kingdom. A third group which includes John Cotton, Nathaniel Stephens, Edward Haughton and Edmund Hall were postmillenialists. This group was similar to the first-category premillenialists except that they believed Christ would not return personally until the end of the thousand year reign. This view though popular in the 1640s and 1650s has its roots in the eschatology of Thomas Brightman. Brightman taught a spiritualized advent and John Cotton developed his teaching. Cotton writes concerning the destruction of Antichrist in 2 Thess 2:8, "And though it be translated ... The Lord shall destroy him with the brightnesse of his coming ... The Lord will destroy Antichrist with the brightnesse of his Presence in his sacred and Civill Ordinances, sundry ages before the brightnesse of his comming to Judgement" (Ball, *Great Expectation*, 161-70).

And what about Hanserd Knollys? We know that he was certainly a millennarian. Commenting on Revelation 20:3 where it teaches that the Devil will be bound for a thousand years, Knollys states, "... that [the thousand years] is, a certain definite time, ... They are not any mystical or prophetical number, but literal" (*Revelation*, 222). He also taught with Nathaniel Homes that the new heavens, new earth, and the new Jerusalem were a vision of the millennial kingdom. He writes, "The WORLD to COME is not that *eternal* State of God's *Kingdom* of GLORY in *Heaven;* but it is the *glorious* and *spiritual State* of the Kingdom of Christ on EARTH ... *That same* WORLD, *even* THAT, *that is* to COME; to wit, The inhabited WORLD to Come, wherein the PEOPLE of God shall build Houses, and inhabit them, according to Gods Promise, *in that day,* when he will *Create* New Heavens, and a new Earth" (*Apocalyptical*, Pt. 3, 15).

Knollys was not only a millennarian but also a postmillennarian? All of his eschatological works seems to point in this direction but it is most explicit in his work entitled, *The Parable of the Kingdom of Heaven Expounded* written in 1674. According to Knollys this parable from Matthew 25:1-13 is concerned with the coming of Christ before the millennium. He called this coming a "virtual, spiritual, powerful and glorious appearance in his saints" (*Parable*, 78-79). According to Knollys this spiritual coming is also taught in *Revelation* 11:15, 16, 17; 19:1, 4, 6, 7, 8, 9, 16; and 20:4-9. Following this coming Christ will reign spiritually for a thousand years in His saints who are alive when he comes. At the end of the millennium he will come visibly and personally for the second time (Heb 9:28) (*Parable*, 75-77). This is when he comes with all his saints, both resurrected and living (1 Thess 4:13-18). At this time the eternal judgment will take place, the heavens and earth will be dissolved as the Apostle Peter taught (2 Pet 3:12), and the eternal kingdom will begin (*Parable*, 72). See Dennis Bustin for an argument that Knollys was a premillenialist and not a postmillennialist, *Paradox and Perseverance*, 214-28. It is clear that he is a postmillennialist in the *Parable*, and upon further reflection on this subject, in particular my rereading of Knollys" *Expostion of*

Revelation, I still maintain that he was a postmillennialist. I have come to this conclusion based on his use of "second coming" in the final two chapters of his *Exposition*. For Knollys, these chapters address the millennial kingdom in which the continuity between the dispensation of grace (the world that now is) and the millennial kingdom (the world that is to come) is much greater than either are to the eternal kingdom. The key difference is that Christ and his saints rule in the millennial kingdom. See *World*, Pt. 2, 24–29. Consequently, his comments on the second coming in chapters 21–22 refer to his postmillennial coming. For example, he writes on Rev. 22:11, "Here are two sorts of persons, of whom Christ testifies will be found in the same state and condition of the soul at the second coming, as they were under the dispensation of the Gospel of the grace of God" (239–40). And again, when commenting on, "Behold, I come quickly," he writes,: this is his second appearance and coming of Jesus Christ . . . The Lord Jesus Christ will give a reward to the wicked and ungodly, according to the merit and desert of their works; and he will also give to the righteous and godly a reward of Grace according to their good Works" (240). This is the final judgment which, for Knollys, occurs after the millennial reign, and is confirmed by his comment on the Rev 20:11–14, the great white throne, "Here John had a vision and revelation of the Day of Judgment . . . which signifies the Glory and majesty of our Lord Jesus Christ at his second coming, Heb. 9.28. which will be with power and great Glory, Matt. 24:30, then we shall all stand before the Judgment-seat of Christ whom John saw sit upon the white throne . . . By Sea, Death, and Hell, here we are to understand the places where the Bodies or Souls of the Dead were held and kept until this Day of Judgment. This lake of fire is that Gehenna, into which the Dragon, the Beast and the false Prophet were cast" (225–26). For Knollys the dragon is not thrown into the lake of fire until after the millennium at the Day of Judgment. Consequently, Knollys is referring to a postmillennial return in this context. In addition, commenting on Rev 22:6 where it says, "And the spirit and the Bride say, Come," Knollys writes, "By the Bride here, we are to understand the new Jerusalem, who shall come down out of heaven as a Bride adorned for her Husband . . . the Church of God, and the holy spirit of God, and all converted persons, do invite all sorts of sinners, especially, thirsty sinners, without exception against any persons, that are willing, and without any price, to take Christ freely" (241–42). This is a call to sinners during the millennial period after the New Jerusalem has come down out of heaven. Consequently, I conclude from this evidence that Knollys's final eschatological work agrees with his earlier writings in particular his *Parable*, that teaches a postmillennial return of Christ. This however, does not answer why his *World that now is* seems to teach a premillennial return. One possible answer is that the historical context of *World that now is* (1681) demanded that Knollys emphasize the coming of Christ before the millennium with little regard for the coming after the millennium. Current issues were pressing him to address the present church (the world that now is), in order to prepare for the coming of the millennial reign (the world that is to come), e.g., voting down of the Exclusion Bill by Parliament in 1681. He still maintained his postmillennial position he espoused in *Parable* (1674), but emphasized the coming of Christ before the millennium in *World* because of this context. Preachers do this all the time as well as most apocalyptical writers. Further evidence in support of his not changing his mind from *Parable* to *World* are his references in *World*, encouraging the reader to read his 1674 *Parable* concerning the Bridegroom's coming, which clearly taught that the bridegroom comes spiritually at the beginning of the millennium with no retraction of his *Parable* teaching (*World*, Pt. 2, 17, 27). My gratitude to my former colleague Paul Wilson for this insight.

these years the Spirit and the bride call sinners to take Christ freely.[120] Knollys closes his commentary with an invitation to the readers to come out of papal Rome.[121]

Final observations regarding Knollys's Interpretation of the Book of Revelation

1. Anti papal rhetoric throughout — he truly believed that the time of the death of the witnesses was on the horizon and the bowls were about to be poured out on Papal Rome. The time of tribulation for the church was present. The church must not lose sight of the fulfillment of prophecy, the wickedness of Papal Rome, and so contend for the truth as congregational churches
2. The true church is the congregational churches that maintain true doctrine (reformed) and practice (congregational church polity)
3. He believed that the true church will always be under persecution, particularly by the Roman papal church
4. Constant call to faithfulness for the true saints
5. Hope in the millennial kingdom where evil will be destroyed, and Christ and his saints will reign in holiness and conquer evil

Lessons for Our Generation

1. Reminder to keep our eyes on the return of Christ, to be looking for it.
2. The expectancy of the imminent return of Christ in each generation has been around since at least the Protestant Reformation — this is not new for our time as some dispensational eschatologists would have us believe. It also highlights that one can expect the end time events to occur soon without endorsing an "any moment" return of Christ
3. The danger of date-setting is not new — let us learn from history
4. Beware of dogmatism on the interpretation of the Book of Revelation. Knollys was certain of his interpretation, that is, his historicist and symbolical method which included his certainty regarding the Anti-Christ's person. This teaches us to be humble about reading current events into the text of scripture.

---

120. *Revelation*, 242–43.
121. *Revelation*, 243–44.

Select Bibliography

Knollys' Writings in Chronological Order

Knollys, Hanserd. *A Moderate Answer vnto Dr. BASTVVICKS BOOK Called. Independency Gods Ordinance.* London, Printed by Iane Coe. 1645.

Knollys, Hanserd, Benjamin Coxe, and William Kiffin, &c. *A Declaration concerning the Publicke Dispute Which Should have been in the Publike Meeting House of Alderman-Bury, the 3d. of this instant Moneth of December; Concerning Infants-Baptisme.* London, Printed in the Year, 1645.

———. Letter to Mr. John Dutton. 1645. In *The History of the English Baptists, from the Reformation to the Beginning of the Reign of George I*, edited by Thomas Crosby, 1:231–32. London: 1738.

———. *Christ Exalted: A lost sinner Sought, and saved by Christ: Gods people are an Holy people. Being the summe of divers Sermons Preached in Suffolk.* London, Printed by Jane Coe, according to Order. 1646.

———. *The Shining of a Flaming fire in Zion. Or, A clear Answer unto 13. Exceptions, against the Grounds of New Baptism; (so called) in Mr.* Saltmarsh *his Book; Intituled,* The Smoke in the Temple, *p. 15, &c.* London, Printed by Jane Coe, according to Order, 1646.

Knollys Hanserd, et al. *A Confession of Faith of seven Congregations or Churches of Christ in London, which are commonly (but uniustly) called Anabaptists Published For the vindication of the truth, and information of the ignorant; likewise for the taking off of those aspersions which are frequently both in Pulpit and Print unjustly cast upon them. The Second Impression corrected and enlarged. Published according to Order.* London printed by Matth. Simmons, and are to be sold by John Hancock in Popes-head Alley. 1646.

———. "To the Churches of God in London and elsewhere in all places with the Bishops and Deacons." In Robert Garner, *Mysteries Unvailed.* Printed . . . at the black sprad [*sic*] Eagle, at the west end of *Pauls.* 1646.

Knollys, Hanserd, et al. *A Declaration by Congregational Societies in, and about the City of LONDON; as well as those commonly called* Anabaptists, *as others. In a way of* Vindication *of themselves.* 1647. In *Confessions of Faith and other Public*

Documents, Illustrative of the History of the Baptist Churches of England in the 17th Century, edited by E. B. Underhill, 273–87. London: 1854.

———. *The Rudiments of* Hebrew Grammar *in* English. *Published for the benefit of some friends, who being ignorant of the Latine, are desirous to understand the Bible in the Originall TONGUE.* London, Printed by Moses Bell, for William Larner at the Blackmore neere Bishopgate, and George Whittington at the blew Anchor In Cornhill neer the Exchange. 1648.

———. "To the Churches of God in London and elsewhere in all places with the Bishops and Deacons." In [Robert Garner], *Redemption By Jesus Christ Unto lost Sinners, Handled. Also, The Scriptures (alleadged by Mr. Den, Tho. Moor, Thomas Lamb, and others, to prove the Universality of the extent of the death of Christ) are freed from the corrupt sense which is put upon them. With an Epistle to the Churches of God in London, and elsewhere, by Hanserd Knollys.* London, Printed for Giles Calvert, at the black Spread-Eagle at the West-end of Pauls: 1653.

———. *An exposition of the first chapter of the Song of Solomon.* London: 1656.

Knollys, Hanserd, et al. *Address of the Anabaptist Ministers in London to the Lord Protector.* 1657. In *Confessions of Faith and other Public Documents, Illustrative of the History of the Baptist Churches of England in the 17th Century*, edited by E. B. Underhill, 335–38. London: 1854.

———. "Courteous Reader." In *A Christian Womans Experiences of the glorious working of Gods free grace*, by Katherine Sutton. At Rotterdam, Printed by Henry Goddæus, Printer in the Newstreet, Anno 1663.

———. "Recommended to the use of all Parents and Schoolmasters, by H. Knowls." In *Instructions for Children*, by Benjamin Keach. 1664.

———. *Radices simplicium vocum, flexilium maxime, Novi testamenti opera & studio.* Londini: [s.n], 1664.

———. *Grammaticae graecae compendium operâ & studio.* Londini: [s.n], 1664.

———. *Grammaticae Latinae compendium, or, An introduction to the Latine tongue.* London : [s.n], 1664.

———. *Linguae Hebricae delineatio opera & studio.* Londini : [s.n], 1664.

———. *Radices Hebraicae omnes, quae in S. Scriptura, Veteris testamenti occurrunt opera & studio.* Londini : [s.n], 1664.

———. *Grammaticae Latinae, Graecae, & Hebraicae. Compendium. Rhetoricæ adumbratio. Item Radices Græcæ & Hebraicæ omnes quæ in Sacra Scriptura Veteris & Novi Testamenti occurrunt. Opera & studio.* Londini: typis Tho. Roycroft, anno Dom. 1665.

———. *Apocalyptical Mysteries, Touching the Two WITNESSES, the Seven VIALS, and the Two KINGDOMS, to wit, of Christ, and of ANTICHRIST, EXPOUNDED.* London, Printed in Year, 1667.

———. *The Parable of the kingdom of heaven expounded, or an exposition of the first thirteen verses of the 25th chapter of Matthew.* London: printed for Benjamin Harris, and are to be sold at the Stationers Armes in Sweetings Rents, in Cornhill, near the Royal Exchange, 1674.

Knollys, Hanserd, Daniel Dike, Thomas Paul, William Kiffin, and Henry Forty. *The Quakers appeal answer'd, or a full Relation of the Occasion, Progress, and Issue of a Meeting held in Barbican, the 28th of August last past.* Printed for Peter Parker, at the Leg and Star in Cornhil, over against the Royal Exchange, 1674. Where are Sold the three Diologues between a Christian and a Quaker.

Knollys, Hanserd, et al. Letter to Andrew Gifford. 1675. In *History of the English Baptists*, by Joseph Ivimey, 1:417–20. London: Printed for B. J. Holdsworth, 1811–1830.

Knollys, Hanserd, William Kiffin, Dan Dyke, Jo Gosnold, Henry Forty, Thomas Delanne. *The Baptists Answer to Mr. Obed Wills, His appeal against Mr. H. Danvers.* London: printed for Francis Smith, at the Elephant and Castle in Cornhill, near the Royal Exchange, 1675.

Knollys, Hanserd, et al. *Confession of the Faith Put forth by the ELDERS and BRETHREN Of many CONGREGATIONS OF Christians (bapized upon Profession of their Faith)* in London and the Country. Printed in the year, 1677. In *Baptist Confessions of Faith*, edited by William Lumpkin, 241–95. Philadelphia: Judson, 1959.

———. *An Exposition of the Eleventh Chapter of the Revelation. Wherein All those Things therein Revealed, which must shortly come to pass, are Explained.* N.p. Printed, Anno Domini, 1679.

———. *Mystical Babylon Unveiled, Wherein is Proved, I. That* Rome-Papal *is mystical-Babylon. II. That the Pope of* Rome *is the Beast. III. That the Church of* Rome *is the great Whore. IV. That the Roman-Priests are the false Prophet. Also a Call To all the People of God to come out of Babylon.* N.p. Printed Anno Domini, 1679.

———. *The World that now is; and the World that is to come: or the first and second coming of Jesus Christ. Wherein several prophecies not yet fulfilled are expounded.* 1681.

———. *An Exposition of the whole Book of the Revelation. Wherein The Visions and Prophecies of CHRIST Are opened and Expounded: Shewing The great Conquests of our LORD Jesus Christ for his Church over all His and Her Adversaries, PAGAN, ARIAN, and PAPAL; and the glorious State of the Church of God in the New Heavens and New Earth, in these Latter Days.* By Hanserd Knowles, Preacher of the Morning Lecture at Pinners-Hall. Licensed, September 12. 1688. London, Printed for the Author; and are to be Sold by William Barthall, at the Bible in Newgate-street, MDCLXXXIX.

Knollys, Hanserd, et al. "To the Congregation of Baptized Believers in *England* and *Wales*, Grace, Mercy and Peace be multiplied through the saving Knowledge of our Lord Jesus Christ." In [Benjamin Keach], *The Gospel Minister's Maintenance Vindicated. Wherein, A Regular Ministry in the Churches, is first Asserted, and the Objections against a Gospel Maintenance for Ministers, Answered. Also, The Dignity, Necessity, Difficulty, Use and Excellency of the Ministry of Christ is opened. Likewise, The Nature and VVeightiness of that Sacred VVork and Office clearly evinc'd.* London Printed, and are to be sold by John H. . . . at the Harrow, in the Poultrey, 1689.

———. *An Answer to a Brief Discourse concerning singing in the public worship of God in the Gospel-Church by I [Isaac]. M [Marlow].* 1690. 1691.

Knollys, Hanserd, et al. "A General Epistle." In *A Narrative of the proceedings of the General Assembly of the elders and messengers of the baptized Churches . . . of England and Wales.* 1691.

———. *The Life and Death of that old Disciple of Jesus Christ, and eminent Minister of the Gospel, Mr. Hanserd Knollys, who died in the Ninety-third year of his age written with his own hand to the year 1672; and continued in general in an epistle by Mr. W. K. To which is added his last Legacy to the Church.* 1692; rpt. London: E. Huntington, High Street, Bloomsbury, 1812.

Secondary Sources

Ball, Bryan W. *A Great Expectation: Eschatological Thought in English Protestantism to 1660.* Leiden: Brill, 1975.
Belcher, Richard P., and Anthony Mattia. *A Discussion of the Seventeenth Century Particular Baptist Confessions of Faith.* Southbridge, MA: Crowne, 1990.
Brackney, William H., ed. *Baptist Life and Thought 1600-1980.* Valley Forge, PA: Judson, 1983.
———. *The Baptists.* Westport, CT: Greenwood, 1988.
Brady, David. "The Number of the Beast in Seventeenth- and Eighteenth-Century England." *The Evangelical Quarterly* 45 (1973) 219-40.
Brown, J. Newton. "Hanserd Knollys, 1638-1641." In *Annals of the American Baptist Pulpit,* edited by William B. Sprague, 1–7. New York: 1860.
Brown, Louise F. *The Political Activities of the Baptists and the Fifth Monarchy Men in England During the Interregnum.* Washington, DC: American Historical Association, 1912.
Burrage, Champlain. *The Early English Dissenters.* 2 vols. Cambridge: Cambridge University Press, 1912.
———. "The Restoration of Immersion by the English Anabaptists and Baptists (1640-1700)." *The American Journal of Theology* 16 (1912) 70–89.
Bustin, Dennis. *Paradox and Perseverance: Hanserd Knollys, Particular Baptist Pioneer in Seventeenth-Century England.* Carlisle: Paternoster, 2006.
Cameron, James K. "The Commentary on the Book of Revelation by James Durham (1622–58)." In *Prophecy and Eschatology,* edited by Michael Wilks, 123–29. Oxford: Blackwell, 1994.
Capp, B. S. *The Fifth Monarchy Men: A Study in Seventeenth-Century English Millenarianism.* London: Faber and Faber, 1972.
Christianson, Paul. *Reformers and Babylon: English Apocalyptic Visions from the Reformation to the Eve of the Civil War.* Toronto: University of Toronto Press, 1978.
Clements, K. W. "The Significance of 1679." *The Baptist Quarterly* 28 (1979–80) 2–6.
Clouse, Robert. "The Apocalyptic Interpretation of Thomas Brightman and Joseph Mede." *Bulletin of the Evangelical Theological Society* 11 (1968) 181–93.
———. "John Napier and Apocalyptic Thought." *Sixteenth Century Journal* 5 (1974) 101–14.
Cohen, Alfred. "Two Roads to the Puritan Millenium: William Erbury and Vavasor Powell." *Church History* 32 (1963) 322–38.
Cohn, Norman. "Medieval Millenarism: Its Bearing on the Comparative Study of Millenarian Movements." In *Millenial Dreams in Action: Essays in Comparative Study,* edited by Sylvia L. Thrupp, 31–43. The Hague: Mouton, 1962.
———. *The Pursuit of the Millenium.* Rev. ed. New York: Oxford University Press, 1970.
Cooper, Brian G. "The Academic Re-Discovery of Apocalyptic Ideas in the Seventeenth Century." *The Baptist Quarterly* 18 (1960) 351–62.
Crosby, Thomas. *The History of the English Baptists, from the Reformation to the Beginning of the Reign of George I.* 4 vols. London: 1738.
Culross, James. *Hanserd Knollys "A Minister and Witness of Jesus Christ 1598 1691."* London: Alexander and Shepheard, 1895.
Dawson, Jane E. A. "The Apocalyptic Thinking of the Marian Exiles." In *Prophecy and Eschatology,* edited by Michael Wilks, 75–91. Oxford: Blackwell, 1994.

Duncan, Pope A. *Hanserd Knollys: Seventeenth-Century Baptist*. Nashville: Broadman, 1965.
Emmerson, Richard K., and Bernard McGinn, eds. *The Apocalypse in the Middle Ages*. Ithaca: Cornell University Press, 1992.
Estep, William. "On the Origins of English Baptists." *Baptist History and Heritage* 22/2 (1987) 19–26.
———. "The Nature and Use of Biblical Authority in Baptist Confessions of Faith, 1610–1963." *Baptist History and Heritage* 22/4 (1987) 3–16.
Firth, Katherine R. *The Apocalyptic Tradition in Reformation Britain, 1530–1645*. Oxford: Oxford University Press, 1979.
Froom, L. E. *The Prophetic Faith of our Fathers*. 4 vols. Washington, DC: Review and Herald, 1948.
Garrett, James Leo, Jr. "Restitution and Dissent Among Early English Baptists: Part II— Representative Late Sixteenth and Early Seventeenth Century Sources." *Baptist Heritage and History* 13 (1978) 11–27.
George, Timothy. "The Reformation Roots of the Baptist Tradition." *Review and Expositor* 86 (1989) 9–22.
George, Timothy, and David S. Dockery. *Baptist Theologians*. Nashville: Broadman, 1990.
Gritz, Paul Linton. "Samuel Richardson and the Religious and Political Controversies Confronting the London Particular Baptists, 1643 to 1658." PhD diss., Southwestern Baptist Theological Seminary, 1987.
Hannen, Robert B. "Historical Notes on the Name 'Baptist.'" *Foundations* 8 (1965) 62–71.
———. "A Suggested Source of Some Expressions in the Baptist Confession of Faith, London 1644." *The Baptist Quarterly* 12 (1948) 389–99.
Hayden, Roger. *English Baptist History and Heritage*. N.p.: The Baptist Union of Great Britain, 1990.
———. "The Particular Baptist Confession 1689 and Baptists Today." *The Baptist Quarterly* 32 (1987–88) 403–17.
Haykin, Michael A. G., ed. *The British Particular Baptists 1638–1910*. Springfield, MO: Particular Baptist, 1998.
———. "Hanserd Knollys (ca. 1599–1691) on the Gifts of the Spirit." *Westminster Theological Journal* 54 (1992) 99–113.
———. "The Nature and Purpose of the Lord's Supper According to Early Calvinistic Baptist Thought." Unpublished paper, 1995.
———. *Recovering Our English Baptist Heritage: Kiffin, Knollys and Keach*. Leeds: Reformation Today Trust, 1996.
———. "The 1689 Confession: A Tercentennial Appreciation." *Reformation Canada* 13/4 (1990) 13–28.
———. "The 1689 Confession: A Tercentennial Appreciation." *Reformation Canada* 14/1 (1991) 11–25.
———. "The 1689 Confession: A Tercentennial Appreciation." *Reformation Canada* 14/2 (1991) 10–18.
Hill, Christopher. *Antichrist in Seventeenth-Century England*. London: Verso, 1990.
Horle, Craig W. "Quakers and Baptists 1647–1660." *The Baptist Quarterly* 26 (1975–76) 344–62.
How Samuel. *The Sufficiencie of the Spirits Teaching without Human Learning*. Seen, Allowed and Printed by us etc, 1640.

Howson, Barry H. *Erroneous and Schismatical Opinions: The Question of Orthodoxy Regarding the Theology of Hanserd Knollys (c. 1599-1691).* Leiden: Brill, 2001.

———. "Hanserd Knollys and the Book of Revelation." Forthcoming in a collection of essays from the Andrew Fuller Conference (2007).

———. "Hanserd Knollys (c.1598-1691)." In *English Particular Baptists 1638-1910*, edited by Michael Haykin and Trevor Wolever, 59-85. Rev. ed. Springfield, MO: Particular Baptist, 2009.

Hudson, W. S. "Who Were the Baptists?" *The Baptist Quarterly* 16 (1956) 303-12.

———, ed. *Baptist Concepts of the Church.* Philadelphia: Judson, 1959.

Hutton, Sarah. "Henry More and the Apocalypse." In *Prophecy and Eschatology*, edited by Michael Wilks, 131-40. Oxford: Blackwell, 1994.

Ivimey, Joseph. *A History of the English Baptists.* 4 vols. London: Printed for B. J. Holdsworth, 1811-1830.

James, Muriel. *Religious Liberty on Trial: Hanserd Knollys—Early Baptist Hero.* Franklin, TN: Providence, 1997.

Kingsley, Gordon. "Opposition to Early Baptists (1638-1645)." *Baptist History and Heritage* 4 (1969) 18-30, 66.

Klaiber, Ashley J. *The Story of the Suffolk Baptists.* London: Kingsgate, 1931.

Korshin, Paul J. "Queuing and Waiting: The Apocalypse in England, 1660-1750." In *The Apocalypse in English Renaissance Thought and Literature: Patterns, Antecedents and Repercussions*, edited by C. A Patrides and Joseph Wittreich, 240-65. Manchester: Manchester University Press, 1984.

Kromminga, D. H. *The Millennium in the Church.* Grand Rapids: Eerdmans, 1945.

Lamont, William. "Richard Baxter, The Apocalypse and the Mad Major." *Past and Present* 55 (1972) 68-90.

Land, Richard D. "Doctrinal Controversies of English Particular Baptists (1644-1691) as Illustrated by the career and Writings of Thomas Collier." DPhil diss., Oxford University, 1979.

Langley, Arthur S. "Seventeenth Century Baptist Disputations." *Transactions of the Baptist Historical Society* 6 (1919) 216-43.

Lea, Thomas D. "A Survey of the Doctrine of the Return of Christ in the Ante-Nicene Fathers." *Journal of the Evangelical Theological Society* 29 (1986) 163-77.

Leonard, Bill J. *Baptist Ways: A History.* Valley Forge, PA: Judson, 2003.

Lindberg, Richard. "The Westminster and Second London Baptist Confessions of Faith: A Historical-Theological Comparison." MTh thesis, Westminster Theological Seminary, 1980.

Lumpkin, William L. *Baptist Confessions of Faith.* Philadelphia: Judson, 1959.

———. "The Nature and Authority of Baptist Confessions of Faith." *Review and Expositor* 76 (1979) 17-28.

MacDonald, M. D. "London Calvinistic Baptists 1689-1727: Tensions within a Dissenting Community under Toleration." DPhil diss., University of Oxford, 1982.

Manley, Kenneth Ross. "Origins of the Baptists: The Case for Development from Puritanism-Separatism." *Baptist History and Heritage* 22/4 (1987) 34-46.

McBeth, H. Leon. *The Baptist Heritage.* Nashville: Broadman, 1987.

———. *English Baptist Literature on Religious Liberty to 1689.* New York: Arno, 1980.

———. *A Sourcebook for Baptist Heritage.* Nashville: Broadman, 1990.

McGlothlin, W. J. *Baptist Confessions of Faith.* London: Baptist Historical Society, 1911.

———. "Dr. Daniel Featley and the First Calvinistic Baptist Confession." *The Review and Expositor* 6 (1909) 579-89.

———. "Sources of the First Calvinistic Baptist Confession of Faith." *The Review and Expositor* 13 (1916) 500-507.
Murray, Iain. *The Puritan Hope*. Edinburgh: Banner of Truth Trust, 1971.
Murrin, Michael. "Revelation and Two Seventeenth-Century Commentators." In *The Apocalypse in English Renaissance Thought and Literature: Patterns, Antecedents and Repercussions*, edited by C. A Patrides and Joseph Wittreich, 125-46. Manchester: Manchester University Press, 1984.
Naylor, Peter. *Picking up a Pin for the Lord: English Particular Baptists from 1688 to the Early Nineteenth Century*. London: Grace Publications Trust, 1992.
Nelson, Stanley A. "Reflecting on Baptist Origins: The London Confession of Faith of 1644." *Baptist History and Heritage* 29/2 (1994) 33-46.
Nettles, Thomas J. *By His Grace and for His Glory: A Historical, Theological and Practical Study of the Doctrines of Grace in Baptist Life*. Grand Rapids: Baker, 1986.
Novak, Michael J. "'Thy Will Be Done': The Theology of the English Particular Baptists, 1638-1660." PhD diss., Harvard University, 1979.
Oliver, Robert. "Baptist Confession Making 1644 and 1689." Paper from the Strict Baptist Historical Society, March, 1989.
Parratt, J. K. "An Early Baptist on the Laying on of Hands." *The Baptist Quarterly* 21 (1965-66) 325-27, 320.
Pater, Calvin. *Karlstadt as the Father of the Baptist Movements: The Emergence of Lay Protestantism*. Toronto: University of Toronto Press, 1984.
Patterson, W. Morgan. "The Lord's Supper in Baptist History." *Review and Expositor* 66 (1969) 25-34.
Payne, Ernest A. "Contacts Between Mennonites and Baptists." *Foundations* 4 (1961) 39-55.
———. "Who Were the Baptists?" *The Baptist Quarterly* 26 (1956) 339-42.
Prall, Stuart E. *Church and State in Tudor and Stuart England*. Arlington Heights, IL: Harlan Davidson, 1993.
———. "More about the Sabbatarian Baptists." *The Baptist Quarterly* 14 (1951-52) 161-66.
Reeves, Marjorie. "The Development of Apocalyptic Thought: Medieval Attitudes." In *The Apocalypse in English Renaissance Thought and Literature: Patterns, Antecedents and Repercussions*, edited by C. A Patrides and Joseph Wittreich, 40-72. Manchester: Manchester University Press, 1984.
———. *The Influence of Prophecy in the Later Middle Ages*. Oxford: Oxford University Press, 1969.
Roberts, R. Philip. *Continuity and Change: London Calvinistic Baptists and the Evangelical Revival, 1760-1820*. Wheaton, IL: Richard Owen Roberts, 1989.
Rogers, P. G. *The Fifth Monarchy Men*. Oxford: Oxford University Press, 1966.
Solt, Leo F. "The Fifth Monarchy Men: Politics and the Millennium." *Church History* 30 (1961) 314-24.
Starr, C. E. *A Baptist Bibliography*. 25 vols. Philadelphia and Rochester: 1947-1976.
Stassen, Glen H. "Anabaptist Influence in the Origin of The Particular Baptists." *The Mennonite Quarterly Review* 36 (1962) 322-48.
———. "Opening Menno Simons's *Foundation Book* and Finding the Father of Baptist Origins Alongside the Mother—Calvinist Congregationalism." *Baptist History and Heritage* 33/1 (1998) 34-44.

———. "Revisioning Baptist Identity by Naming Our Origin and Character Rightly." *Baptist History and Heritage* 33/1 (1998) 45-54.

Stephen, Leslie, and Sidney Lee, eds. "Knollys, Hanserd." In *Dictionary of National Biography*, 11:279-81. Oxford: Oxford University Press, 1921-22.

Tolmie, Murray. "General and Particular Baptists in the Puritan Revolution." PhD diss., Harvard University, 1960.

———. *The Triumph of the Saints*. Cambridge: Cambridge University Press, 1977.

Toon, Peter. *The Emergence of Hyper-Calvinism in English Non-Conformity, 1689-1765*. London: Olive Tree, 1967.

———. "A Message of Hope for the Rump Parliament." *The Evangelical Quarterly* 43 (1971) 82-96.

———, ed. *Puritans, the Millenium and the Future of Israel*. Cambridge: J. Clarke, 1970.

Torbet, Robert G. *A History of the Baptists*. Philadelphia: Judson, 1955.

Torrance, T. F., and J. K. S. Reid, eds. *Eschatology*. Edinburgh: Oliver and Boyd, n.d.

Tuveson, Ernest Lee. *Millenium and Utopia: A Study in the Background of the Idea of Progress*. Berkeley: University of California Press, 1949.

Underhill, E. B., ed. *Confessions of Faith, and other Public Documents . . . of the Baptist Churches of England in the 17th Century*. London: Printed for the Hanserd Knollys Society by Haddon, Brothers, and Co., 1854.

Underwood, A. C. *A History of the English Baptists*. London: Carey Kingsgate, 1947.

Walker, Michael J. "Baptist Theology of Infancy." *The Baptist Quarterly* 21 (1965-66) 251-62.

Wamble, Hugh. "Early English Baptist Sectarianism." *Review and Expositor* 55 (1958) 59-69.

———. "The Beginning of Associationalism Among English Baptists." *Review and Expositor* 54 (1957) 545-59.

———. "Inter-relations of Seventeenth Century English Baptists." *Review and Expositor* 54 (1957) 407-25.

Watts, Michael R. *The Dissenters*. Vol. 1. Oxford: Clarendon, 1978.

White, B. R., "Baptist Beginnings and the Kiffin Manuscript." *Baptist History and Heritage* 2/1 (1967) 27-39.

———. "The Doctrine of the Church in the Particular Baptist Confession of 1644." *Journal of Theological Studies* N.S. 19 (1968) 570-90.

———. "Early Baptist Arguments for Religious Freedom: Their Overlooked Agenda." *Baptist History and Heritage* 24/4 (1989) 3-10.

———. *The English Baptists of the Seventeenth Century*. London: Baptist Historical Society, 1983.

———. "The English Particular Baptists and the Great Rebellion." *Baptist History and Heritage* 9/1 (1974) 16-29.

———. *The English Separatist Tradition*. Oxford: Oxford University Press, 1971.

———. "The Frontiers of Fellowship between English Baptists, 1609-1660." *Foundations* 11 (1968): 244-56.

———. *Hanserd Knollys and Radical Dissent in the Seventeenth Century*. London: Dr. Williams's Trust, 1977.

———. "Henry Jessey in the Great Rebellion." In *Reformation Conformity and Dissent*, edited by R. Buick Knox, 132-53. London: Epworth, 1977.

———. "How Did William Kiffin Join the Baptists?" *The Baptist Quarterly* 23 (1970) 201-7.

———. "Knollys, Hanserd (c. 1599-1691)." In *Biographical Dictionary of British Radicals in the Seventeenth Century*, edited by Richard L. Greaves and Robert Zaller, 2:160–62. Brighton: Harvester, 1982-84.

———. "John Pendavres, the Calvinistic Baptists and the Fifth Monarchy." *The Baptist Quarterly* 25 (1974) 251–71.

———. "The London Calvinistic Baptist Leadership 1644–1660." *The Baptist Quarterly* 32 (1987-88) s34–45.

———. "The Origins and Convictions of the First Calvinistic Baptists." *Baptist History and Heritage* 25/4 (1990) 39–47.

———. "Organization of the Particular Baptists, 1644–1660." *Journal of Ecclesiastical History* 17 (1966) 209–26.

———. "Samuel Eaton (d. 1639) Particular Baptist Pioneer." *The Baptist Quarterly* 24 (1971-72) 10–21.

———. "Thomas Collier and Gangraena Edwards." *The Baptist Quarterly* 24 (1971-72) 99–110.

———. "Who Really Wrote the 'Kiffin Manuscript'?" *Baptist History and Heritage* 1/3 (1966) 3–10, 14.

———., ed. *Association Records of the Particular Baptists of England, Wales and Ireland to 1660*. London: The Baptist Historical Society, n.d.

Whitley, W. T., "Baptist Churches till 1660." *Transactions of the Baptist Historical Society* 2 (1911) 236–54.

———. "Baptist Meetings in the City of London." *Transactions of the Baptist Historical Society* 5 (1916) 74–82.

———. *The Baptists of London: 1612–1928*. London: Kingsgate, 1928.

———. "Debate on Infant Baptism, 1643." *Transactions of the Baptist Historical Society* 1 (1910) 237–45.

———. "Dissent in Worcestershire during the Seventeenth Century." *Transactions of the Baptist Historical Society* 7 (1920) 1–12.

———. *A History of British Baptists*. London: Charles Griffin, 1923

———. "An Index to Notable Baptists, Whose Careers Began within the British Empire before 1850." *Transactions of the Baptist Historical Society* 7 (1921) 182–239.

———. "The Jacob-Jessey Church, 1616–1678." *Transactions of the Baptist Historical Society* 1 (1910) 246–56.

———. "John Tombes as a Correspondent." *Transactions of the Baptist Historical Society* 7 (1920) 13–18.

———. "Militant Baptists 1660–1672." *Transactions of the Baptist Historical Society* 1 (1909) 148–55.

———. *Pulpit in Parliament: Puritanism during the English Civil Wars, 1640–1648*. Princeton: Princeton University Press, 1969.

———. "Records of the Jacob-Lathrop-Jessey Church 1616–1641." *Transactions of the Baptist Historical Society* 1 (1910) 203–25.

———. "The Relation of Baptists to the Ejectment." In *The Enactment of 1662 and the Free churches*, 75–96. London: National Council of Evangelical Free Churches, n.d.

———. "Rise of the Particular Baptists in London, 1633–1644." *Transactions of the Baptist Historical Society* 1 (1910) 226–36.

———. "The Seven Churches of London." *The Review and Expositor* 7 (1910) 384–413.

———., ed. *A Baptist Bibliography*. London: Kingsgate, 1916.

Wilson, Walter. *The History and Antiquities of Dissenting Churches and Meeting Houses*. London: 1808.

Winter, E. P. "Calvinist and Zwinglian Views of the Lord's Supper among the Baptists of the Seventeenth Century." *The Baptist Quarterly* 15 (1953–54) 323–29.

Woodman, Simon. "Stoned in the Pulpit: The Provocative Preaching of Hanserd Knollys." *The Baptist Quarterly* 45 (April 2014) 327–28.

Yarbrough, Sladen A. "The Origins of Baptist Associations Among English Particular Baptists." *Baptist History and Heritage* 23/2 (1988) 14–25.

www.ingramcontent.com/pod-product-compliance
Lightning Source LLC
Chambersburg PA
CBHW050847230426
43667CB00012B/2181